BY PURE LUCK

A Memoir

by
Fela Igielnik

Edited by Curtiss Short

"By Pure Luck" ISBN 978-1-62137-003-1 (softcover); 978-1-60264-982-8 (hardcover) 978-1-60264-983-5 (electronic version).

Library of Congress Control Number: 2012903349

Published 2012 by Virtualbookworm.com Publishing Inc., P.O. Box 9949, College Station, TX , 77842, US. ©2012 Fela Igielnik.
Manufactured in the United States of America.

Table of Contents

Author's Note

After six dreadful years, the war that devastated a large part of the world and left in its path destruction, death, suffering, and sorrow, came to an end. With it also ended the period known as the Holocaust—the deliberate, premeditated murder of million of Jews, Gypsies, and other "undesirables."

For years, I kept a box full of notes containing my eyewitness accounts of this grievous period. All along I knew that those of us who had survived this horror had a moral obligation to inform the world of this tragedy; that it was our responsibility, not to scare, but to warn future generations to be vigilant. That they must learn how to separate facts from propaganda, and to be able to prevent a reoccurrence. Despite the survivor's motto, "Never Again," the world still settles disputes by the sword—ploughshares are nowhere to be seen. We still use stereotypes and scapegoats, racism and bigotry, ethnic cleansing, prejudice, hatred. The ingredients that laid the foundation for the Holocaust are still with us and, regretfully, doing quite well. This is my third attempt at writing an account, and, I hope, it will be the last. I am determined finally to put all my notes together—all those boxes full of records and notes that have been piling up throughout the years.

We survivors are now on the endangered species list. A few years from now, we'll belong to history. But our legacy must go on; our message must not die. Every survivor has his or her own story. I am glad that I survived and am able to convey the message, the plight, of the millions who weren't so lucky. How else can one make people aware that such hideous crimes could be possible in a so-called civilized world?

I would like to express my heartfelt thanks to those who fought the Nazis on all fronts, who struggled in the forests, in underground movements, and those who resisted the Nazis by disobeying their orders. I feel indebted to all my liberators—governments and individuals—who fought to protect the world from the Nazi plague and who helped to bring this horror to an end before my death sentence was carried out. My deepest gratitude also goes to the relief organizations— the Red Cross, the Salvation Army, HIAS-Joint—which helped me during my recovery from this ordeal.

To my husband, children, and grandchildren, I would like to say: *Thanks for your love and support. Without your encouragement, my notes would still be in the box.*

I. Refugees

I was twelve years old when, while walking home from school, I saw some people gathered by the entrance of Krasinskich Park across the street from where I lived. Curious, I pushed my way into the center of the gathering where a boy and a girl, about eight and nine years old, in oversized but clean and nicely pressed clothes, were giving a concert. The boy, the older of the two, was playing the violin, the girl singing a children's song in a foreign language. The tin can in front of them was quickly filling up with coins. I heard a woman in the audience say, "They must be refugee kids." When I told Mama about these kids she said that the woman was probably right. "They must be German Jews recently expelled by the German ruler."

Soon, more refugees began arriving in Warsaw. It was 1939.

There was a girl in my sister's class who needed help in learning Polish. And there was Mama's Onkel Harry, who with his Gentile wife, Tante Trude, had been expelled from Berlin. Sis and I first met them in Aunt Rachel's home. We used to visit there quite often because of Fredzia and Renia, who besides being our relatives were also our best friends. All of us liked Tante Trude. Even though she spoke hardly any Polish, we communicated quite well. With the help of Onkel Harry, whom we used as a translator, she told us many interesting stories and taught us some songs. She talked about the wonderful German countryside, about the good life that she and her husband had enjoyed in Berlin, and about the places they had visited before being expelled.

But the stories Onkel Harry and Tante Trude told the adults weren't exactly the same. Once we kids overheard such an adult conversation. They were talking about some things called "Nuremberg Laws," something about a *"Kristallnacht,"* some weird camps, among other such strange things that were happening in Germany.[1] Onkel Harry also spoke about Tante Trude. "She could have remained in Germany," he said, "but she chose to evacuate with me, even when I told her that it would be dangerous and, at best, very difficult."

Life for the refugees was hard. When they were expelled, they were allowed to take very little money, and only a few belongings. They were transported to the "neutral zone" between Poland and Germany.[2] No country, he said, wanted them. Those who were finally accepted into Poland were of Polish origin. Once the government let them in, they were distributed to many cities. The burden of supporting them, even those without family or friends, would fall solely on the Jewish community (in which housing and employment were a problem even long before the refugees began coming).

The adults, besides discussing all these events, also talked about the latest news being reported in the mass media. They talked about uncertain times, about a war that could or couldn't be prevented, about the German dictator named Hitler, the head of the Nazi party who was very wicked and who hated Jews and other minorities. All these stories meant very little to us kids. We kept playing our games while eavesdropping on the adult conversations.

II. Rumors of War

These adult conversations became more meaningful when we returned from our summer vacation in mid-August. Arriving in Warsaw, we found people busy taping up windows, digging trenches, and preparing air-raid shelters. Newspapers were being grabbed up as soon as they could be printed. Crowds gathered around all bulletin boards and under loudspeakers that had been installed at all major intersections. "Will there be war or peace?" This was the major concern.

Rumors in the crowds had it that Hitler was simply making idle threats so that Poland would hand over the Corridor.[3] Some heard that France and Great Britain had promised to help in case of a German invasion. Others said that "'the insane painter' can bark as much as he wants, but he'll never get an inch of our land."[4] Also there were those who received their news from God. They heard that God would help, if only people would pray and obey. These were mostly Hasidic Jews with connections to God.[5]

While all of this talk was going on, Germany and Poland were mobilizing their military and reserves.

Not paying attention to obvious signs, the mass media kept reporting that "encouraging" progress was being made at the negotiations. The assurances designed to calm the population didn't help much. People reading between the lines saw that the situation was grim. The more affluent began stocking up on essential goods. Those without money stood helplessly by and watched all vital supplies disappearing from store shelves.

Other indications that something was wrong were the merchants and suppliers drastically raising commodity prices. Despite warnings of severe punishments for such deeds, prices were soaring. Encouraging speeches on radio and mood-boosting articles in papers did not help, either. People's optimism was dwindling. The seriousness of the situation became even more apparent when an order was issued to all men ages sixteen to twenty who weren't yet in, or not fit for, military service, to report to induction centers for duty in the OPL, a civil defense organization that was to help with the civilian population in case of air-raids.

I found all of this very exciting. After hearing many stories from adults about World War I (1914-1918), which had ended only twenty-one years before, I really wanted to see a war. September was quickly approaching, and school was about to start. But on September first, instead of school beginning, German planes began roaring through the skies and German troops started crossing the Polish border.

I was going to see a real war.

III. The Bomb Shelter

It was not long before I became acquainted with our so-called bomb shelter, which was really just a dark, damp, dismal cellar, with sewer and water pipes running along the walls, and a dirt floor below. Here and there an electric bulb was suspended from a wooden ceiling beam. When it became obvious that our stay in this place would be longer than we had expected, one of the neighbors installed an electric socket into which he plugged a radio that had been donated to the shelter by another neighbor. The OPL workers, helped by a few young teens, got some chairs and benches so that the older people had a place to sit. The younger folks and the kids would sit on blankets spread out on the dirt.

One day, during a raid, I started a conversation with a girl sitting next to me. We talked about returning to school, and what the assignments would be. We were sure that there would be at least one about the war and the extended vacation. In preparation for that, I started keeping a diary.

The following days provided me with a lot of exciting events to record. One late afternoon during an air-raid, while I was writing about some boring days in the shelter, I felt the ground shake. A few minutes later a young man, about seventeen or eighteen, with a white OPL band on his left upper arm, came running into the cellar, announcing that a bomb had fallen only three buildings away. In a scared, shaky voice he said, "Some people managed to crawl to safety through a hole in the cracked door before the wall caved in. Many are still buried in the basement of the building. The exit is blocked by debris."

The young man was looking for volunteers to help with removing the rubbish. In particular he was looking for Dr. Flanzman, who lived in our building and who was supposedly somewhere in our cellar. "Police, fire trucks, and ambulances are just arriving. We need help to get the victims out." Hearing that, I put away my diary and jumped up to volunteer my service. But Dad, as though reading my mind, turned to Mama, and said, "You had better keep an eye on that girl; she is getting a little out of hand."

After the young man left our shelter, taking with him a few volunteers, a long discussion started among the adults. They talked about the Spanish Civil War and how new bombs had been tried out there, about how most people just could not believe that one bomb could destroy a whole building.[6]

Meantime, the radio in the shelter was broadcasting patriotic speeches from Warsaw Station II. The announcer praised the OPL workers and the Polish armed forces, commending their spirit and bravery. "We will keep fighting to the last soldier!" he declared. "Till final victory! To the last drop of blood!...." Reports of defeats were very brief and vague. Many older people said that such talk actually meant defeat, that we were losing. I couldn't understand how they could have come to such a conclusion.

As soon as the "All Clear" signal sounded, I told Sis, "Tell Mama I'll be back shortly," and with three neighbor girls, I ran to explore the bombed-out building.

Outside, in the first courtyard garden where the water fountain had been turned off, we saw *Pani* Wilanowska watering her flowers. We said, *"Dzień dobry!"*—"Good day!"—and ran past her into the street.[7]

By the time we got to the bombed-out building, many people were gathered around the collapsed wall, digging in the rubble, trying to find survivors. Young OPL attendants were carrying people on stretchers. Ambulances were picking up the wounded. Amid the debris we could see arms, legs, and other body parts separated from still-buried torsos. Screams were coming from beneath the wreckage. A woman who did not know what had become of her child was pulling at her hair and screamed pathetically. Another woman in a half-torn dress was carrying one shoe in her hand and holding this crying mother at the waist, trying to calm her down. Police had blocked off the street around the ruined building and were dispersing the curious onlookers.

We ran home to tell everyone about our new experience, our first encounter with a real war, assuming that everyone would be excited. But instead of listening, the adults got angry. Each of us girls got a share of the scolding, and we had to promise never again to venture outside the courtyard gates. I assured Mama and Dad, but my promise was short lived.

Bombing raids became more frequent and more frantic. We were spending a lot of time in the shelter. Many stories were told during the long eerie hours. Old men talked about the First World War. Women usually talked about their families, and about Mr. Greenfarb, the old man who was refusing to come to the cellar, insisting that God would protect him as God had during World War I, when he had fought against the Russians. He had been saved by a miracle, and he strongly believed that "those predestined to be hanged won't drown"—an old Polish proverb. We also got to know many of our neighbors who lived in the three adjacent buildings. There were about a hundred apartments in this complex, and I don't know how many tenants. The only person who knew all of them was Jósef Kowalski, the building custodian.

An especially memorable day was the Eve of Rosh Hashanah, the Jewish New Year. That day the Jewish section of Warsaw was the target of air attacks. Almost one third of the Jewish-owned buildings and businesses were demolished. This deliberate bombing on the High Holidays, especially in the Jewish quarter of town, was made to look accidental. Huge squadrons of Luftwaffe bombers flew low over the buildings.[8] They came in fives, tens, maybe even larger groups. They flew so low that we could almost see the pilots. In the early afternoon, sirens began to blow, informing everyone of an incoming raid. Soon, the roar of falling bombs and the angry barking of the anti-aircraft cannons drowned out the noise of the blowing sirens.

People in the shelter were screaming, crying, cracking their knuckles. Women were beating their breasts, praying, asking God to save their children. Men quietly kept reciting the *Tehillim*.[9]

The radio announcer warned people to stay in shelters and asked that they remain calm. He said that there was good news from the international dispatch: "England and France are coming to help. The aggressors will pay for their belligerence. Long Live Poland!"

Meanwhile, the bombs kept falling. It seemed as though some must have fallen on our building. We just sat and waited for the walls to crumble. Then the earth would shake again. Then all the lights in the cellar went out, and the radio voice died.

When finally the "All Clear" siren sounded, people hugged and kissed. The OPL guards opened the cellar doors. People thanked God Almighty that the raid was over, that the bombs had missed us.

As I got out of the cellar, a great idea flashed through my mind: "Let's go and see how Grandma Ester is doing." I said this to my sister. Our father's seventy-two-year-old, widowed mother lived on Pavia Street, about four or five kilometers away.

Sis agreed, but Dad thought that neither of us should go. We tried bargaining with him, but he wouldn't budge. Meantime, a couple of neighbors started talking to him. I said loudly, "Daddy, we'll be back shortly." I grabbed my sister by the hand, pulled her through the large entrance gate and into the street.

Narrow Swietojerska Street was filled with a continuous crowd of running people. Past Krasinskich Park, emergency vehicles were blocking the way to Nalewki Street. We decided to go around the block. At the corner of Wolowa Street, a mob of young people had gathered around a burning pawnshop. Bricks were still falling from under the partly collapsed roof, and streams of water were pouring from fire hoses. A group of young men and a few women started running into the building and dragging out boxes and bags of goods. Some just loaded their pockets or carried armfuls of soaked loot. Envious onlookers cowardly watched the "courageous" looters getting rich. First aid workers, helped by volunteers, were carrying in their arms wounded men, women, and children; others had lifeless bodies thrown over their shoulders. A group of OPL attendants were trying to reach some people still buried underneath the piles of smoldering rubble.

Closer to Nalewki Street, another building was on fire. Flames blazing through the boarded-up windows were meeting tongues of fire coming from the opposite wall. Curled smoke thrust forward, blinding those who were trying to escape the flames. Frightened people and small children with wet blankets over their heads were running frantically, screaming, trying to cough out the smoke that they had swallowed, rubbing their burning eyes—all running, running aimlessly.

From the people hurrying down Gesia Street, we couldn't make out a clear story of what had happened; it all seemed to be incoherent bits of horror. At first, there was no way to find the house numbers; later it was impossible even to find the street. Dad's business was at Gesia 3; his brother, Uncle Louis, lived at 18. Sis and I got scared.

Loudspeakers on the street corner warned people of the potential risk and told them to keep away from the danger zone. The announcer pleaded with the crowds to disperse, but the people just stood there, cemented to the ground, hopelessly watching as their homes burn, anxious to find out the fate of their loved ones still trapped in the fires.

In a frightened voice, my sister said, "Let's get out of here." She pleaded to go home. Her eyes were filling with tears. I pulled her across the street. For another few moments we watched fire fighters, half engulfed in flames, jerking their heavy fire hoses, climbing their ladders amid the swaying clouds of smoke.

Suddenly, I felt a strong hand from behind grabbing my shoulder. Someone was tugging at my braids. My whole body rocked suddenly as a hand spun me around, knocking my braids into my face. A frantic man's voice was yelling at me. "What are you crazy little bastards doing here? Don't you have

15

anyone watching you? Get the hell out of the God-forsaken street! Go home! If you don't have one, follow me!"

Behind this figure, I saw a man holding a little girl in his arms. His jacket was hanging over the girl's head. The front of his hair had been scorched by fire. I decided to follow the man's advice. Holding Sis with one hand and protecting my eyes with the other, we both ran as fast as we could, elbowing, pushing and shoving, our way through the swelling crowds. As we finally approached our street, I thought, "Another great story for my diary," but I didn't dare say a word.

When we at last reached our building, Dad, Mama, and her sister, Aunt Naomi, accompanied by a few neighbors, were waiting for us at the entrance. We were sure that we would be scolded. We were still scared from our adventure, and now we didn't know what to expect at home. But they were so happy to see us alive that no one yelled at us; no one even said an unkind word.

I ran upstairs to the apartment to try to change my wet, smoke-stained clothes. On the second floor of the stairway, Moshe, the Hasidic son of Cantor Goldberg, was busy inspecting mezuzahs on Jewish doorposts to see if they had been disturbed by the raids.[10] Mrs. Gurfinkel, our next-door neighbor, was walking down the steps, carrying a towel-covered basket. "Where in the world have you kids been?" she asked, handing me a potato pancake from the basket. Before I could tell her my story, she said, "Eat, my child. That's all I can offer you; thank God you're okay," and she continued walking downstairs. *"Baruch Hasham.* Praised be the Almighty," mumbled Moshe, drawing out his words into a chant.

That evening, while lighting the High Holiday candles—and they had to be lit in the cellar because of another air-raid—I saw hardly a dry eye. These candles were the only reminder of the holiday, and they provided the only light for the otherwise dark cellar. Our holiday meal consisted of some lukewarm potato soup that Mama had cooked between raids, and a few slices of old bread. Other families didn't eat any better.

Most of the following days and nights were spent in the shelter. Many people started acting strange: The smallest disturbance would provoke high tension, any slight irritation uncontrollable tears. Mrs. Ziegler, a widow whose husband was killed fighting in World War I, became a complete nuisance. She kept screaming and calling for her dead husband to come back. "She is mad, poor soul," a woman said. Some men put a damp cloth on her forehead to calm her down, but her screams couldn't be stopped.

With electricity out, and no radio, we were cut off from the outside world. There were more irritated people, and Mrs. Ziegler's screams worsened. Another woman, known only as *"Oy Veh,"* whose two sons were on the frontline, cried day and night.[11] Outside, shells were exploding, buildings collapsing, and people screaming. There were more corpses of burned, smoke-choked children, and more orphans whose parents' bodies were still buried under the rubble, and widows whose husbands had fallen in defense of the country. Many soldiers still fighting on the front did not know that their wives had been killed while trying to save their children. As always, there were many mothers of missing sons and daughters.

Swiectego Jana Bozego, the St. John Church on Bonifraterska Street, and the adjacent mental hospital, had now been converted to a field hospital. Nuns were tending to the wounded. All mentally ill patients had been transferred to a state mental facility in Pruszkow, an institution from which no one was ever known to come back alive. School buildings were being used as infirmaries; churches, synagogues, and public buildings had been transformed into shelters and filled up with those who were left homeless by the bombings.

Park Krasinskich had also been converted. Until the bombings, it had been a French-style park with a small lake ornamented with dignified swimming swans, carefully manicured flower beds, and long wooden benches under the shade of old trees. It was surrounded on three sides by a twelve-foot-high iron fence railing mounted on a five-foot cement foundation and on the fourth side by the federal court building. It had now become a stop-over for the hungry, wounded, exhausted soldiers. Their dismounted nags, tied to fences, were chewing on tree bark now that all the grass had been consumed.

About two weeks had passed since the first German troops crossed the Polish border. Most of Poland was now occupied. The western part was taken by the Germans, the eastern part by the Soviet Union (whom we called the "Russians"). Poland's two neighbors, the Germans and the Russians, had signed a "non-aggression treaty" which divided Poland between themselves. Only the city of Warsaw was still fighting, "defending the country's honor."

"We will never surrender! Never give up our beloved capital!" the official radio broadcasted through the speakers on every street corner. "We will fight to the last soldier! Long live Poland! Long live Warsaw, the heart of our Homeland!"

The German army surrounded the city. The Polish anti-aircraft guns were being silenced by German cannons, which were bombarding day and night. From the Zoliborz suburbs, artillery thunder burst the ears; fire lit the sky; combined with a rain of shells and bullets, it felt like a wild metallic thunderstorm.

Polish military men were fleeing the defense lines. Soldiers were running all over the city. Every park, every street, every courtyard, was filled with retreating Polish troops. Weary, wounded, worried soldiers were dragging themselves through the debris-filled roads, shedding their uniforms and putting on civilian clothes that had been given to them by kindhearted residents. Military vehicles and dead or wounded horses lay abandoned in the streets. Our courtyards, all three of them, were filled with fleeing soldiers. Chained to garden posts, limping horses were chewing on tree bark and eating *Pani* Wilanowska's flowers.

During the night, our street was bombarded by grenades. Though our apartment complex was spared severe damage, we didn't escape the attack. One building was hit by a shell that entered the top floor apartments through a side wall. A few apartments were struck by splinter shells. We knew right away that one of them was ours. Because of the constant heavy bombing, however, we were unable to find out the precise extent of the damage. Seen from the courtyard, the roof seemed to be intact, but the balcony was hanging on the falling plaster. Like devils' horns, sharp chunks of glass were pointing from smashed window panes. The outside walls, though pockmarked by grenade splinters, remained standing upright.

A few days later, while taking advantage of a short interruption in the shelling, Dad decided to take a look at our apartment, assess the damage, and see what, if anything, could be salvaged. I could not resist such an opportunity, and asked him if I, too, could go. To my great surprise, he said yes.

After pushing through the crowded courtyard, we started up the four flights of steps. On the third floor, Neighbor Greenfarb's apartment stood in ruins. A shell had entered through an outside wall. There was an intense odor of gas, sewage, and smoking cinders. Old Greenfarb, who had once believed in predestination, lay dead on the floor.

In our apartment, the parquet floor was covered with a heap of bricks from fallen interior walls. A pile of broken boards and smashed furniture was ornamented with shattered glass. All windows in the apartment had been blown out. Most interior walls dividing the rooms were crumbled, but the outside walls remained intact. What used to be a six-room flat (three rooms, two halls, and a kitchen) had been reduced to an entrance hall, one room, and a large space filled with debris.

Before Dad and I had time to look any further, we heard the sound of sirens: Another bombing.

After a few days, the bombing stopped, but the shelling continued for two more days. During the second night, the central waterworks of Warsaw was destroyed. Other water supply systems, such as wells and pumps, were very scarce in the city; in many neighborhoods, they were non-existent. The situation became catastrophic. All food provisions were exhausted. Medical supplies were almost gone. Fires were raging in most parts of the city. Every available shelter was filled to capacity.

On September 28, 1939, Warsaw surrendered to the Germans.

IV. Surrender

A hush fell on the city. Poland had ceased to exist. All Polish military personnel, from high-ranking officers to privates who hadn't been taken prisoner, cast off their uniforms and put on civilian clothes. OPL attendants removed their armbands and threw them into fires. Important leaders fled the country, or else went into hiding. Those who didn't manage to escape were taken prisoner.

Inhabitants of Warsaw grieved for their city and their country; all Polish citizens grieved along with them. Yet, amid their profound sorrow, they found a slight comfort in knowing that the shelling and killing had finally stopped.

Exhausted, weary, hungry, the civilian population started crawling out of their burrows to look for water and food, for whatever was left of their possessions. They had yet to bury their dead; and they now faced the cleanup job, as well as an unknown future.

Dad and I walked in the street. Looters, many by now quite experienced in the profession, were hard at work. On the other side of the street, not far from our house, some youngsters were filling their bags with anything they could grab from the still smoldering ruins. An older gentleman who was standing next to us started yelling, "Loot, kids, loot!" Then, putting both hands to his mouth, he added through this megaphone, "Take everything you can! Don't leave anything for the German demons!" After shouting this, he turned to my father and said, "Barely twenty years ago, I finished fighting these sons-of-bitches, and here they are, coming again."

Dad and I continued on our way. The destination was Gesia Street. We were going to see what had happened to Dad's business. We found only a heap of rubble. After taking me home, Dad went back there with his partners to see if something could be dug up, if anything could be salvaged.

I think that it was the next day that German troops began marching into the city. Sis, three other girls, and I took off into the streets to see the Germans. Bonifraterska Street was crowded. White surrender flags were hanging out all the windows facing the street. Men, women, old and young, mothers with children in their arms, on their shoulders, by their sides—masses of people, all wearing white kerchiefs or waving pieces of white cloth, were coming from all directions. They were rushing to greet the people who had just finished bombing their city.

In order not to lose one another, we girls were holding on to one another's hand, dress, or braids. We kept pushing our way through the crowds. From the side of the Zoliborz suburbs, we heard some tunes—faint, distant voices, singing in unison. As we pushed farther into the swelling crowd, we began to see columns of soldiers coming over the viaduct. They were moving closer, young handsome soldiers in spotless, tidily pressed grayish-blue uniforms, and shiny boots. They were marching in perfect formation and singing in German. Following the columns of marching soldiers was a long line of military trucks. On each of them a few young, good-looking soldiers were smiling and waving their hands. "What an enemy!" I thought. It was like being somewhere in a foreign country without ever having crossed a border.

It was exciting. It was even more appealing because we girls had come here without our parents' permission. It was like being free. We felt independent. From the crowd, people were calling out a variety of messages. Some yelled, "Glad you're here!" Others tried to scream even louder: "Drop dead, you rotten bastards! Get lost, you German aggressors! Go to hell!" Even: "May God strike you with cholera!"[12]

Pointing to another little boy wearing a kippah, a little Polish boy, about ten or eleven, yelled at the top of his voice, "Mr. German! He is a *Jude!*"[13] He said this in Polish, but the last word in German: *"Yoode."* People were paying little attention to what the others had to say. They were more interested in what was happening on the trucks. At a given signal, the victors started throwing bread from these vehicles. Hundreds of loaves went flying through the air and into the crowd. The soldiers, waving their arms, greeting everybody with friendly smiles, were yelling, *"Brot! Brot!"* They were saying some other words in German, but I couldn't understand.

From the ends of the bread trucks, mounted movie cameras were rolling. They were trying to capture this fantastic greeting of the "Super Race feeding the *Untermenschen,*" the poor sub-humans.[14]

It didn't take us long to figure out why so many people had been so eager to come and "greet" their enemy. The bread give-away had been announced on the radio. My friends and I came out of curiosity; those whose electricity wasn't cut off had heard about the bread on the morning news.

Anyway, the five of us got home with three loaves of fresh bread, which we later divided. We hadn't had for quite some time such a precious commodity.

V. Occupation

As soon as the victors entered the city, they promised an end to the chaos and a beginning of good German Law and Order: They made the Laws; we obeyed the Orders. To assure that no one dared to defy their authority, they took hostages and imposed a curfew. They arrested some prominent citizens—professors, clergy, politicians—and kept them in jail as "protection." Announcements were then made over all available media that if something should happen to any German person, military or civilian, there would be reprisals. For any non-compliance or civil disobedience, the hostages would be killed. A list of the hostages was posted for everyone to see. To top it off, some of these well-known leaders were sent away to so-called detention camps.

Collaborators were quickly found. A new government, under German supervision, was set up, and the new rulers were now in business. Western Poland was annexed to the Third Reich, and the Eastern part was taken over by the Russians.[15] Central Poland would be occupied and governed by the Germans. In the process, Poles lost all their rights; they now had only obligations. Jews no longer counted: They now needed temporary permission to live. Many new regulations were soon announced.

Most of them started with the word *Verboten:* Not, Do Not, Do Not Go Here, Do Not Do That.... Even more frequently, signs read *"Juden Verboten,"* Jews forbidden. Hardly mentioned was anything that people were allowed to do, like where to get water, food, housing, fuel, medicine, or work. Such trivial matters were left to the local authorities.

People carried water from the Wisla River, which was at the time filled with debris and floating human and animal corpses. Some people had to walk many kilometers to reach a source of water, and often this water had to be boiled before it could be used. To boil the polluted water, fuel was needed, but gas and electrical power had been cut off in most places; where they hadn't been, they were rationed. People gathered broken boards and smashed furniture taken from destroyed buildings to use for fuel.

The problem of food was no better. Stores not destroyed by the bombing were ordered to reopen; but their shelves were empty. Although transports with some food and fuel started rolling into the city, it was far too little. Shortages of the necessities were so widespread that there was not anything even to loot or steal. Some people, under great risk, resorted to illegal trading. Those who needed things to survive were forced to pay whatever price was asked in order to feed their children. Ex-looters were becoming entrepreneurs. The black market was booming.[16] Only perishable items could be bought for paper money, which had lost most of its value. It wasn't unusual to get a wallet of goods for a sackful of money. Theft and barter became the means of acquiring goods. Anything edible—and outside of bricks, glass, and nails, everything was considered edible—was traded for jewelry, clothing, musical instruments, among other non-essential commodities. Nothing was wasted. To make sure that the horses didn't die in vain, they were cut up and sold for meat. Horse meat, now considered a luxury, was traded for winter clothes, coal, candles, or gold. Such was also the price for colored salt: blue, green, and red salt, formerly used in industrial plants, was now a food additive.

We soon had to join the bartering crowds, or else face starvation. The flour and rice that we had stored up were coming to an end. These precious items had come from burning warehouses. Aunt Naomi had acquired them the day a bomb fell on the grain elevators and barges by the riverfront in Praga.[17] In this manner, our aunt became a looter. Aunt, along with thousands of other decent citizens, ran across the Kierbedzia Bridge to "save" the rice and flour from burning, ruining, or being taken by the Germans.

Besides the problem of food, we also faced the problem of housing. Places had to be found for thousands of the homeless who were staying in temporary shelters. We were staying with Aunt Sara, our maternal grandfather's widowed sister, who, with her three grown children, lived in the same housing complex we used to. Many of the homeless people, especially the children and the elderly, were getting sick. Only rats, bugs, and black-marketers could thrive. During warm, sunny days, insolent, fat rats would pace the ruins at random. Days passed before the city began the slow, hideous cleanup process. The injured were taken to makeshift hospitals that had been set up in churches, clubhouses, school gymnasiums, warehouses—wherever a place could be found. All permanent hospitals had long since been filled up. The dead were finally being buried. People who had lost many material goods were thankful to God Almighty that they hadn't lose their lives. The poor folk who had never had any material possessions were now boasting about the furs and jewels that they had lost in the fires. There was a great deal of envy and misunderstanding among the people who were forced to live together. After the initial excitement of good will wore off, those who had escaped from the flames with their lives had little respect for dishes, clothing, or knickknacks. Still, these things were cherished by those who used to have them.

When our home was shelled, there was no fire. We found many usable items under the rubble. After cleaning up the one room and the adjacent hall, we established residency for the five of us: my mother, father, sister, Aunt Naomi, and myself. For three reasons this small, crowded, pathetic living space turned out to be a great bargain for us. First of all, we didn't have to live with relatives, friends, or in a shelter. Second, we weren't assigned to take in any of the refugees who were pouring into Warsaw from other cities and towns and being put up in many of the larger, intact homes. Third, because this apartment was so damaged, we didn't have to pay full rent.

Ever since the German troops entered the city, there wasn't a day without new developments. The handsome and friendly bread-givers, our humanitarian occupiers, started showing their real identity. Almost every day, new laws or decrees were announced. The new regulations affected every Polish citizen but were especially hard on Jews. Roadblocks were being set up on the streets, and men were being rounded up and loaded onto trucks and shipped away. Without warning, people began to disappear off the streets. While most Jews seized in these roundups were taken to forced labor brigades inside and outside of the city, many Poles were being swept up by Gestapo raids and shipped off to Germany to work in the fields or in munitions factories.[18] I saw thousands of refugees coming into Warsaw from cities and towns that had been annexed to the Third Reich. These territories were to be *"Judenrein"*—free of Jews. All refugees coming from these places were wearing yellow stars sewn to the front and back of their outer garments.[19]

Every day, street posters announced new ordinances. One read, "Anyone found guilty of crimes against the Third Reich will be hanged or shot on the spot." For Jews, an offense against the Third Reich could be anything from smuggling a loaf of bread to such an abominable crime as crossing in front of a German guard.

Like most Jewish kids, I was instructed not to go to parks, public libraries, movies, or theaters, because these were *"Für Juden verboten"*—forbidden to Jews. Jews were instructed to step off sidewalks whenever a German was walking there. Jewish men had to take off their hats whenever passing a German soldier (even though a head-covering for Jewish men was required by their religion).

Anti-Semitism wasn't a new phenomenon to Polish Jews. Long before there was a Hitler in Germany, prejudice and injustice flourished in Poland. Jews were discriminated against, blamed for every misfortune, excluded from government jobs, barred from living in certain areas, not allowed into many schools and universities. These practices weren't part of official Polish law but simply came from a common understanding that Jews weren't allowed to participate as equal citizens. At some universities where Jews were admitted, Jewish students had to sit, or stand, in the back of the class. In general, there was a kind of mistrust between the Gentiles and the Jews.

Yet, amazingly, amid the prejudice and mistrust, Jewish culture in Poland prospered. Even though the majority of Jews lived in poverty, they were culturally rich. Through the centuries, Jews somehow had managed to cope with discrimination and poverty. They had established their own way of life: They had their own schools, libraries, and theaters. There were Jewish self-supporting organizations—orphanages, hospitals, geriatric centers, synagogues, cemeteries. And, astonishingly, on an individual basis, Jews and Gentiles seemed to get along quite well. Some were neighbors, friends, business partners, and even, occasionally, would intermarry.

Since the Germans came, however, propaganda campaigns led to unbearable conditions. My first encounter with the new laws came the day that Dad was one of those trapped in a street roundup. Along with about a hundred other Jewish men, he was caught in the street and taken away. He just disappeared. No one heard a word from or about these captured men until after five days, when Dad showed up, exhausted, unshaven, and dirty. His clothes were torn; he was heartbroken. He told us some gruesome stories about his experience. When he was caught in the roundup, he was not really scared. He knew the Germans, and he knew their language quite well. During World War I, Dad had been sent to work in Germany, where he was treated fairly. When he was taken off the street, he was sure that he would be all right, and that we would be notified of his whereabouts.

But these weren't the Germans many of these captured men remembered. These were Nazis. No one told the men what was going to happen to them, or when, if at all, they would be released. They slept only three hours a night; the remaining time they worked cleaning up debris, scrubbing sidewalks, and unloading military trucks. They were preparing the King's Palace for German occupancy.[20] It wasn't the work that made their experience so terrible; it was the treatment they received. Dad saw old men being beaten and dragged by their feet when they could not walk; he saw one of the men have his beard forcibly cut off, and another one shot to death. Dad talked about his experience for days. Whenever he wanted to tell the more gruesome parts of the events, he would tell Sis and me to go out and play in the yard.

After this first encounter with the "New Germans," or rather with the Nazis, he was reluctant to leave the house. He was forty-three, in very good physical condition, and of a happy disposition. He could run up and down four flights of steps faster than I could at the age of twelve—and I was fast. After his return, however, he was weak, his faculties were numbed, and he looked sick. Yet he still insisted that the Germans were good, civilized people, that he had only encountered a bad bunch of them, that it had been a freak incident. The guards responsible for holding him had been young, know-nothing punks; and "one cannot judge all Germans by the misbehavior of a few." Yes, he did know about Hitler, the Nazis, the Nuremberg Laws, and about the expelled Jews, but he believed that this chaos would soon pass. Not everyone thought the way Dad did.

VI. *Exodus to the USSR*

With all these changes, people started evaluating the situation and assessing their own options. Many, in order to avoid the grim reality, chose to deny the danger. "It's only a passing trend," they reasoned. "Eventually, conditions will improve.... We learn to coexist with the enemy, and then they will not bother us." Others, mostly the young and impatient, decided instead to take a chance and run. The only possible place to go was the territory then being occupied by the Russians. In order to get there, one had to take a chance and illegally cross the Bug River, which had become the new Polish-Russian border. Assuming that this venture turned out successfully, there was still no guarantee of being accepted in that country.

My only worries, at that time, were how to fill my stomach and how to have more adventures. School hadn't yet resumed. I was still keeping my diary, and I needed new materials for it.

One rainy day, our neighbor, young Mrs. Gurfinkel, asked me if I could watch her two-year-old girl because both she and her husband had things to do. I liked little Sarenka, so I gladly went.

In the living room, a couple of packed suitcases were standing against the wall. Mr. Gurfinkel was busy packing a knapsack. "Tell your father," he said, without looking up, "that we are leaving for Russia tomorrow morning. Only the three of us. The old folks and sister Masha have decided to stay." Then turning to his wife, he added, "It's going to get worse; just wait and see."

That afternoon I had a nice talk with my father. The reason I remember it so well is that it was the longest and deepest conversation I recall ever having with him. Dad was always busy, working long hours, or else was too tired and impatient to listen to my stories. But that day I told him about young Mr. Gurfinkel, and asked him if we, too, could go to Russia.

Dad gave me a very funny look, then a whole list of excuses. He said that he knew people who were going, but he didn't think that it was the right thing to do. From his answer, it was obvious that he had already thought about it. He told me that many people who left were turned back at the crossing; many others were swindled out of their money by fraudulent border guides. I was surprised by how much Dad knew about the exodus to Russia. I had thought that he would be hearing about it now for the first time. After a few seconds of silence, he looked at me and added, "Besides being dangerous, Mama and I worry about you kids, getting sick on the way or getting separated."

All of this sounded like excuses. I just wanted to go. It was a great opportunity to see a foreign country, to have new adventures. I had never been outside of Poland; as a matter of fact, the only places I had ever been were the villages where we used to spend the summers. So I kept reasoning with Dad to leave for Russia.

Slowly, Dad walked over to the window. It was raining even harder now than it had been in the morning. He stood there staring for a while, watching the rain fall. The deep wrinkle in his forehead became even deeper.

"What do you know about life?" he said, after a long pause, in answer to my question. "Don't we have enough problems without looking for more? When will you grow up?"

VII. First Year

Food supplies were dwindling. There were shortages of everything except decrees, debris, and misery. Endless bread lines were becoming a normal occurrence. Sometimes people would stand in line, taking turns, all night, not knowing whether bread would even arrive. On the black market, we bartered jewelry, clothes, and pillows in order to get food.

While thousands of people were standing in lines worrying, complaining, and praying, those with access to food supplies, and those with connections to new government officials, or with ties to the underworld, were doing a booming business on the black market. It was the first time I heard the saying, *"Podczas wichury, śmieci dó góry"*—"During a windstorm, trash flies to the top." Poland had always been a highly class-conscious society. For the rabble to be taking over the market was against the natural order. People knew, certainly, that such chaos couldn't last very long, but in the meantime, those who had the means were stocking up on everything and thereby creating more shortages and running up prices.

Most established businesspeople couldn't function in such eccentric conditions, so the black market became the "new economy." Legitimate jobs were scarce. Some people between the ages of sixteen and forty and with the right connections or bribe money, found legal jobs in a few German-run shops which were producing military uniforms, brooms, brushes, and other textile items. It often took a lot of illegal money to get one of these legal jobs. With small home workshops almost extinguished and factories bombed out or closed due to lack of materials, the normal way of sustaining life had been almost eliminated. People started working from their homes, legally or not. Under certain conditions one either adjusts or dies. We learned that lesson quickly.

It must have been mid-November when it was announced that primary school children would be returning to school. The 1939-40 school year was to have been my last in elementary school. After the sixth grade, I applied for and had passed the entrance exam for high-school. (Compulsory education was required only through seventh grade. Students who were continuing on could skip the seventh grade and go directly to high-school. All schooling after that was voluntary, and expensive.) After such a prolonged vacation, I was glad to be going back to the seventh grade.

My happiness, however, was short lived. The second day of school, during math class, two Polish police officers walked into our classroom. They whispered something to the teacher and then walked out. Miss Braff, our teacher, turned pale; she was speechless. After regaining her composure, she told us that German gendarmes had surrounded the school; the building was to be vacated immediately. It was to be used as barracks for the German military.

"Don't panic," she said calmly. "Don't run! Go straight home, all of you. We'll let you know when to come back and where we'll be meeting."

This was the end of my formal schooling, but not of my education, in Poland.

It seemed as if everything bad that could happen, did. After a while even the rumors became more optimistic. "These odd conditions will not last very long; the world is watching. These are not the Dark Ages. In these Modern Times, with telephone, telegraph, radio, and movies, with newspapers, magazines, and reporters everywhere, people must behave in a civilized manner."

Those with more pessimistic views maintained that "This madness could last for months, maybe even for as long as a year. So don't be surprised if it isn't over soon."

In daily life there were no indications that anything would change. If it did, it was not going to be soon, and surely not for the better. There were more beggars in the streets asking for alms and more singers walking from one courtyard to another chanting songs of lamentation and begging for money or food.

But somehow—I never figured out the reason—hope was running high. People had faith in the future. Maybe by repeating their wishful thinking often enough, they could believe that it would come to pass; or maybe it was their faith in God that kept Jews optimistic. Anyway, for better or worse, life kept going on.

A *Judenrat*, a Jewish council, was appointed by the Germans. New, self-help organizations sprang up in the city, supported by the still wealthy and the newly rich. They set up soup kitchens and shelters for the poor, the homeless, and the refugees who still kept pouring in from other towns.

Conditions in our household reflected the general situation. We had no income, very few items left to trade, and all of us were too proud to ask for help. With the schools closed and no room in the house, Sis and I were looking for things to do. Before the war started, Sis and I used to play games, do homework, read books, listen to the radio, visit friends, and go to movies, libraries, parks, and ice-skating; we played hopscotch, and we attended social gatherings. We also had extracurricular activities: drama and sports. And there were theaters, shopping, and sleigh riding. In summer, when we weren't out of town, we would go to the riverbank and visit special recreation facilities for children; or, we would take short, one-day trips. Now, with most of these activities gone, Sis and I started exploring new territories, looking for some excitement and adventure. But neither of us was experienced in roaming aimlessly around town, so we started new ventures by visiting relatives. Almost all of Mama's and Dad's relatives lived in Warsaw, and we had our friends; there was no shortage of places to go.

Our first venture was to Grandma Ester. She wasn't doing well. Ever since she returned from the bomb shelter, she had been ill. I knew something was wrong with her when, after the bombing, I went with Dad to see her, and she didn't greet us at the door. Next time, when I came with Sis, she was bedridden. The house was crowded. Aunt Sara, Dad's widowed sister who was always poor, had been bombed out, and, with her fourteen-year-old son, Sheye, and ten-year-old daughter, Golda, was now living with Grandma. Sara's stepson Marek was taken into service when the war started. The last we heard, he was in a German POW camp. Stepdaughter Rosa, about twenty, was staying with an aunt. Aunt Bella, with her husband Yitche and two teenaged daughters, Balka and Franya, were living with Grandma, too, as was Aunt Polla, the youngest of

Dad's five siblings. She was in her mid-thirties and still looking for a proper man.

Uncle Louis, Dad's only brother, still had his apartment intact. His son, Cousin Shlomo, had fled to Russia; Cousin Abram, Shlomo's younger brother (who had lost his left leg during the bombardment while on OPL duty), was dying of an infection. Jadzia, their sister, was fourteen. She was helping around the house, waiting on her mother, our Aunt Tova, who was sick and heartbroken.

We didn't visit Aunt Leah, Dad's oldest sister, nor her married daughter, Shanna. They all lived far from us. We heard that they were managing. Sara's baby girl was growing, and her husband was back from the service.

Sis and I became the family messengers. We visited other aunts and uncles, most of whom weren't any better off than we were. I heard that three of Mama's cousins—Haim, Moniek, and Shmulek (with his new wife, Mollie)—had fled to Russia. Another cousin, Laib, was supposedly getting rich on the black market; everyone tried to borrow money from him. There were a few other cousins on Mama's side of the family who hadn't yet used up all of their wealth. But most of the other relatives were getting poorer by the day.

All the people we visited were very nice to us. On Mama's side of the family, there were only three children of our generation: Sis and I, and a five-year-old, Cousin Romka. The three of us were being spoiled by all the adults.

The person we liked to visit best was Grandma Ruth, Mama's stepmother. Grandpa married her sometime during World War I, after Mama's birth-mother died. It was after Grandpa's death that I found out this story. It didn't matter very much to me, because Grandma Ruth was always very good to us; she spoiled us a lot. Everybody had been happy to see Grandma having a nice life with her new husband. Only Sis and I had had a problem: What should we call her new husband? To call him Grandfather or Grandpa was unthinkable, because we loved our grandfather too much. After long debates with Sis, we decided to call him *"Pan Dziadzius"*—Mr. Granddaddy.

Grandma and Mr. Granddaddy survived the bombing with little damage. Not only was their home intact but they also had food. One of Mr. Granddaddy's sons, Gersh, was a miller who lived in Sandomierz, a small town on the Wisla River in Southern Poland. He was sending them food parcels. We were all very happy that Grandma didn't have to suffer. Mama told us not to go to Grandma Ruth too often. She didn't want her to think that we needed feeding. But we would drop in, anyway.

We also used to visit Uncle Harry and Tante Trude. They were translating papers and documents for the newly founded *Judenrat*. We visited a few of our schoolmates, even some teachers who lived not too far from us. Mama didn't like us to roam the streets, but there was little else for us to do. We didn't even need to help around the house: There was nothing to make it dirty. The only thing we could do was read. Both Mama and Dad insisted that we did so. But from books I gained no stories for my diary.

One day on our venture we stopped to see our cousin-friends, Fredzia and Renia. They, too, were out of school. They told us about their new plan: They were going to help their father with his luggage business. "Suitcases," they explained, "are now in big demand, and if, through some connections and bribes, Father manages to get some materials, he can reopen his workshop. Father will make the luggage, as he always did, and we can take it to market." The girls also told us that their oldest sister, Luba, had fled with some friends to Russia, and that their seventeen-year-old sister, Ida, had found a job in a German brush shop.

I brought home the news and told Mama that I wanted to do something like Fredzia and Renia, or at least to help out the girls in their new venture. I kind of guessed that her answer would be "No."

The girls' plan worked out better than they expected. Not only were suitcases in great demand by the general public, but as it turned out, German soldiers were their best customers. Unfortunately, Aunt Rachel and Uncle Yakov didn't think that it was a good idea for me to go with their daughters. I was very disappointed. Without telling anyone, I followed the girls to the market.

To my surprise, I found many teenage boys and girls selling and delivering goods. Many kids were now turning to enterprise. Bored with doing nothing, I started nagging Dad to let me do something worthwhile. A few days later, Dad came up with an idea. Due to his experience with the forced work, he was afraid to go into the street. He thought that I could deliver some of the fabric that he had saved from the store to garment manufacturing customers who were now running small tailor shops out of their homes. But I could do it on one condition: I would have to obey all the rules set by Mama and Dad. I had to take my sister with me (but not to walk next to her); and we had to go by streetcar while carrying the merchandise. We weren't to talk to strangers. If anything unusual happened, one of us should be able to give an account of the incident. I didn't like all the rules, but I agreed to the deal.

Most of Dad's customers—tailors—lived all the way across town, in Mokotow, around Plac Trzech Krzyzy, which gave me a chance to visit other parts of town. My enterprise went quite well. I was happy, and I obeyed most of the rules Dad had set; but sometimes I went off my prescribed route in order to visit some friends, and to explore new places.

On Swietokrzyska Street, I stopped outside Aunt Bella's haberdashery store. I remembered visiting there many times before, usually during the Christmas season, when we would help Aunt Bella decorate the display window. One time, about a year before the War, I saw a picket line of Polish youths standing in front of some Jewish stores who were warning prospective customers that the owner was a Jew. They were carrying signs that read, "Don't beat Jews. Boycotting is okay." This I found out was the slogan of moderate Jew-haters. The radical anti-Semites called for beating up Jews and smashing windows. I never went back. The store now was locked. The broken display window was boarded up. No one was in front of the store nor inside it. It looked scary, abandoned. I was passing by on the way to Dad's customers. They worked in their private homes and were hard to find because they had taken their name plates off the doors. I learned to knock only on doors that still had their mezuzahs on the doorposts.

I really enjoyed my newly acquired freedom of movement. Never before had I been allowed to run the streets as I did now. My diary was filling up with new adventures. When Dad's few rolls of fabric came to an end, though, my career in the delivery business was over.

I started looking for new things to do. For quite some time, I suspected that Aunt Naomi was doing something, but I wasn't sure what it was. With her looting experience and her Aryan looks, she could have been doing a number of things.[21] She never talked about her adventures whenever Sis and I were at home. But I knew that the small amounts of food that had been lately trickling into our home were coming from her. So I asked her if she would take me along to wherever she was going. The answer was "No."

Many people were now trading with farmers, with craftsmen, and even with the Germans who were stationed in Poland. Numerous stores reopened.

After a while, I found a new job. My new enterprise was selling candy. It brought me not only a little money but a lot of education, fun, and, of course, adventures with which to fill many pages of my diary. It all started on my thirteenth birthday.

Then, in Eastern Europe, Jewish girls didn't celebrate a bat-mitzvah.[22] The bar-mitzvah honor was reserved for boys only. Girls did have a special birthday at the age of twelve or thirteen, however, and my birthday was always special because I was born on Hanukkah.[23] All the years until now, whenever the third Hanukkah candle was lit, we would celebrate my birthday. It had become a family tradition to celebrate the holiday, my birthday, and my sister's birthday at the same time (even though my sister, who was one year younger, was born at the beginning of January). Each year friends, uncles, aunts, grandparents, and cousins would gather at our house for a Hanukkah party. For this particular birthday, however, because of the curfew, only those who lived very close to us showed up. I got a few useful gifts—a pair of woolen socks wrapped in a newspaper, a skirt, and a sweater that my cousin Zosia had grown out of, two books, and a game—all secondhand items. Sis got some things, too. Then we both got some *Hanukkah Gelt*, a whole bunch of devaluated paper money.[24] Usually our Hanukkah started with a special dinner, then we would have latkes (potato pancakes fried in oil and traditionally served with "sugar and spice and everything nice"), but now we had only the latkes, which were naturally sweetened from the frozen potatoes; we also drank hot tea. Everybody enjoyed the meal, and we all sang Hanukkah songs.

Through the window, which was slightly open, an icy breeze was blowing the flickering candles. We closed the window to save the light. Although the room filled up with choking smoke from the wet wood, the burning candles, and the frying oil, we continued to sing, play games, and tell stories. With occasional naps, we sat up till dawn. When the curfew hours were over, the guests left.

From one of the guests I found out about Gucia and her candy workshop. Gucia was a hunchbacked orphaned woman, who for many years had lived with Aunt Dora (my dead grandmother's sister). A couple of years before the War, that poor, inconsequential woman, at the age of forty-five, married a well-to-do widower with five children moved into his apartment on Krochmalna Street, where "they all lived happily till the War started."

We saw Gucia occasionally at Aunt Dora's house whenever she was visiting there. Now Gucia and her family were running a candy workshop out of their home. I told Fredzia and Renia about Gucia's business, that I would like to sell candy, but I had no idea how to go about it. They offered to help. If my parents would let me, they said, I could go with them while they delivered their luggage, and they would show me the enormous closed-in glass-roofed bazaar at Plac Zelaznej Bramy, and how to go about the selling. I persuaded Mama to go with me to Gucia to investigate the candy business.

The kitchen of Gucia's second-floor apartment had been converted into a factory. Gucia, her husband, all five children, ranging in age from seven to eighteen, as well as three cousins, were all busy working. Even the youngest boy was helping. When Mama and I came in he was licking sugar from his fingers and watching the cat. "When the weather is warm," he told us proudly, "my job is swatting flies."

After a lengthy discussion with Gucia, and a debate with Dad, I was allowed to start my own candy business. As with the fabric delivery, I had to obey some rules. I had to follow Gucia's instructions and get acquainted with the other kids in the business. I would not be able to start working until spring, and if school started before then, the whole deal was off.

As soon as the weather got warm, I started working. I had to be home between one and two o'clock—whether I sold anything or not. The candy I was selling was sugared dough flavored with artificial fruit drops. I was selling the stuff as fast as I could get it to the market. As a matter of fact, I was soon going to have to find a partner.

Sis, meantime, found herself a babysitting job, watching a three-year-old boy. She wasn't getting much money, but she did get all the food she could eat, and she was happy.

During the eight days of the Passover holiday I stayed home.[25] Already weeks before, I saw Dad meeting with friends from a charitable organization, which, among other things, was making sure that every Jew in town had matzo and kosher food for Passover. As in all the years before, the organization members were planning the collection and distribution of food for the needy. The ancient tradition was to be observed strictly during good times and bad. All who didn't receive from the institution gave to it. I remember once asking my grandfather if some people I knew were receiving the food coupons for the holidays. His answer: "Talking about people you help and bragging about yourself is not nice; it is not Jewish."

We always had guests for the first Passover Seder.[26] For this first Seder of the War, Dad's sister Sara and her two children came over. Aunt Naomi was with us, and an older couple from Lodz who lived in the refugee shelter located in our apartment complex. Usually Mama needed a lot of preparations for this holiday: Guests had to be invited, the house had to be spotless, and the traditional meal cooked. This year the preparations were easy. We only had one room to worry about, and there weren't many choices of food to think about. We had potatoes, matzo, and even fish and cake. We celebrated with a cherry wine from a glass carboy that was miraculously saved from the bombs. Dad read from the Haggadah, and Cousin Sheye asked the "Four Questions"; even though he wasn't the youngest as prescribed by law, all of us younger kids were girls, so the honor had to be awarded to a him. Sheye asked all the "Why" questions, and after Dad answered them according to the Haggadah, everybody at the table talked about the parting of the Red Sea and the freeing of the Jews from slavery.[27] We all knew that God would soon perform such a miracle again and free us from the Nazis the way the Almighty had freed our ancestors from Egypt. We wished each other *"L'shana haba b'Yerushalaim"*— "Next year in Jerusalem." The old couple went home, and all the others stayed until morning. Some slept on the beds, some on the floor.

After Passover, Sala, my classmate and friend, became my business partner. Every morning we went to Gucia's home to pick up the candy, then from there to the marketplace. Sometimes we met there with Fredzia and Renia while they were delivering their luggage. We would have a chat or buy a bagel. One day, a market guard walked over and asked us if we had a permit to sell our stuff. We really didn't know what he was asking for, but whatever it was, we did not have it. It had really scared both of us when we saw him approach. We thought that he was going to ask about the white armbands embroidered with a blue star of David, which all Jews over the age of twelve were required to wear.

(These armbands, like the yellow stars in the Third Reich, were to tell Jews apart from the Gentile population. It was hard to figure out why Hasidic Jews needed such special identification.[28] Long before the Nazi armbands and yellow stars came up, these men made sure that they would never be mistaken for Gentiles, or anyone else. That was why they dressed in traditional apparel. One could easily see their ritual garments with knotted fringes showing from underneath their gabardine coats. They wore beards, earlocks, and special head-coverings. Some, especially those in religious groups, wore satin robes, white hose, and low-cut black shoes. Their identification didn't come on their thirteenth birthday, but on the eighth day after birth.[29] Hasidic women, too, could be easily identified: They covered their bodies, wore long dresses and long sleeves. Married women wore head-coverings or wigs. Now the new law said that they needed armbands for special identification. These ordinances must have been designed to give equal rights to secular Jews.)

After the license incident, Sala and I were careful not to linger too long around that market. We ventured into nearby streets, then into other neighborhoods. As we walked, we would tell each other stories. Sometimes we would pass some familiar places and reminisce about our school days, friends, teachers. Other times we would sing songs—school songs, folksongs, forbidden songs. While in the candy business, I not only enjoyed my freedom but I also learned things from Sala as well as from other sources, things which the teachers at school never taught us. I heard about the "birds and the bees," and about things that weren't even in my biology book. I was meeting other teens. Sala turned out to be a great resource. I was the youngest in our class and the oldest at home. She was almost a year older—the oldest in class and the youngest at home. Even though I wasn't an envious kid, I always yearned for older siblings. These kids had access to "special" information. They usually knew about adult movies and dances, about songs and dating and other such important things. Sala's stories were even more informative than the ones I would hear from Fredzia and Renia. I felt so grown up. I promised not to reveal the source of my information to anyone. I just broke my promise!

We had a good time together. I talked to her about my childhood, when I was little and had a nanny. I told her of how I used to give my gift dolls to my sister because I would rather play ball, skate, or climb trees with the boys, than play house. I liked to walk barefooted, and to run after Gypsy wagons.[30] She told me that her father died when she was little, and that her older siblings had to work to help keep the family together.

One day we walked through Pilsudski Square, named after Marshal Józef Pilsudski, a World War I hero who fought for Polish independence. He was especially respected by Jews for his liberal policies. After his death, anti-Semitism increased considerably. Now the Square had been renamed "Hitlerplatz." The eternal flame that had once burned on the grave of the Unknown Soldier had been extinguished. There was no one guarding that honorable grave. German soldiers now occupied the buildings where government offices used to be.

Sala and I walked by a building where two gendarmes were standing guard. They looked at us and at the candy trays suspended over our necks, but said nothing. Then, one gendarme who was standing on the other side of the gate came over. He said something to us in German. "I don't understand German," said Sala in Polish. She pulled the cover off her candy try. "Bonbon," she said in German and, taking some money out of her pocket, showed it to the gendarmes, adding, "This much for candy."

Both gendarmes smiled. The one who had come from the other side switched his rifle to the other shoulder, took some change from his pocket, and asked, *"Dobrze?"* ("Good?") He gave her some German pfennigs and said in half-Polish, half-German, "This good Deutsch money."

Sala looked at me with questioning eyes. "Should we take it? How much is this?" she asked me.

"How should I know? Let's take what he gives us, and let's get out of here!"

Through a second-floor window, soldiers were watching this extraordinary transaction. One by one, they started coming out of the building. They bought all of our candy. "Tomorrow you come!" said one of them in broken Polish, "and bringen much candy."

Sala and I thanked them, saying *"dziękuję bardzo"* and *"Danke schön,"* and then we left.

On the way home, we stopped in a gateway and counted our pfennigs. We still weren't sure whether taking the German money was a good deal or not. Later, we found out that it was more than we had asked for.

We went back to the German quarters the next day, and a few more days after that, until we were finally stopped by our parents when they found out. They didn't think that it was a very good idea.

It wasn't long after our soldier adventure that a new ordinance came into effect. It said that all Jews living in certain ethnically mixed sections of town had to move out by a specified date, and that they had to relocate to the mostly Jewish section of town. No explanation was given.

We started taking different routes each day in order to avoid the streets where all the moving was going on; we were looking for new customers, and trying to break the monotony. On Bielanska Street we stopped at the place called "Automaty." It was a confectionery shop that operated like a vending machine. It used to be packed with young people, always full of life. It was now a shelter.

Another day, while on the way home, we passed Plac Zamkowy . I told Sala about the roundup and Dad's encounter with the Germans, how afraid he still was to walk the streets. Sala told me that the roundups had subsided quite a bit because there was a new way to provide free labor for the Germans. Some Germans continued their seizure of Jews in the streets; many, however, were now getting their workers through the *Judenrat,* which had been assigned to deliver a certain quota of people daily to the Germans. To solve the problem, the *Judenrat* would send out notices to Jews, who were to report for the job on a rotating basis. Rich and influential Jews could usually buy their way out. The *Judenrat* would then use that money to hire replacements. For many young and poor boys, subbing for the rich became a way to earn some badly needed money. Sala knew all of this because her brother was one of the proxies. One more thing I learned from Sala.

One summer morning, like many times before, we met Fredzia and Renia near the Bazaar. The first question Fredzia asked me was if I had seen our Uncle Sruel lately. "Well," I said, "why would I want to see him?" Fredzia didn't answer. I repeated my question. "Okay," she said, "you should see the way he looks without his beard." She giggled, then continued excitedly: "He looks really funny. Two days ago, some German punks caught three traditionally dressed Jews and cut off their beards. It was right on Nalewki Street, with all people watching. The soldiers even took photographs."

"I hope nothing like that ever happens to your father," I said, and promised to see our uncle.

Around Plac Zelaznej Bramy, near the Bazaar, new announcements were posted. Names of streets that were to be *"Judenrein"* were listed and dates were given. Those Jews who had to move, crowded into the Jewish section of town (which was already overcrowded). This time the move was explained.: It was necessary for protection because of some anti-Semitic outbreaks in the Gentile neighborhoods. It was to prevent Jews from being harmed. The Jews were given no choice in the matter, so they did as they were told.

On streets bordering the Jewish section, eight-foot brick walls were being constructed, "so that traffic can be rerouted because of congestion." A narrow wall was built across the street from our house, next to the thoroughfare, in order to protect the German occupiers stationed at the courthouse on Plac Krasinskich and in the adjacent park. On our candy route we found other walls that had sprouted up overnight.

Walking the streets with Sala, we saw more refugees with babies in their arms and children at their sides, pushing belongings on handcarts and two-wheelers. Amid this exodus we saw happy children jumping rope, playing ball and hopscotch in the streets, and some restaurants filled with people sitting at window tables eating; and we saw people lined up at soup kitchens and those who could no longer stand up lying on the sidewalks against buildings. And we saw vendors and merchants and peddlers, along with beggars and clowns and street-singers.

And there was the blind singer, led by a boy, who walked from one courtyard to another playing his fiddle and chanting songs. That was how for many years he had earned his living. People liked him because he usually composed songs about current events. Many people would wait for him at their windows, and almost everyone would wrap some money in paper and throw it into the yard, where the boy would pick it up and put it into a small locked can that the blind man carried under his coat.

Now the blind man had a new song called, "I Want to Go Home." In it a man describes the terrible conditions in the refugee shelter, but not the shelters of deteriorating Warsaw—rather, the ones in the Russian-occupied territories, in which most of the people who ran away from the Germans were being kept. The lyrics spoke of the inadequate food, the poor sanitary conditions, and the uncertain future. The refrain went something like this:

> *I want to return to Warsaw, for that's where I came from;*
> *I'm not used to life over here; I want to go home.*
> *Thanks but no thanks for your promises of the golden dome;*
> *Oh, please, dear brothers, I just want to return home.*

This song soon became very popular. It sounded funny; it actually made people laugh to keep from crying. It reflected the disappointment not only in the physical conditions in Russian refugee camps but also in the whole new social system to which millions of disillusioned people had looked for new hope.[31] It seemed as though the escapees were running from the frying pan and into the fire and could no decide which was worse. Among the returnees were our two cousins, Haim and Moniek. Their families were happy to see them back. Happy too were those who had no trust in the Communist system, especially the Hasidim. They had warned the runaways all along about the "Godless Society."[32] Now they were saying, "Well, we told you so."

The returnees, on the other hand, seeing the changes that had taken place while they were gone, were disappointed anew. They hadn't known about the shortages in all necessities, the ID armbands, the unemployment, the moving of Jews out of Gentile neighborhoods, the walled-off intersections. They had known only that it was bad and getting worse. On returning home, for example, many found their rooms or even their beds rented out. After many streets in the Gentile sections became *Judenrein,* the Gentiles living in the Jewish part of town were ordered to move out. This order included the Gentile building custodians who had for years lived and worked in the Jewish buildings. It was hard to imagine our building without Józef. He knew everyone in the complex, and was everybody's friend. It was a sad day when Józef had to move. Besides Josef we also lost other neighbors. A few of them we were glad to see move out, but for most of them we felt very sorry, and we were heartbroken to see them go. As for our family, we missed our next-door neighbor, *Pan* Rys. He was a government official, but since the occupation he had been assigned odd jobs. His last words to us, before departing, were, "We'll see each other as soon as this mess is over. This cannot last too long." We all knew that it would not, but in the meantime conditions deteriorated day by day. Even rumors were scary.

All winter we were hoping and praying for the spring to come. But things did not turn out the way we expected. Of course, we were thankful for the shorter nights and longer curfew hours. But with the sun and warm weather came bugs, lice, and a typhus epidemic. Food became scarcer instead of more abundant. More people became depressed. Hardly a day went by without new ordinances and new decrees. I do not remember all the different laws that were passed, but probably the one that affected the most people, and in the worst way, was the one that had separated the city into officially Jewish and Gentile sections.

Sala and I were still running our candy business. We worked every day till noon. It felt good to get out into the streets after being cooped up during the long winter curfew hours. It had been a while since we had seen Fredzia and Renia. One day, Sala asked me about the girls, and she wanted to know if I ever went to see Uncle Sruel, the one with the cut-off beard.

"I'm sorry, Sala dear," I said, "I just forgot to tell you. The next Sabbath after we met the girls, Mama, Sis, and I went to visit Uncle Sruel. Mama hadn't seen him or Aunt Hanna for quite some time. I hadn't told her about the beard. When we walked through the door Uncle was sitting at the table reading a paper. I looked at him curiously. Actually I liked him much better without the beard. I used to think of him as being a very old man, but now he looked younger.

"'Nice of you to come,' he said to us. Mama glanced at his face. 'Well, you see what has happened to me.' He sounded like a broken man. Tears filled his eyes. He was trying to hold them back, but they began dropping down his cheeks and into the rugged whiskers that were leftovers of his beard.

"Mama said she was sorry for what had happened. Sis and I didn't say a word; we weren't sure what to say. In his gabardine coat without the beard, he looked funny."

Aunt Hanna gave Mama a detailed account of the whole beard-cutting incident. She said that Uncle was lucky, that one of the three men caught in the incident had protested, so he was beaten; the soldier who did the cutting hacked out a chunk of the protesting man's face along with the beard. Then Aunt gave each of us a glass of tea and a piece of homemade cake and started talking about her son. Ever since Mordekhei left for Palestine she has been crying constantly, lamenting his absence.[33] She was sure that he had done the wrong thing by leaving his home and venturing into the world to work in a kibbutz.[34] She wasn't sure if she would ever see him again. He missed his sister's elaborate wedding, and didn't even get to see his nephew. But now, turning to Mama, she said loud and clear, "Do you know, my dear, I am glad Mordekhei is not here to see what is going on in this forlorn place."

We went to visit Fredzia and Renia, who lived nearby. A refugee family was living with them now. Aunt Rachel showed Mama a postcard she had received from her daughter Luba. It came from some remote place in central Asia, from one of the Soviet republics. It read, "I am fine. I am going to school learning to be a nurse. Don't worry about me. Give my best regards to all. See you soon." "We miss her so much," Aunt Rachel said. From the way she cried when she read that card, you would have thought that her daughter had just died.

Later, while we girls played a word game, the two women talked about the situation in Warsaw. Many more streets were being blocked off, and the Jewish labor brigades were being forced to do this work. Aunt Rachel and Mama would talk about were their memories of years past and their hopes for the future. They just knew that things would get better. They parted on a hopeful note.

A few days later, our family was struck by a personal tragedy. Cousin Balka, one of Dad's nieces, was run over by a truck. People were saying that it was an accident. Others were insisting that it was a suicide, that she purposely had run into the truck. Those who said that Balka committed suicide wouldn't say whether her deed had any relation to the War or to some personal condition. The sad fact was that at the age of nineteen, she was dead.

Due to the thousands of deaths and the crowded cemeteries, dealing with funeral arrangements was a nightmare. Besides, according to Jewish law, there were different rules for burial as well as for sitting shiva for those who hadn't died of natural causes. The cause of death had to be established not only for the sake of Jewish rules but also for the police. Polish law required that all unnatural deaths be reported and that the bodies undergo autopsies—a procedure forbidden by Jewish tradition.

Workers from the "Jewish Death Watchers" cruised the streets to make sure that this organization, and not the Polish police, claimed the bodies. During the whole tumult, I found out that Balka and her sister, Fronia, were Uncle Yitche's children. Aunt Bella, like her sister Sara, had married a widower and adopted the girls. To me it made no difference. Balka was my cousin, and I really liked her. I was sick and heartbroken.

Neither my sister nor I was at the funeral. Our family thought that we were too young, but we did get to visit the family during the mourning period. Both Uncle Yitche and Aunt Bella were sitting on low stools. The mirror was covered with a white sheet. A candle was burning on a small table in the corner of the room.

Balka's sister, Fronia, who with her boyfriend and a group of other people had fled to Russia, was spared the pain of ever finding out.

VIII. Typhus

W hen the typhus epidemic hit, it affected mostly the young. A large part of the population over the age of twenty had developed some immunity to this dreadful disease during the World War I typhus epidemic. Trying to prevent further spread of the disease, authorities ordered special procedures that had to be followed: All cases of typhus had to be reported to the health department. All patients diagnosed with the disease had to be taken immediately to a hospital. All apartments in the building from which the diseased person had been taken had to undergo a thorough disinfecting. All tenants had to be checked for lice and then be sprayed with antiseptic powder. The entrance gate to the apartment complex was to be sealed off during a ten- to fourteen-day quarantine period. The families of the sick and the unexposed alike were to be imprisoned in their homes.

The first typhus case in our building complex was Masha, our neighbor's eighteen-year-old daughter. Her parents didn't report her illness for fear that she would be taken to a hospital, and die there. The percentage of patients being cured in the hospital and the makeshift infirmaries designated for Jews was known to be negligible. They were overcrowded, understaffed, under-equipped, short on food, and lacking in medicine. Most patients were taken there to die.

After a week, Masha died at home. When the news spread, the front gate of our building was locked. Guards were placed on the outside of the gate to prevent anyone from leaving or entering the buildings. The inhabitants were stuck without food or basic necessities.

(It became routine for relatives and friends to bring by some food and pass it through the gate railings. Sometimes, black-marketeers would stop by and take advantage of the quarantined people by charging even higher prices than they normally did. The underground exit which was originally dug out as an escape route during the bombing period was now used for passing food.)

The disinfecting process began as soon as the building complex was locked up. The powder used on people could kill not only the germs but those carrying them. Men, women, and children were taken into designated rooms to be sprayed and checked for lice. Sis, Mama, and I walked through the Ladies' control stations. At the exit door, as we were getting our documents stamped, a young man from the sanitation department glanced at Mama. He stopped her, touched her long, just-unbraided hair with his fingertips, and told her to braid it up. Then without saying a word, he quickly took a pair of large scissors and cut off the thick, heavy braid hanging down her back. He put it on the table and, with a smile, said, "Gorgeous, isn't it?"

We walked out heartbroken, not only because of the lost hair, which would eventually grow back, but because of the way he had cut it off. By now, anybody could do anything to a Jew without any retribution, without any concern for justice. It was open season on Jews.

I had never seen Mama with short hair before. She had always worn it in a Grecian knot. Now, she looked strange. I looked at her saddened face carefully. I had never before paid that close attention to her looks; to me she always looked like "my mother." I knew, of course, that she had lost weight since the War started. Now, with short hair and a slimmer body, she actually looked younger and better, I thought.

Anyway, our irritation with the hair incident didn't last very long. Next morning, I woke up with a headache and fever. The first thought, of course, was "typhus."

Mama put her hand on my forehead, then the thermometer under my arm. The temperature was 103 degrees. She gave me a pill that she had been keeping for an emergency, and said, "If the fever is not down by morning, we'll have to hide you somewhere. Our apartment is scheduled for disinfecting tomorrow." Then she sent Sis down to Aunt Sara, not knowing whether she had already been infected. Mama looked fearful. Two doctors lived in our building, and at least one of them would come if asked. But there was always the danger that he might be seen and followed. Besides, there was very little he could do with his bare hands.

Lying in bed with a wet towel over my aching head, I saw Mama blotting tears with a handkerchief. Her voice broke as she tried to say something. When she saw me looking, she quickly turned to hide the tears, but still she had difficulty repressing her sobs. She turned her face away from me and walked into the hallway.

That night we went to see Dr. Flanzman. He was an older gentleman who, like my dad, was afraid to go into the streets for fear of being caught in a roundup, or being dragged away by the occupiers.

Remember, when the Germans first came into Warsaw, they shot a few doctors along with some professors, clergymen, and other intellectuals. His fears were well founded.

Anyway, Dr. Flanzman looked me over, shook his head, and said to Mama, "I am not sure what your daughter has, but it does not look like typhus. Watch to see if she develops a rash. It might be scarlet fever."

By morning, I still had a fever, but I felt well enough to leave the room when the sanitation workers arrived. My illness continued for a few more days, then it was gone.

IX. The Ghetto

More than a year had now passed since the Germans began their occupation of Warsaw, a fearful, distressing year in which many grievous decrees had been passed. I don't remember the exact order, but those concerning Jews stated that:

- Jews had to be identified by a white armband or a yellow star.
- "Jews Forbidden" signs had to be placed on buildings and in public places.
- Jews could be forced to work for the Germans without pay.
- Jews had to tip their hats before Germans, and get off the sidewalk when passing one.
- Jewish children were banned from schools
- Jews had no rights to assemble or pray.
- Jews had to move out of Gentile neighborhoods and into a section of town designated "For Jews Only."

Luckily, we didn't have to move, for our building was the last one on the block at the Jewish side of the dividing line. On one side was Bonifraterska

Street, also known as the new East-West Thoroughfare, and across the street was Krasinskich Park. From the front windows of our building we could observe German soldiers stationed in the Park. Every street beyond the Park and the Thoroughfare now belonged to the Gentile neighborhood. Between the end of the Park and the next building, which housed government offices and courts, was an alley leading to Krasinskich Square. This alley was now blocked off by an eight-foot brick wall topped with broken glass and an entanglement of barbed wire. It had been put up recently, built on the order of the German authorities with Jewish forced labor. It was constructed from bricks and topped with glass that had been found in the rubble of burned-out houses.

At first little attention was paid to that wall or to any other walls that were springing up all over the city. Adjacent to this wall, across from our house, was the block-long Appeals Court building, which featured an archway through which ran the East-West Thoroughfare. Every day, thousand of people passed under that arch to go from the Zoliborz suburbs to Castle Square and to the Kierbedzia Bridge, which crossed the Wisla River, connecting Warsaw proper with the Praga suburbs. When selling candy, I used to go through this archway almost every day, usually on my way home.

One day, something had changed at the arch. I know that it was a Jewish Holiday, perhaps Sukkoth, so I didn't go on my candy route. It was at that time hard to tell since there were no tabernacles, and synagogues were filled with refugees, not worshippers.[35] (Even if they had been accessible, Jews weren't allowed to assemble. To conduct prayers Jewish men had to meet in private homes.[36] That day, I remember, it was Dad's turn to hold services in our house, so when the men arrived Sis and I had to go for a walk.) Across from our building, next to the archway, was an unusually large gathering of people. They were talking emotionally, flapping their arms, some nervously walking back and forth, cracking their knuckles. "Let's go over there," I said to my sister.

Two Jewish men were standing near the archway. "Where do you girls think you are going?" one of them asked.

Before we had a chance to answer, we saw, on the other side of the arch, two Polish police officers, two German gendarmes, and a huge German Shepherd. A woman pulled me by the arm. "You can't go there. The gate is closed today," she said, and walked off.

No one seemed to know what had happened, but all were asking the guards the same question: "When will the road reopen?" No answer was given.

Sis and I ran home. I told the man who opened the door that I had something very important to tell Dad. The man didn't answer; he kept on praying. (At the time, I didn't know that this was a prayer that could not be interrupted.) I was angry. I was anxious to tell Dad about the Jewish policemen who were standing guard at the gate. They weren't wearing uniforms, but people said that these cops could be identified by a lapel pin. They were called "The Thirteens"—*"Trzynastka"*—because their main office was located on Leszno Street 13; they belonged to a newly formed Jewish police force. But no one in this crowded prayer room wanted to listen to what I had to say; the men didn't even let me in.

Finally, Dad came out of the room, put his forefinger over his mouth, and whispered, "Ssh...ssh.... Be quiet. The service will be over in ten minutes. Go get Mama; she is downstairs at Aunt Sara's."

Mama said that she had already heard about it, and told us not to worry. There were other streets open if we needed to go to the bridge.

All kinds of rumors had been going around since Rosh Hashanah. It was the Jewish New Year, on the anniversary of the terrible bombing, that the Nazis officially proclaimed the establishment of a specific city section designated for Jews.

The road across from our house never reopened. To the contrary, more roads were closed daily, till one drizzly November day, without warning, all entrances to the Jewish section were closed. The ghetto was sealed off.

At first, the Nazis had tried to disguise the ghetto as a quarantine operation to prevent the spread of the typhus epidemic that was getting worse daily. Then, other excuses would be given in order to keep the population from panicking, protesting, or resisting. Once all Jews were in the ghetto, however, there were no longer any more excuses. Only more decrees.

Gradually, the walled-off city became a separate world, self-administered by the *Judenrat,* with no German troops or Polish police inside it (these had been placed outside the walls at each entrance point). The ghetto had its own police force, sanitation department, even its own bus service. It seemed odd to see Jews in these jobs and positions. Because of discriminatory hiring practices, very few Jews had ever held government jobs. Now Jews were running their own economy and welfare system. Ignoring German orders, the *Judenrat* set up more soup kitchens, more medical facilities, more mortuaries, and many clandestine education centers—free of charge for those who couldn't pay.

But every time they found ways to cope, the situation would worsen. There were more decrees and stricter guards, less food and more dying. The ghetto became a pit of human suffering. There was depression, epidemics, isolation, starvation, a feeling of world rejection and indifference, a feeling of complete hopelessness. Other than dying, everything was prohibited. Against all odds, Jews tried to adjust to the circumstances that they couldn't change. Against expectations, people were holding on to life. Of course, there were some who lost hope, and some who committed suicide, and some who just gave up; but these all were in the minority. The majority didn't want to give the enemy the satisfaction of dying on command, or on Nazi terms. Besides, suicide was against Jewish law.

During the autumn months, right after the ghetto was sealed off, a dying person in the street would attract a lot of attention. Passersby would gather around the motionless but still breathing body and try to help. Sometimes an onlooker would give a piece of bread, a glass of water, or would offer to take the dying person to a shelter. By the time winter set in, however, people weren't only starving but also freezing to death. Then it was no longer unusual to see men, women, even children, dead or dying in the streets.

Hunger drove some people to madness and many to death. Those who died in their homes were no better off than those who died in the streets. Sometimes the bodies of the deceased who died at home were hidden for long periods of time, so that the families could collect the precious food card allotted to their loved ones. Those who died in the streets had their ID cards stolen for the same reason. So many bodies soon to be corpses lined the streets that, after a while, those who were still able to walk no longer bothered to stop. Besides, there was hardly anything one could do but stare. Many faces of the deceased were distorted beyond recognition. Even if someone did recognize a friend or a relative among the rows of corpses, he or she wouldn't acknowledge it, in order to spare the family the high cost and complicated procedures of the burial.

Occasionally, an observant Jew, if he wasn't a Kohen, would stop and cover the corpse with its outer garment or with a newspaper, if he could find one.[37] He would then weigh down the covering with a brick so that the wind would not blow it off, and, with a few passersby, he would form a minyan and recite the *Kaddish*, the prayers for the dead.[38]

When it was finished, all assembled would say, "Amen," and with a sigh or a tear, continue on to their destination. Sometimes, one could hear a worshipper say to himself, "Dear God, when, oh when will it all end?"

One time I was standing with Sala as I watched the *Kaddish* being recited over a little boy's body. I whispered to Sala, "You know, we all prayed a lot in the bomb shelter, and it didn't help a bit. Old Mr. Greenfarb, who hoped God would help him, well, he got killed."

One of the men in the minyan, a traditionally dressed, bearded Jew, must have overheard what I said because, right after he said "Amen," he turned to me and, focusing his eyes to the ground to avoid looking at me (by now I was developing feminine features[39]), said very politely, "Let me tell you something, young lady. The great rabbis tell us that it is men's duty to praise God for all the evil that befalls us as well as for the good."

I wasn't very impressed with what he had to say. The only reason I even remember the incident at all is because for the first time, somebody had called me *Panienka*, "Young Lady." Before going away, he added, "I hope you remember that God tests all of us. You must know the story of Job."[40] Well, I did not know the story, so I shook my head and said nothing.

Besides the *Kaddish* reciters, two other kinds of people would stop at a dead body: those who undressed it so that they could wear or trade its clothes, and those who were employed by the Pinkert Burial Organization. Both of them had to work fast. The first had to make sure that the boots came off before the legs swelled; the second had to load the corpses onto their *jinrikishas* (trailered three-wheeler bikes) and get to the cemetery before curfew hours.

A large number of those fading away in the streets were refugees who had nothing to trade and no connections. Having connections and having knowledge of bribery procedures were very helpful for obtaining life necessities; sometimes they could even assure a job in a German workshop, where one couldn't only get some pay but also receive special ID cards that would enable the person to avoid forced labor or being shipped to one of the labor or concentration camps that were being established all over the country.

Many people resorted to smuggling. Those who did everything by the law, by God's commandments, or by German rules, had hardly a chance of surviving. They were starving and freezing, condemned to die. To defy the legal system was to become a sinner or a criminal. Besides trading, smuggling, like other illegal activities, was punishable by death. Execution on the spot—even for children. Severity of punishments depended a lot on individual guards, their discretion and mood. They didn't have to answer for their actions to anyone if their victims happened to be Jewish. The choice between doing everything by German law—which meant to die—or resorting to some forbidden action, was whether to starve or to be shot.

For the ultra-Orthodox Jews, the answer was "God."

"If it is God's will that we suffer," the pious reasoned, "we should not defy God's Divine Wisdom and His Judgment."

For others, however, making such decisions was more difficult. Our Aunt Naomi made hers early on: She decided to fight the system. Before the War, she had shared a ladies' corset shop with two of her cousins. Aunt Naomi was tall, fairly slim, and, like Grandpa and most relatives on Mama's side of the family, had blue eyes and light brown hair. Taking advantage of her Aryan looks, looting experience, and familiarity with the black market, she began traveling in and out of the ghetto, trading with farmers and Gentile smugglers.

Like many other established and new black-marketeers, Aunt Naomi was doing quite well financially. These black-marketeers didn't see their job as wrong; they saw it as a legitimate business. According to their view, the only crime that they were committing was refusing to die of starvation. As for the ghetto population, they were providing most of the necessities and also the raw materials for the artisans, who were keeping busy making shoes, clothes, luggage, and other items that were in demand outside the ghetto. They were also bringing in information, news that wouldn't come through the censored media. Black marketeering took a lot of knowledge and skill, and Aunt Naomi learned many tricks of the trade.

Fredzia and Renia were still trading luggage; Sala and I were still selling our candies. We even added a new department to our business. We were bringing sugar and candles into the ghetto. We became small entrepreneurs. We were crossing the border through gates that, at this time, weren't too well guarded, sometimes slipping through friendly crossing points where the guards weren't doing their jobs properly, or going through places where the guards were regularly paid off. Many of these things we did without our parents' knowledge. Usually, when we made it through the crossing, we felt quite safe. Without the armbands, no one could tell us apart from the general population—unless, of course, we were stopped for questioning, as often happened, even to the non-Jewish traders.

Again, like all times before, as long as there were no new decrees, people would adjust to their troubles as they constantly repeated the old Jewish saying: "O Lord, do not inflict upon us all that we may be able to endure." No sooner had the people found a way to cope with prevailing conditions than new decrees would be issued. "Better," more reliable guards were put on crossing points and many underground passages boarded up. Each passing day, it became riskier for us to get out of the ghetto. Finally Sala and I had to give up our entrepreneurship. Fredzia and Renia stopped theirs, too. Smuggling and black marketeering were no longer for amateurs. Only the big operators could stay in business. The higher prices they now charged were justified by the enormous risks involved and the high operational costs, including bribery. Everybody down the line, from the people who sold the goods to those who helped transport them, even guards—Germans, Polish police, the Jewish patrol—everyone from the bottom distributor to the highest-ranking officer, all had to be paid off. Often even people on either side of the ghetto who just happened to see or know of the transactions, wanted a piece of the action. They extracted money for not informing the authorities. Aunt Naomi explained all the tricks of the trade, and the dangers involved.

After quitting my business, I found a job in our building complex. It was a combination of babysitting and instruction. I was watching four six-year-olds, three girls and a boy. I taught them some elementary reading, numbers, and songs. The curriculum was given to me by their parents. I worked six days a week. Each day we assembled in a different kid's apartment. Each day I was fed lunch by one of the host families. I also got a little money and, occasionally, a bit of leftover food.

Yes, during this period of starvation there were some people who still had some food. In our house, the food supply was going through different stages, depending on Aunt Naomi's luck, and on black market prices. Some days, we had a little food; often we had nothing. I remember how one day we feasted on a raw onion, the only edible thing in the house. Looking at each other, we could see tears rolling down faces and an occasional mouth bend into what could be considered a cry or a smile as the nutrients slid down throats. This meal was among those recorded in my diary. Those days, even the drinking water wasn't a simple matter because it had to be boiled before it could be consumed. Since boards from bombed-out houses and broken furniture that we used for firewood were slowly coming to an end, even a drink of water became a precious item.

We didn't use much water anyway. Our house was clean most of the time: There was no garbage, no trash, no dirty dishes, no bugs. We could open the window and enjoy the fresh air without worrying about flies or bees coming in. Even the usual smoke from factories that used to blow in had ceased to exist. After a while, even the mice and rats that used to visit frequently after the bombing had disappeared. Housewives became very inventive seamstresses and also very proficient cooks. As the saying goes, "If you don't have what you like, you learn to like what you have." These housewives learned to patch garments and to prepare meals out of the available food, the so-called "hot foods"—perishable items occasionally attainable on the market for more-or-less affordable prices. One time such an item was rotting cabbage. We ate it for a week. When it was gone, there followed weeks of absolutely nothing.

Another time, frozen potatoes, like the ones we had had for my birthday pancakes, came on the market; but the most memorable item, by far, was one we called "stinkies." It was a component of the seafood family that looked something like the waste from fish processing plants. The largest piece in this mess was the size of a broken sardine. This stuff, too solid to pour and too mushy to pick up by hand, was doled out with a ladle. One kilogram, including the water, was allotted per customer. Whenever a shipment of this delicacy arrived in the stores—and the aroma spread throughout the neighborhood—it lured thousands of people out of their homes and into long lines. It was the only source of protein available to those who were lucky enough to get it.

Preparation of this delicacy usually developed into a joint effort of a few families. One provided the "stinkies," one the fuel, another one the bread crumbs or flour, salt or spices, or whatever one could contribute. Small patties were made out of the mess. Whenever this gourmet food was served, we would have a party.

On the days when we did have a bite of food, it was my job to take some of it to Grandma Ester. For years, Dad, his brother, and his two sisters, had contributed to Grandma's support. Aunt Sara, who was the poorest and Aunt Polla, who was single, were excluded. Grandma was now bedridden. Only her mind was still intact. She appreciated the food I brought, and she continued to ask about our family. When she saw me leaving she would say, "Be careful going home, my child. You must survive this madness."

On the way home from Grandma's house, I would stop to visit with Fredzia and Renia. Their father and mother were sick, their luggage shop was shriveling; a professional smuggler was now taking the manufactured pieces of luggage to market and bringing in raw materials. They were struggling. Yet, every time I came over, Aunt Rachel would give me something to eat.

On the way home I would sometimes stop to see some other relatives and friends. Dad's brother, Uncle Louis, had had to move from his Gesia Street apartment. I don't remember where he moved to, but I can still see the one small room and the iron bed in which Aunt Tova use to lie sick. Before the bombing, Aunt Tova had been a vigorous woman in her mid-forties. Since her son Abram died of an infection that had set into the thigh where his leg had been amputated, and since her son Shlomo was somewhere in Russia, she had become a listless woman without any interest in living. By the time Shlomo decided to return home from his Russian adventure, she was dead.

From Aunt Sara, we never expected any good news, but one time we did get some. Her stepson, Marek, along with a few other Jewish war prisoners, had been released from a German POW camp.[41] It was the only time since her husband died that I ever saw Aunt Sara smiling.

Coming home from these visits, I used to report what I had seen and heard. As the news grew gradually worse, I would hardly speak; I would only answer questions, letting my face say the rest. Soon even the questions ceased.

On Mama's side of the family, things were looking a bit better. Grandma Ruth and Mr. Granddaddy were still receiving food parcels from Mr. Granddaddy's son, Gersh, the Sandomierz miller. Even though most packages were now arriving opened, and part of the food missing, there was still always something left for them, and some to tip the mailman. (We called such tipping "live and let live.") Whenever I visited Grandma Ruth, I always got something to eat, sometimes even a bit to take home.

Aunt Devora, my deceased grandpa's sister, was doing well. From her second husband, she had inherited some money, which she was now using to help her daughter and granddaughter. One day she was pouring rendered fat from the pan into containers. She offered me a few cracklings and a slice of bread. I hadn't seen such luxury items for quite some time.

My sister was getting along well under the circumstances. She liked her job and the little boy she was babysitting. She wasn't an adventurous type. She liked nice clothes, playing with dolls, and staying close to home; yet, we liked to play together. The only common friends we had were Fredzia and Renia. Other than those two, each of us had our own friends.

Halinka was one of Sis's school friends. She used to visit us quite often. On one of these visits, she asked if my sister would like to join a class that Miss Alla was now forming. Miss Alla was Halinka's older sister, a third-year university student, who, like all Jewish scholars, had been thrown out of school. She had decided to give private lessons in her home to elementary and high-school students. Miss Alla was going to take my sister into one of her classes free of charge.

Ever since our school was closed and Jewish kids expelled from all schools,, Mama had tried to teach Sis and me at home. Mama was a teacher by profession. After Sis and I were born, she quit working. She was now trying to give us home instruction. But Mama was often worried, sometimes even in a depressed mood. And now Sis and I were fighting over homework and grades. It had been a long time since we had been in school; worse yet, no one could predict when we would return.

Sis gladly accepted Halinka's offer. Everybody was happy for her, and so was I. Mama wrote a nice appreciation letter to Miss Alla thanking her for that generous action, and offered to help if the need came up.

Before starting her class, Sis asked me for my last year's textbooks. It was then that I realized that she would soon catch up with me in school. She was thirteen months younger and always a class lower. Such disgrace must never come to pass, I thought. So I organized six of my peers and formed a class. We went to Miss Alla for lessons. She was giving "discounts" to those who couldn't afford to pay the full price. The first sentence I learned in my French class was, *"Donnez-moi un morceau de pain, s'il vous plait."* "Give me a piece of bread, please." This sentence wasn't in my French book, but it was the most appropriate one for me at the time.

Working half-days and going to class took away most of my free time. All my homework had to be done during daylight hours; kerosene was scarce and candles very expensive.

In history class we studied the Holy Crusades, Genghis Khan, the Tartar Invasion, and the plague during the Middle Ages. "Is this war, too, going to be history?" asked Riva, the smallest girl in our group. All of a sudden, our eyes lit up. "Hey! We are living through real history! Our stories will be in history books!" we screamed almost simultaneously. "What is our period going to be called, Miss Alla?" asked Malka with a smile. The discussion made us feel important. Our troubles weren't in vain.

In late fall the days were getting shorter, the curfew hours longer, and the cold winds kept entering the ghetto streets and blowing the coverings spread over the corpses, often exposing the naked bodies that had been stripped of their clothes. Then came the rains and snow and more misery.

On the way to my class, the view is shocking. Every day an increasing number of bodies line the streets. I pass small children sitting by a fading body of a mother or father. These children don't cry; they don't talk; often their eyes are closed. When their eyes are open, you can read in them what the child is unable to say. Once in a while a stranger stops, maybe covers the body. No fuss. A policeman sometimes comes over and takes the still breathing child to an already overcrowded orphanage on Grzybowska Street. The policeman writes something in his notebook.

I come home and record this in my diary.

People just keep on walking. Now dead bodies in the streets are disregarded. A vehicle from the Pinkert Burial Organization comes by. The men pick up the body and pile it on top of the other corpses. The cart rocks slightly. The bodies shake as though they are still alive. I think I am getting immune to the sight of corpses. But I never really do. Not to the sight of dead or dying children, to those skinny toothpick legs and distended stomachs. I ignore them in self-defense. Sometimes I even stop to say a good word or share a crumb.

Pinkert's carts circle the streets from curfew to curfew, picking up as many corpses as they can handle. They can hardly keep up with the accumulation. Jewish law requiring that a body be buried within twenty-four hours of death is being completely ignored. The bodies picked off the streets are buried in mass graves at the Brudno Cemetery in Praga, a place outside the ghetto walls. The Jewish cemetery on Okopowa Street inside the ghetto is almost filled to capacity. Without large sums of money and special connections, no one is buried there any longer.

The Praga cemetery outside the ghetto has many drawbacks. Families are prevented from attending the burials, and they are barred from visiting the gravesites. Often the bodies are buried in mass graves. On the other hand, burying people outside the ghetto has one advantage: It provides a new smuggling route. Horse-drawn hearses never go empty. They often bring in food, fuel, soap, and medicine for those who simply refuse to die. The hearses go through the gates, often unchecked. With good bribes, they just show their papers and get them stamped.

Soon snow covers the streets and the dead and the still living. In Poland, winter comes early and is often quite long. Everyone, inside and outside the ghetto, even the rich and influential, dread it. Snowed-in highways, impassable roads, frozen pipes, and illnesses—everybody is affected. But, somehow, most people believe that "Things must get better, because they can't get any worse." We live on a diet of hope and new rumors. "Shipments of food are on the way," but no one knows on the way from where to where. "Things must change; it can't stay this way." Well, they are right; things have been changing all along: It is getting worse day by day. But people believe what they must believe in order to survive.

It was just before Hanukkah that the House Tenant Committee, which was organized during the quarantine period to deal with common problems, started meeting again. They discussed what could be done in case of frozen pipes, broken latrines, and the heaps of snow. These problems had come up last winter, when there was more fuel. This year, however, the committee didn't have to worry about rats, mice, or bugs; if these creatures wanted to survive the winter, they had better move out of the ghetto.

The committee decided to hold a potluck Hanukkah party for all the teens in the complex. One of the apartments was designated and prepared for the party. The tenants of the designated apartment squeezed in with their neighbors for the evening.

It was the first time that I had ever gone to a party without my parents or my sister or an official chaperon. I was a little scared and, at the same time, very excited. The party started with the lighting of the Hanukkah candles. We ate some bread slices, boiled potatoes, and some cabbage. We danced to accordion tunes and to recorded music. We sang and told jokes. We talked about Pinkert's Burial Company's booming business, about the advantages of living in crowded conditions, where there was no place to undress but there was always a warm body next to yours. We talked about Hitler's funeral, and what the world would look like after this mess was over. One guy said that peace would come to the world only after "the widow of General Franco came to a dying Stalin to announce that Mussolini had suffered a fatal heart attack at Hitler's funeral."[42]

This was my fourteenth birthday.

On an old crank-up phonograph we scratched out many hit songs from the record collection. I met many teenagers, some as old as nineteen, who because of the curfew were locked in their buildings. That night, I had my first dance with a boy, Jerzyk. He was attending first year of *Tarbut*, a Jewish day school for boys. We talked about school. He said that he, too, was taking private classes, but his were taught by a rabbi. I didn't know what else to talk about with a boy, so we stayed on the subject of school—teachers, secular versus religious education, books, trips. Then each of us had a cookie and a glass of lemonade. For a while, at least, we forgot about the freezing winter and the hunger. It was the first time that winter that I ever warmed up. We even had to open the window to get some fresh air.

We sang, danced, and enjoyed the evening. It was agreed beforehand that the party could last only as long as there was kerosene in the lamp and the candles kept burning. When it was time to leave, Jerzyk, shyly, and in an unskilled manner, moved my hand to his lips and, imitating a gentleman, kissed the top of it. I thought that I would die of embarrassment.

It was almost midnight when I walked into our dark, cold room. I knew then that the party was over.

A few days later, at about nine in the morning, Cousin Khava showed up at our door. "Grandma Ester died during the night," said the fifteen-year-old girl in a voice mixed with yawning. Holding her hand over her mouth, she added, "Sorry. I didn't get much sleep. I just had to wait till the curfew was over." Khava and her mother, Dad's oldest sister, Leah, had stayed the night with Grandma. There were also two other sisters, Aunt Bella and Aunt Polla, who were living in the house.

Dad knew his mother hadn't been doing well. He had visited her only a few days before and taken her some food. She was feeling badly, but her mind was still intact. She was still worrying about her children, especially her sons, whose visits made her nervous. She didn't think that it was safe for her boys to be in the streets.

Dad knew that it was now his job, and that of his brother, to make funeral arrangements. He said that if it weren't for Uncle Louis, who within a year had already buried his son and his wife (and therefore had some experience in these matters), Dad alone couldn't have made the preparations.

Grandma Ester was to be buried the afternoon of the following day, in the Brudno Cemetery. This meant that no one, not even her sons or daughters, would be allowed to attend the burial. The funeral procession would be able to escort the hearse to the ghetto gate only. It was agreed that Grandma would be buried in an individual grave, and that a temporary marker would be put up.

In the afternoon we all went to Grandma's home. Her two sisters, her nieces and nephews, and her friends came. It was cold outside, and some snow was on the ground. Her apartment and that of her two neighbors were full of people. Grandma's body lay in the living room, the floor covered with straw, her body draped with a black pall, her feet toward the door. Two candles were burning at her head. The mirror was covered with a white sheet. An old, bearded man was sitting on a low stool, chanting prayers.

Next morning a few women came and washed Grandma's body, then dressed it in shroud—a ritual that used to be done at the mortuary—in preparation for burial. The rabbi came, said some prayers, executed *Kriya*, talked with the mourners, and performed all the other prescribed rituals.[43] Late afternoon, four hours behind schedule, a horse-drawn hearse arrived. Grandma's body was placed in a box for transportation to the cemetery. It was then to be taken out of the box for burial. We walked behind the hearse for only a few blocks, to Zamenhofa Street. There, some more bodies were picked up and put into the hearse. All four of Grandma's daughters wept as the hearse moved away.

To keep the traditional shiva period, the sons and daughters should have stayed in Grandma's house for seven days; however, the rabbis had modified some laws and let mourners stay only from curfew to curfew. During the day, all mourners sat on low stools. Aunt Leah took off her shoes as taught by Orthodox tradition. Dad had stopped shaving the day Grandma died. Uncle Louis always wore a small goatee, so his appearance hadn't changed. But Dad looked funny. Every morning and evening, a minyan of men gathered for *Kaddish* services. During the day, friends and relatives brought bits of food. Tradition wouldn't be broken.

Everyone spoke Grandma's hard but honorable life. She had married at the age of sixteen, and had lost two children in childbirth. One of her sons and her husband had both been killed in World War I. I met many of Dad's relatives whom I hadn't known before. Out of the fifteen first cousins, there were only four my age; all the others were older. When Aunt Polla was born, her oldest sister, Leah, was already a mother. I knew all my aunts and uncles, and all my first cousins, with the exception of two very religious ones who wouldn't look at girls.

I knew Grandma's two sisters and some of their families. I never could remember how many other relatives Dad had. I know that when Grandma died, they came in bunches. Most of them kept asking me how old I was, what grade I was in before the schools had been closed, what I wanted to become when I grew up. Some told me how much I had grown; others asked how come a good Jewish girl did not speak Yiddish.[44] I found out two reasons why Grandma hadn't visited us very often: One, it was difficult for her to climb the stairs; two, she was skeptical of Mama's kashrut—her kosher-keeping practice.[45] In the ghetto, after the rabbis relaxed some restrictions because of *"Pikuach Nefesh"*— "regard for human life," the duty to save an

79

endangered life, which temporarily overrides existing commandments—only then had Grandma started eating Mama's food.

It was shortly before Grandma's death that we found out that Gucia had switched from her candy business to producing apple jam, a product more suitable for ghetto consumption. Because of Grandma's death, we had postponed meeting Gucia and checking out the new enterprise. When we finally visited her, she wanted to know if we would be interested in selling her product. Mama and Dad didn't want me to do any more selling, but Mama came up with an idea: She was going to try her own luck in the business world. When we returned from Gucia's house, Mom and Dad were still discussing the new offer. They talked late into the night. Mama said that she was no longer willing to sit idly by and watch us starve, or to keep selling our possessions for nothing. The only items left by this time were heirlooms given to her by her mother and father; some were even from her grandparents. She was getting tired of spending her days in food lines and fighting over bread or a potato.

(I remember Mama, her voice breaking, telling Dad of one such experience from having to stand in one of the bread lines: "I was so glad that day to finally get a half-loaf of bread," she said, "and this guy grabbed it out of my hand. I think I screamed; but deep inside I felt sorry for the poor soul in his tattered, snow-covered clothes. Icicles were hanging from his unshaven face, and his feet were wrapped in rags." She sighed. "Yes, I think I did scream, because a Jewish policeman came over to ask what happened. But before the cop had time to look around, that poor fellow stuffed the bread into his mouth, and like a snake, he swallowed it while everyone was looking.")

She looked straight into Dad's face. "I am going to do something about our hopeless situation, whether it be legal or not." Then, in a really strong voice, she said, "If it's illegal to live, that's too bad! I'm not ready to die, at least not yet!"

I had never heard Mama talk that way before. Even Dad seemed shocked. "I can't believe it's you," he said. "Quiet down, please; you'll end up with another migraine."

They continued talking, now about the horrifying ghetto conditions, the few months of winter that were still left before spring came, and other depressing things. Mama said, "Aren't we fortunate that at least our kids are being fed at work?" Dad listened but said nothing. He must have been feeling guilty for not being able to do anything about the situation.

Mama had always been a quiet person. She had a small circle of friends, and not even the abhorrent conditions would make her take part in gossip or idle talk. Many of our neighbors she had met for the first time in the bomb shelter. She spent her free time in libraries picking out books for herself and for us, as well as magazines for Dad. We took busses, streetcars, or sometimes a *droshka* to visit friends and relatives.[46] She took us to movies and theaters, and, during the Christmas season, when the display windows were artistically decorated, we would go window-shopping. In nice weather, we used to go to parks and on small trips.

Now Mama sounded like a strange person. Influenced by Gucia's talk, she decided to become a business person. "I am not going to hope for miracles any longer," she said in a reassuring, resolute voice. "I am going to do something constructive. At least, I am going to try."

Mama knew more people now than ever before. From the building tenants, her new war acquaintances, relatives, and friends, she compiled a list of potential customers. In the ghetto, one didn't have to be a salesperson in order to sell; food at affordable prices was enough to lure customers.

Gucia gave Mama the first earthen pot of her jam on credit, on a "Pay after you sell" account, something which she had never done for any of her other customers. Slowly but surely, in snow and sleet and blowing wind, Mama started going to Gucia's house to get the jam. She went by public transportation, a ghetto bus, one with a Star of David that circled only inside the ghetto. (Streetcars that carried Gentile passengers never stopped in the ghetto; they only zoomed through on a few designated streets. Gentile buses in general went around the ghetto.)

It wasn't long before Mama established a nice business. After a while, however, picking up the pots of jam from Gucia's home became a very difficult chore, and dangerous, too. Besides, Mama didn't care about going across town, especially not to Krochmalna Street. Sometimes Dad helped, but it was unsafe for him to be in the streets. He was pushing his luck too far as it was.

Once, after a long conference with Gucia and her husband, Mama and Dad decided that it would be better and safer if Mama learned how to make her jam at home. Gucia was going to teach her the tricks of the trade, but only with the condition that Mama would buy the ingredients only from Gucia and her husband. Mama agreed. There was one other condition: The apples and sugar needed for the jam had to be prepaid. So Mama sold another one of her cherished heirlooms and got into her first-ever enterprise. She finally was doing something constructive, something that made her feel useful and happy. Still, it didn't stop her from crying: The only thing that she had left to sell to raise money with was her wedding ring.

The night we cooked the first pot of jam, everyone helped. Sis, Mama, and I cleaned and cut the apples. It took a lot of willpower not to eat them. It was also the first time I had ever seen Dad wearing an apron. He looked funny. His job was to tend to the fire and to mix the jam in the heavy caldron that we had borrowed from a friend.

It was past midnight before the apples were cooked and poured into smaller containers. It was the first time during that winter that our room was warm and we did not have to blow out the candles and sit in the dark. Finally, Sis and I went to sleep. When we went to bed, we knew that the stuff that looked and tasted like applesauce would jell by morning.

Next morning, the stuff that was to be jam still looked like red applesauce. Mama looked worried. In the afternoon, when we came from work, we found Mama sitting on a stool looking into one of the "jam" containers. It was still applesauce. Mama was pale. Red circles under her eyes suggested she hadn't slept much the previous night. She might have been crying, too. She was certain that she had written down and followed all Gucia's instructions. But now everything was gone: the heirlooms, the money, surely the customers; most of all, her hope.

We ate some of the applesauce, and we sold some of it for very low prices to customers who, for the most part, were friends and relatives who bought the stuff out of pity. We felt forever obliged to them for not letting us down by helping us recover from the losses and disappointment.

After the initial shock, Mama went to Gucia, taking with her a sample of the "stuff." The mystery was solved in no time at all. One of the ingredients was missing. Mama hadn't put in the gelatin. It wasn't on her list. She did not know how it had been omitted. Anyway, that was how Mama learned to make jam. She charged off the losses as a payment for education, or, as it is said in Yiddish, to pay *"Rabbe Gelt."*[47] The next batch of jam was perfect, and Mama was in the jam-making business. She was very happy. We were all happy and proud of her.

As before, whenever things settled down and people started adjusting to the conditions, new ordinances came up. The source of apples was cut off. The apples that did occasionally trickle into the ghetto were frozen and too expensive. We were out of business again. However, we had managed to save up some food and fuel, enough to last a few weeks. Luckily, neither Sis nor I quit our job, and we knew that if we could just make it to spring, things would improve.

Spring finally did come. We had made it. We were the lucky ones; thousands had not. The only thing that improved with spring was the weather. We were no longer freezing, and the days were getting longer.

In Krasinskich Park, we could see the trees budding and green blades of grass peeping out from underneath the melting snow. The warm sun rays warmed our frozen bodies and gave us new hope. Still, conditions didn't improve. To the contrary, there were more shortages, more deaths, more rumors. Yet the optimists had the ability never to lose hope. Disregarding reality, they kept believing in propaganda, in rumors, that "Mr. X said that he heard from Mrs. Y about Mr. Z, who knows...." They tried to believe in dreams, in hopes, in a utopia. They wanted to believe in miracles, in fairytales, in God. So in spring, we lived on a diet of sunrays, rumors, and hope. Lice, bedbugs, and rats were returning. Whether they were Aryan or Jewish, whether they needed special permits to enter the ghetto, we did not know. They were just coming back to keep us company.

Passover holidays were approaching, and Jews started preparing whatever they could find to make the days special. The rabbis, now even the Orthodox ones, were making many adjustments. Under the pretext of *"Pikuach Nefesh,"* they now were allowing many previously forbidden foods such as beans, peas, and some cereals, to be eaten during the holidays. Bread, though, was still considered non-kosher, not pure for consumption.

Aunt Naomi came. We invited Aunt Sara and her two grown daughters, Mirka and Natka, who lived in our building complex and so didn't have to worry about the curfew. We also had our next-door neighbors over. Their daughter now dead, and their son with his family in Russia, they were very depressed. The refugee family who had settled in their home were spending Passover at a shelter house where a Seder was being prepared for those who couldn't otherwise have one. Charity organizations were no longer giving out matzo coupons to the poor; instead, they were inviting those without food for Passover to join in a common Seder.

We still managed to put together a meal, which consisted of a few matzos, some turnips, and a soup made of salted water and some parsley. We still had some cherry wine from that decanter that was saved from the bombing. (We always tried to save some of that wine for good luck, for the next year, hoping to celebrate the holiday under better conditions.) Dad, as always, read from the Haggadah, and talked about the miracle of the Red Sea, and how God directed Moses to take Jews out of Egypt. Mrs. Gurfinkel and Aunt Sara cried. Aunt Naomi and the two cousins talked about the Miracle, but in their voices and smiles was some irony, a sense of skepticism. Sis and I talked about the times when we used to look forward to this special spring holiday, when we used to get new clothes; when the house was specially cleaned and decorated, when we used our Passover dishes, the ones Mama's brother, Uncle Mendel, had given us when he returned from his trip to China and Palestine. Uncle Mendel and Aunt Helen had no children. They owned a textile workshop specializing in knitted sweaters and shawls. They traveled halfway around the world, often for business, sometimes for pleasure. They settled in Palestine next to Cousin Mordehkei. Just before the War broke out, they came back to Poland because Uncle wanted to fulfill his obligation as a son by putting a headstone on his father's grave (he was overseas when Grandpa died, and he missed the funeral). When the War started, he and his wife were stuck in Warsaw.

As at previous Seders, we sat till late into the night chanting songs and telling stories. Mama had a surprise for us: She had baked a potato cake for dessert. We prayed and thanked God for the miracles and the wonders, and for the infinite wisdom that benefits all of us. As the candles burned down, we sang praises: "God is One, There is no other...." The Seder ended with new hope. Next morning, we saw men walking to services that were taking place in neighborhood apartments. "The holidays must go on. Jews must pray."

During the rest of the spring and into the summer, many political events took place, but the main one was the surprise German invasion of Russia.[48] News from the Front began to come in daily. It suggested that German troops were penetrating deep into the Russian territories. Newspapers were announcing the achievements of the "Super Race." No one really knew which part was propaganda and which part fact, but many Poles coming from the East would confirm German victories. The Nazis considered Russia a backward country. The Poles were next on the list of inferiority; Jews and Gypsies weren't even regarded as human. And as the news of German victories was coming in, more Jews were shot, more were sent away to various camps. Even the greatest optimists would no longer dare to predict when this phase would end.

Right after the German troops crossed the Russian frontier, life in the ghetto got even worse. Hunger grew so widespread that even those who had survived the winter—and had thought that nothing worse could happen—were now not only starving but losing hope and their will to fight on. Corpses from the streets were being gathered like rubbish, thrown aboard hand-drawn carts and buried in mass graves. People no longer worried about where and how to bury the street dead. The perplexed *Judenrat* had been issued orders by the ruthless Nazi commander to clean the streets, bury the dead, take a census of the Jewish population by age, sex, and occupation, and provide the Germans with workers. In addition, the *Judenrat* was to account for all non-productive people—the old, the sick, and children. The Germans made sure that everything was done punctually, and in exact order.

Jews were now ordered to surrender all their tangible belongings: gold, silver, furs, even such small items as fur collars, cuffs, and muffs. Germans needed money for the Front, and their soldiers needed warm clothes for the soon-approaching Russian winter. Some of these Jewish possessions were forwarded to Germany, to the German wives, sisters, and mothers whose men were out fighting for the "honor of their country." For the Jews, there was a death penalty for non-compliance with the new ordinance. Later, pianos, sewing machines, cameras, and rugs also had to be turned in. All these items had to be taken to an assigned point, where trucks were waiting to haul them away. Prices of these commodities kept falling. And those Jews and Poles who wanted to risk their lives to buy up these "forbidden" items were looking for bargains.

When the occupying forces entered Poland everybody—Poles and Jews alike—had to surrender their weapons. It was understood that this was for the protection of the occupiers. But what was happening now was outright robbery, and people were astounded. Many started burning their small items instead of giving them to the Germans. Some were even giving things away to smugglers who would take them to the Aryan side. What was one to do with such items like machines, musical instruments, rugs, factory equipment? Was it worth risking one's life over such things? Most people complied with the order.

Before we had adjusted to this new ordinance, another one was on the way. Jews were to report to the authorities all non-Jews who were inside the ghetto. The Germans were looking for communists, criminals, political opponents, and instigators who were supposedly in hiding. Strict enforcement of this law was announced; everyone in the ghetto would pay the consequences for non-compliance.

There was no end to the decrees and the torments. Mama walked around with an expressionless face. It was strange that her migraines would subside, for by all logical reasoning her headaches should have been getting worse. Mama had changed. She was no longer interested in reading. She was losing weight.

I had lost one of my kids. Little Lucia was sick. Bolek was still coming, but his parents could no longer feed me lunch. Only Hada and Roza were still relatively well off; they were among the few I knew who had some food.

The loss of hope was also having its effect on Dad. I never remembered him being sick. Now he was walking slowly, looking helpless and depressed. Aunt Naomi was working on some new strategies before resuming her "business" ventures. We suffered not only from our own problems, devastating though they were, but also from seeing our relatives and friends go down hill in enduring so much pain. We had to stand by, helpless, and watch people around us die. We could no longer cry; most of us had used up all our tears. Those who could still cry were lucky.

Older people took it much harder than did the younger generation. Even on empty stomachs the young were falling in love and dreaming of a bright future. For the young, there were still gatherings and parties, songs and jokes. A dangerous, unsuccessful smuggling trip would be turned into a joke. One about German gendarmes sticking their cold hands under the garments of women smugglers, with a pretense of looking for contraband, brought a lot of laughter to the young.

One evening, coming home from a teen gathering in our courtyard, I walked in on a discussion Mama was having with Dad. "What do you want me to do?" Dad was saying. "People are dying in the streets; I have no place to go.... I have borrowed money and food everywhere I can. I have no idea how to pay any of it back."

Dad stopped taking for a minute when he heard me walk in. Then he continued: "At forty-four I am too old to even apply for any job. To do any business nowadays one has to be rough, strong, dishonest, a downright crook or a soulless devil. One needs to rob and lie and push and bribe...." He stopped, took a deep breath, and looked at me. "The people who can still make it the honest way are few and far between; they are very lucky." He was talking nervously but not angrily.

Mama sighed and started crying. I left the room. In the hall, I heard her say, "I am glad the girls have at least something to eat, but who knows how long that will last?"

It was about a week after that conversation that Mama and I went to visit Grandma Ruth. She was looking well. She showed us a letter that she had received from Sandomierz. It was from Mr. Granddaddy's son, Gersh the Miller. Grandma served us some tea and cookies. She brought a bowl of groats and handed it to Mama. "We just got it a few days ago. Take some of it home." Then looking at a picture of Gersh the Miller that hung on the wall, she added, "If it weren't for him, God bless his soul, we'd be starving in the streets."

A few days later I overheard Mama talking to Aunt Naomi. She spoke in Yiddish, not mentioning common names, hoping that I wouldn't understand. "We are making arrangements to leave the ghetto," she was saying. "We are taking a chance. Anything will be better than this godforsaken place. If we are caught, it will all be over, easier and faster."

"Who is going? Where? When?" Naomi asked, almost shocked. "Are you taking the girls with you?"

"No," Mama said. "The little one is staying here with her dad. Polla and you can help. If things work out according to plan, all of you can join us later. I am going to take the big one with me. She is tougher and more resilient. She always liked adventures. She can expect some on this trip." Then she pulled over a chair and asked Naomi to sit next to her, face to face. "Naomi," Mama said, "we will need your help. I know you have some experience with border crossings, maybe even some police connections....?"

"I understand," Naomi said, "but you will need more than connections. You will need money and instructions. You still didn't tell me where, when, and how you are going."

"Well, my dear sister, I hope you can help me with the instructions. As for the money, I am trying to get together as much of it as I can. I hid my wedding band, but I am selling it now. I talked to my dentist. He is buying my gold crowns. I am selling everything that can be moved...." She sighed. "Now let me tell you about the trip. We are going to Sandomierz. Grandma Ruth wrote to Gersh; you know, her stepson, Gersh the Miller. He said he would help us get established if we could get there. She gave us the address of Gersh's friend, Isaak Schneider, who lives near the city market. He will put us in touch with Gersh."

"Why did you pick a place that is almost at the end of Poland? Sandomierz is so far away. It's almost in the Carpathian Mountains."

"Well, we hardly know anyone outside Warsaw," Mama said. "We surely can't get to our old relatives in Great Britain, or to Mordekhei in Palestine, or to those expelled from Germany who were sent away to who knows where. In this country we have no one outside this city. Cousin Haskel with his family—well, you know Grodno City was taken over by the Russians; there is a war going on. In Sandomierz, I heard, they don't even live in a ghetto, at least not yet. If we could make some connections through Otwock, it would help a lot. Mrs. Lonia lives there. The whole family is on Aryan papers. Maybe they can help us get to the boat."

"Oh!" said Naomi, wiping perspiration from her forehead. "It's going to be a long and risky journey. Good luck, Sis!"

X. The Boat

It took some weeks before all "legal" preparations were made. During that time we didn't talk about our plans to anyone so that no one could accidentally say, "There are people in our family who refuse to die here in the ghetto." Anyway, Sis and I pretended that we did not hear whatever was talked about in our house, while the grownups pretended not to have secrets from us. Suffering was the only thing to share; silence was the best prevention against spreading it.

Soon before the departure date, Sis and I were officially informed about the plan. We were told that Mama and I would be leaving the ghetto soon, and that other members of the family might join later. We weren't told any details. We talked till late into the night reminiscing about the good old times when food was plentiful and the only things we kids were afraid of was the barking of a loose dog. Talking about the past made us feel good. The present and the upcoming trip were scary and depressing, the future unpredictable.

The night before the departure, we didn't even talk. We just heard one other sigh and the squeaks of the iron beds as we kept tossing and turning. As soon as the first ray of the sun peeked through the window, all of us got up. Everything Mama and I were to take with us had already been packed the night before. That morning we just bundled up in our clothes: I put on my whole wardrobe, an outgrown dress, a skirt, and a sweater. Mama wore whatever she still had. It made her look somewhat bulky, but it was better than carrying extra bags. She looked very good for a woman over forty. Maybe it was due to my getting older that I was paying more attention to Mama's appearance; or maybe I was beginning to realize that from now on she would be the only person I would be able to talk to, to rely on.

I don't recall parting with my sister or Aunt Naomi. I was waiting for Mama in the hall outside the door while she was bidding farewell to the two of them. When she came out of the room she was wiping her eyes. Dad followed her. He accompanied us to the ghetto's hidden exit. I walked in front of Mama and Dad, thinking about the upcoming "adventure." Mama and Dad kept talking with each another the whole way.

The underground crossing through which we were to pass was somewhere on Przejazd Place by Mylna Street, behind a movie theater called *Promien*—"The Ray." Two young men were waiting for us a block from the theater. A young woman was standing a few meters away. She asked Mama for the password, then winked at Dad to disappear. He turned around, waved his hand at shoulder height, and walked away without ever glancing back.

The woman scratched her upper left arm: a sign for us to remove our armbands. She led us into a large courtyard where a group of Jewish escapees, and a few Gentile smugglers, were already waiting. She then led us to a basement apartment, then through it to a door where one of the men appeared again. He led us into a long, dark tunnel. We held on to each other. In front of us were a young couple with a little girl, about five or six years old, and the guide; all the others were behind us. Once the door was locked behind us, there was no light either at the beginning or at the end of the long tunnel.

Growing used to the darkness, I saw pipes on both sides of the narrow tunnel. Soft drops of water dripping from the pipes onto the dirt floor sounded like marching boots stepping over hard asphalt. After a time, our guide gave a quick flicker with his flashlight: We were nearing the end of the tunnel. A door opened, and we walked into an unoccupied basement apartment. A Polish guide then took over. He escorted us through some courtyards to a gate that lead to somewhere around Bielanska and Leszno Streets. He wished us *"Szczęśliwej Podróży"*—"Bon voyage"—and turned back to the direction from which he had come, most likely to pick up more "clients." Equipped with train tickets, a few zlotys, and our Sandomierz connection, Mama and I ventured into the world.

On the Gentile side of the tunnel, the sidewalk was lined with people. There were a few adults, but mostly it was teenage boys and girls. They were waiting for us with stretched-out hands, and in a "trick-or-treat" manner, they were saying to everyone coming out of the tunnel, "Give us money, or we'll call the police." To the Jews, they yelled, "Hey, kikes, the *Schwabs* will kill you if you're caught!"[49]

We had been warned, and we were now prepared; it was all part of Naomi's instructions: Everyone would put some cash into each squealer's hand. Those who refused were followed and yelled at until they paid up.

We took a streetcar to Dworzec Wschodni—the Eastern Train Station in Praga. We sat in the back of the car, separately. Even when we transferred streetcars we tried to stay apart but within sight of each other.

The Eastern Station was crowded with men and women. Groups of German soldiers loaded with their gear were waiting for a military train. They were smoking cigarettes and singing songs. We walked past the long lines of people at the cashier window; with tickets in hand, we went right to the gate.

The steam engine train that now had replaced the electric one was crowded with people carrying bags, boxes, sacks, baskets, and packages of every imaginable kind. We were heading for Otwock, a small resort town about seventy-five kilometers southeast of Warsaw, from where a boat would take us to Sandomierz. Otwock was the last stop on a line of about eight small resort towns. We were squeezed in the car so that we could hardly move, which was just fine since fewer passengers would be able to start the usual trip conversations.

The distant view of green fields and forests was refreshing after the gray, tall ghetto buildings, the crowded streets, and the barbed-wired brick walls. As the train stopped in the village of Miedzeszyn, the conductor got into our car. He was barely able to squeeze through the crowd. I handed him my ticket; he punched it, then pushed himself forward. I glanced at Mama. Her ticket had also been punched. "Great," I thought. "A few more stops, and we'll be in Otwock. Hopefully, there won't be checks by the gendarmes who often board the train to look for smugglers and spies."

As we passed by the villages, I thought of the summers we used to spend out here, of the carefree times we once enjoyed. I looked at Mama standing across the car. I was sure her thoughts were of the same. One of the places we passed was the village where, a few summers before, I had met Fräulein Hilda, from whom I was to learn some German songs.

A few of Dad's relatives who had a whole lot of kids lived in the next village down the road. I remembered when I had first met them. They tried to be very nice to us, but the kids once told me that Dad without a beard, and Mama without a wig, and Sis and I wearing short, sleeveless dresses, looked very strange to them. I knew only the girls; the boys wouldn't play with us. As the train proceeded to the next village, I thought of the time, when I was about seven or eight, and Cousin Mordekhei, just before leaving for Palestine, spent a summer with us. His parents, who lived in the next villa, had a new phonograph that would go late into the night whenever he and his sister were visiting. I remember when my sister and I fought over whose turn it was to crank it up. I remembered the theater music for the opera lovers, cantorial arias for the older folks, pop dances for the younger generation. I liked to watch the people dance....

The train screeched to a halt. "Otwock!" announced the conductor. "Everybody out." The memories disappeared.

Mrs. Lonia was supposed to meet us at the station, but instead we were met by her mother, a woman in her fifties, with grayish hair. This family was from Warsaw but had moved to this place right after their house was destroyed by a bomb. Their Aryan documents seemed to work; thus far, no one had bothered them, even though all Jews who lived in these villages had long before been sent off to various ghettos and to unknown destinations. Mrs. Lonia had been one of Mama's private students. I don't know how Mama had gotten in touch with her. I had known her when she with her husband and twin daughters used to live in Warsaw.

Mrs. Lonia's mother picked us up and took us to a prearranged place. She led us through almost deserted side streets, where only here and there we could see a peasant woman walking with a basket of vegetables or a bucket of water. The old lady took us to an apartment which, except for a couple of wooden benches set against the wall, was empty. After dark, Mrs. Lonia came over with her kids. They brought us some soup and bread. While Mama talked with Mrs. Lonia, I played with the girls, who were about six years old.

I overheard Mama reminisce about Otwock; she talked about her mother, my grandmother, who was buried there. I found out that Grandmother had died during World War I because there was no way to get her medications, and, when she died, that there had been no way to take her to Warsaw for burial.

Happier memories of this lovely resort town were those of the Mozhitzer Rabbi, who was well known for composing music for prayer services. Dad used to sing in this Rabbi's choir. We used to accompany Dad and hear him sing. Mama liked to go there so that she could visit Grandmother's grave. Now this rabbi was gone, and so was the Jewish population. Mama asked about the cemetery and was told "not to look for trouble." After a while Mrs. Lonia and the girls bade us farewell and left.

We sat in total darkness, looking through the window, counting the stars, waiting for the next step of our journey.

At dawn, an old farmer in a horse-drawn cart came to pick us up. Mama talked to him for a few minutes. She put something into his hand; he then tipped his hat politely and told us to get in and lie on the floor of the cart under some old coats, empty potato sacks, and some straw. We had no idea which route he would be taking to the river. He explained that for safety reasons he often had to change roads. Looking through the holes in the floor, we could only see the cobblestones passing under the metal-covered wheels. The cart rocked and shook and tossed us about. I began to wonder if this adventure was really going to be that exciting. I only knew that I was with my mother in Aryan territory, riding in an Aryan wagon being driven by an Aryan coachman and pulled by an Aryan horse. We weren't sure if the coachman knew who we were, or why we were going to the river. He specialized in transporting professional smugglers from the villages to the Swiderek, from where his business partner, a young fisherman, paddled them in a rowboat to the steamboat dock on the Wisla River, only a few kilometers away.

Our coachman dropped us off at an old fishing cabin where an old woman, maybe his wife, was waiting. We stayed there till nightfall, then, under the cover of darkness, we got on the small fishing boat. There were already a few people on it. In the darkness it was hard to make out who these people were. Mama gave an agreed amount of money to the young boatman, who then told us to sit down on the floor. When the boat pulled away from the bank, we heard the men and women give each other business instructions: What to do and what to say in case of a raid or an inspection. One woman was talking about the time she had spent in a Polish jail for smuggling, and how she had gotten out by pretending that she was pregnant.

The conversation died down as we reached our destination. It was about midnight when we arrived to the riverboat stop. Even though the ticket office wasn't to open till morning, the place was already filled with travelers. Since the War started, riverboats had become the best means of transportation between cities located on riverbanks.

When the fishing boat let us off, Mama and I sat down on a tree stump and listened to the stories of the professional smugglers. We didn't talk to them, and only very little to each other.

Mama had already told me that if anything should happen to her on the way, or if we got separated, I should try to get to Sandomierz or to any other place on the river. "Go to farmers; maybe you can work there for food. For God's sake, do not try to return to the ghetto." I assured her that I would do as I was told, that I would be okay. In reality, however, I was scared even to think about being alone. I was almost sure that I wouldn't know what to do if Mama wasn't around.

At about six in the morning a cashier, an information clerk, and four Polish guards showed up for work. The passengers lined up at the ticket window. Our tickets had been arranged earlier, so we were allowed onto the pier. This by no means guaranteed a place on the boat, but it did give us a better chance.

The waiting passengers became worried when the riverboat finally arrived already packed with travelers. Their worries proved well justified because the rule was that the number of passengers allowed onboard the steamer was the same as the number to depart from it. Mama and I were lucky. We were the first to get on. The next boat, we heard, could show up within six to twelve hours.

The voyage to Sandomierz was to take about three or four days, with five scheduled stops (and usually a number of unscheduled ones, if the boat was stopped and searched). Some of the people we met on board had been there three or four days already, many sleeping on benches or on the floor. Some asked us if they could buy any food at this stop; they were disappointed to learn that there was none.

Mama and I got onto the middle deck, where we found a couple of vacant spaces on the floor. We had taken some bread, jam, and a two-liter bottle of boiled cold drinking water, all of which was to last us until some food was available. Despite deciding not to do so, we sat next to each other, anyway. We tried not to talk. As soon as we left home we put all our troubles into the proper perspective. We sorted out what was important for our immediate survival, leaving all other problems, those of the past and those we had no power to change, behind the ghetto walls. We decided not to talk about things that could have or should have been done better, or differently. We were preparing for new unknown problems. We had recalled an old Yiddish song whose refrain went something like:

> *Yesterday will never return,*
> *And who knows what tomorrow can bring,*
> *Today is the only day that belongs to us,*
> *So be happy and enjoy it.*

In these uncertain times, making plans for the future was just as meaningless as thinking of changing the past. We learned to take things day-by-day, and to make decisions on the spot. Only a filled stomach and a safe place to put down one's head were worth worrying about. Everything else was trivial.

The boat whistle that signaled departures didn't go off. It was only when we saw the gray smoke dissipating into the clear sky, did we know that the boat was soon to move. The sun was rising. The gangplank was pulled away. The black water widened between the boat and the shore. The boat began swaying. "God spare us," whispered a woman next to us, crossing herself. We stood up to look at the river and the slowly receding boat stop. We enjoyed the breeze of the fresh, warm air and the view of people working in the fields. It had been a long time since we were allowed such luxury as fresh air. The ghetto boundaries had been drawn to exclude all parks and playgrounds.

The steamboat sailed southward up the murky Wisla River. We passed orchards and forests; we watched huts with thatched roofs peeking from behind budding trees. I looked at Mama. She had tears in her eyes. She sighed heavily. I wasn't sure if it was the view, the fresh air, some pleasant memory, or the sadness of leaving her home and family, that made her cry.

I kept forgetting where I was and why I was there. Then a feeling of panic, like a flash of lightening, ran through my body, and a weird thought hit my brain: "What if Mama and I get separated?" I looked at her. She was now listening to the conversation of the people next to us, who were talking about the searches that happened quite often on the boat. Among them were regular travelers, refugees, and some professional smugglers. They had many things to say. The only things that we were smuggling were deep in our minds: the names and addresses of the two men we were to meet in Sandomierz.

We had no IDs. If caught, it was safer to have "lost" one's ID than to have one that said *"Jude."* Smuggling, like traveling without a permit, was a big offense, punishable by confiscation of merchandise, jail sentences, forced labor in Germany, or even time in some *Konzentrationslager*—a concentration camp. Punishment for being Jewish was torture and death.

At twilight, the steamer halted at a boat stop. We bought some bread and a small paper bag of sunflower seeds, and filled our bottle with boiled water. Some passengers got off, others got on, and the boat was on its way again. We slept very little that night. Besides the excitement that did not let us sleep, there was a middle-aged, unshaven man drinking some stinking alcoholic beverage from a bottle, who was telling some incoherent stories about his smuggling adventures and about Jews being kicked, beaten, or taken off boats and trains. He had even seen some shot. He seemed to be enjoying his stories. He told a few anti-Semitic jokes; some people laughed. Then he dropped to the floor and began to snore so loudly that he must have awakened some fish in the river.

A couple of days later, at dawn, the boat halted in Kazimierz. The gorgeous little town on rolling hills overlooking the river bank was altogether different from anything I had ever seen on the Mazowsze Plateau, where Warsaw is located. The only places I had seen such a beautiful view was in black-and-white movies or color picture books. It was so overwhelming that I wanted to scream for joy. Then I remembered the rule: *Don't talk if you don't have to.*

Mama went out to get some food while I kept our place on the crowded deck. As in every harbor, people were departing and boarding. When Mama returned she brought with her a new supply of water, a paper funnel of garbanzo beans, and some bad news: "People on the pier were saying that there is going to be an inspection onboard." Then in a shaky voice she added, "I would have stayed in the harbor if I hadn't left you here."

As she was talking we saw four good-looking German gendarmes blocking the entrance to the gangplank. They were letting people get on, but not off. Followed by three Polish policemen and two young SS soldiers, they entered the boat. One of the officers announced an inspection, and started explaining to the young soldiers, who seemed to be apprentices in this trade, some of the procedures for searching and reporting seizures.

By Pure Luck

As soon as the gangplank was pulled away, the German gendarmes, accompanied by a Polish police translator, walked up and down the aisle, picking out suspicious passengers and pushing them to one side of the deck. One of the gendarmes glanced at me. He moved away. Another stopped next to Mama. For a few seconds he looked at her, then he stepped back, looked at me, and asked through an interpreter, "Are you two together?"

Mama looked him straight in the face, and said, "No, sir, I am alone." With a hand gesture, he indicated that she should follow him. Soon, all selected people—there must have been sixty or more—were told to take their belongings with them and get down into the hold. The Polish policemen were keeping order on the deck, where tensions were rising by the minute.

From the first few people who returned, we heard that each of them had been taken into a small, closed-up room, questioned, and then searched. One of the women said that the Germans had undressed her, searched all her bags, and confiscated all of her better things and all of her money. While she was talking I thought of all the things Mama had told me before we left home and at the stop near Otwock. "What if Mama gets arrested?" I thought.

After some time—what seemed like hours— Mama came back on deck, looking pale and shaken. She still had her wicker basket, the one that she had taken with her to the inspection. I was so confused when they took her away that I hadn't even noticed that she had left the small bag next to me on the floor. Actually, it didn't matter; no one would try to take it way, surely not during a search. I didn't know what the searchers did to her since I couldn't ask, but I was relieved to know that she was still with me.

The search went on for a few hours. We knew that it was over when the gendarmes and police left the boat at the next stop. It was then that Mama and I got to say our first words to each other. She told me that whatever the gendarmes asked her, she replied, *"Nicht sprechen deutsch"*—"I no speaking German" (although she remembered quite a bit of the language that she had learned during World War I). Then she worried that she might slip and say something wrong, or answer an untranslated question. By then it would have been too late to change a statement. In addition, she said, she was worried about me. In confusion, she almost forgot about being Jewish. With all the Gentiles around her, she began to think that she was one of them. Again, luck had been on our side. These gendarmes were assigned to look for smugglers, not for Jews. They were only doing their job. Even so, the process usually depended on each individual searcher's mood on that day. Whether he would or wouldn't harm his victim was up to his discretion. Germans were allowed to do with the Poles as they wished. In German eyes, any person outside of the "Master Race," especially a person from occupied territories—be he Pole, Russian, Greek, Hungarian, whatever—wasn't worthy of consideration. Gypsies and Jews, of course, had forfeited their right to life. To think otherwise was insane. So, when one of the "apprentice searchers" told Mama to take her *"verfluchte Korb und raus!* [damned basket and get out!],"* she almost started running, but luckily caught herself in time, and waited for the translator. In her head, she knew she was safe—at least for the time being. A long time passed before Mama could utter another word. She wasn't sure whether she really remembered all that had happened to her in that little room. She did, however, remember coming face-to-face with the gendarmes and fearing that one might ask her for identification papers. None did. "They were looking for smugglers," Mama said. "I saw them taking away cigarettes, ham, money; some even took flour, grits, and other less expensive items. I watched them stuffing their own pockets with confiscated money. They took the money I had on me. Good thing that we still have some in that little bag I left here. Anyway, I was lucky they weren't hunting for Jews." She breathed a sigh of relief. "Some of the guys seemed to be having a good time. I saw them dividing things and cigarettes among themselves. One of the younger ones took a small chain with a cross off a woman's neck and stuck it in his pocket." Mama paused for a minute, then asked, "Do you remember that drunk who was snoring all night? Well, they arrested him. They also took away a woman who carried some saccharine under her dress...."

The rest of our voyage to Sandomierz went by uneventfully. We again enjoyed the scenery and the fresh air. We got into a conversation with couples who had already been on the boat when we boarded it. We were glad to hear that these friendly people were going all the way to Krakow, not getting off in Sandomierz with us. One told us that they had made a few trips before and had never had an uneventful journey. The husband was arrested once, but after a few days, and through special connections, he was let out of the Polish jail. "After each trip," said the lady, "we keep telling ourselves that it would be the last one. But somehow we always seem to go again." Mama told her that our house in Warsaw had been bombed out during the invasion, and that we were now going to live with some relatives on a farm.

We arrived in Sandomierz during the night. We waited at the harbor till morning. At dawn, we admired the breathtaking view of green hills being illuminated by the rising sun. The clear waters of the upstream Wisla were really refreshing. We could have stayed there for hours. But after a while, we started walking toward town.

There was still no end in sight to my education.

XI. Sandomierz

As Mama and I walked down the unpaved path on the side of a hilly road, we watched horse-drawn wagons loaded with goods going toward town. Everything around us seemed very peaceful, calm. Closer to the city we watched some merchants opening their shops. We passed a few old bearded Jews dressed in their traditional clothes, wearing the blue-starred armbands. Mama stopped one of them and asked for directions to the city market. Before he showed us the way, he told us about life in Sandomierz, how much people, especially Jews, had suffered since the War. He said that the synagogue had been burned down. He talked about the many people killed by the SS invaders and other terrible things that had befallen that small, peaceful town. When Mama told him that we came from Warsaw, he stopped talking about the problems of Sandomierz. He said that he had heard many rumors about the troubles in the big cities. He explained that life in his *shtetl* wouldn't be a picnic for us, but that it should be better than what we had had in Warsaw.[50] He then changed the conversation to his personal problems. He told us that his wife had died a year ago because Jews weren't admitted to the hospital. Two of his sons had left for the USSR with a group of other young men. "You can't talk to these young people nowadays. I asked them to stay home with us; they wouldn't listen." Thus far, he hadn't gotten any letters from them, but he had learned through others that one of his sons was in the Red Army.[51] He gave us directions to the city market.

Sandomierz was a completely new experience for me. That small southern town on the Wisla River at the foothills of the Carpathian Mountains, was geographically and culturally very different from Warsaw. People seemed calmer; they moved at a slower pace, stopping to chat, saying "Hello," even to strangers.

Mama explained that people in small towns lived differently from those in larger cities, that they were more trusting and friendlier. In these towns, or *shtetlekh,* as they were called in Yiddish, one didn't even need a proper name or address in order to find somebody: People knew each other by their first names and surnames which were usually determined by the profession or a characteristic—Mosze Fryzjer (Mike the Barber) or Malka Garbus (Mollie the Hunchback), for example. She also told me a bit of history regarding this region, known as Galicia; how before World War I, it had been occupied by the Austro-Hungarian Empire; and why some of the customs and pronunciation differed from ours. Another surprise to me was the houses that were built on hills; a three-story building here was only two stories high on the next street up the hill. I was so amazed; I even remember writing about it on my first postcard home. I also mentioned it in my new diary, the one I started writing the day we came to Sandomierz. (My first diary I had left in Dad's care. I told him to make sure that it didn't get lost. He promised to watch it, and even asked, in one of his postcards, if he was allowed to read it.) Once we reached the market, we had no problem finding Isaak Schneider's apartment on Zydowska Street. A mezuzah on the doorpost, and the whirling of a sewing machine, indicated that we were in the right place. We were warmly greeted by the two tailors who were working in the small room. "Peace be with you," said the younger one in Galician Yiddish. "I see you made it. I am sorry I didn't get up to let you in. I should have known it was a stranger; our people don't knock at the door; they just walk in. How is life in the big city? Gersh the Miller told me to expect you, but he had no idea when. Come right in, meet my father, and feel at home."

An older lady entered the room. *"Baruch Hashem,"* she said in a very friendly voice. "Praised be the Almighty." She smiled, showing her few scattered teeth. The large mole by the left corner of her mouth enhanced her peasant look. She pushed her flowered bandana away from her forehead and said, "Oh! So you are the ladies from the big city. Nice to have you here."

Before Mama had a chance to say one word, the old woman announced in an uncertain voice that food would be ready soon. "You are going to eat with us and sleep in our house tonight." Then, turning to her son, she said, "Isaak, go and bring the straw mattress from your brother's bed and put it here on the kitchen floor." She took Mama aside and showed her a covered night bucket in the corner behind the door. Then she removed the clothes and sewing equipment that were cluttering the long table, stretched a sheet over it, and put some bread in the center.

During the meal, we found out that Gersh Mlynarz and his family had fled into hiding after the Germans rounded up some prominent businesspeople and hanged them in the city square. Gersh was hiding somewhere, either in the forest with a guerilla group or, by using Aryan papers, on a farm. In any case, his whereabouts were either unknown or a secret. Isaak was married, and lived with his twenty-four-year-old pregnant wife, Sheyndele, and her parents, a few blocks away.

We stayed with Isaak's parents for a few days, then we found a place to live in the same building. Our quarters consisted of an iron bed with a straw mattress, a feather bed, a goose down pillow, and part of a chest of drawers, located between our bed and the bed of our "landlady," Roza.

The original tenants of this two-room apartment were Roza's in-laws, a man in his fifties who looked seventy, and her mother-in-law, who was working as a cleaning lady for some well-to-do families. The bed we were renting was where Roza's husband had slept before he ran away to Russia. Her twelve-year-old son, Hershel, had then slept in it until we came. From now on he had to sleep with his mother. Baby Moszele, who was born after his father left, slept in a cradle. Roza was a woman in her early thirties who, as the result of a childhood accident, was lame and walked with a cane. Despite her disability, she was obsessed with cleanliness, which, by the way, didn't prevent lice and bedbugs from entering her otherwise spotless home. Her pastime was looking through her children's clothes and cracking lice. She was quite skilled at it.

During the first few days in Sandomierz, Mama and I explored the neighborhood, the town, and the possibilities of survival. We found the refugee center with its soup kitchen, an institution that proved to be of great moral and physical support to us. This place, which we called "The Club," became our source of nourishment, information, and entertainment. It was also a center for news and rumors.

Almost every day, new people were arriving, some having escaped from the horrifying conditions in the big-city ghettos, others having come from nearby villages from which they had been expelled.

The chief entertainer in "The Club" was a blind, middle-aged woman named Fräulein Else. She had come to Sandomierz in 1938 when the first Jews were deported from Germany. She sang in Yiddish, German, and Polish; she played the piano and told jokes. One of Else's songs was *"Vo Ahin Zoll Ich Geh'n"*:

> *Whereto shall I go when there is no place for me?*
> *Whereto shall I go when all doors are closed to me?*
> *Wherever I go, I am told to stop....*

Whenever she spoke in German, she reminded me of Fräulein Hilde and Tante Trude.

This refugee center turned out to be a great educational place for me, a new learning experience, an endless supply of entries for my diary. Even though we volunteered in the kitchen and did all the cleanup, we appreciated everything that was done for us. We were even thankful for the garbage. (It must be hard to comprehend that having garbage is a privilege denied to many.) It had been a long time since we had had any. But standing in line for free food made us feel like beggars. It was depressing. After a while I found a job babysitting for a six-month-old girl of a well-to-do Jewish family. Mama, too, found work. She started a new profession peddling sewing supplies, candles, socks, and aprons, which she would take to nearby farms and trade for food. Later, I quit my job and helped Mama carry the produce home.

For us, Sandomierz was a blessing. Of course, like most of Poland, this city wasn't immune from suffering. Many intellectuals were being arrested, many public buildings were being occupied by the Storm Troopers, many goods were being confiscated and shipped to Germany; taxes were very high. There were evacuations, deportations, hangings, shootings, and so forth. But the city hadn't been bombed, and there was no wall around the Jewish quarter. The only wall in this old town was part of the medieval ramparts. The Jews who lived in predominantly Gentile neighborhoods had remained in their homes, but they still had to wear their ID armbands.

Jews were barred from certain streets and public places, but these laws, like those of the armbands, were seldom enforced. Signs in the shop windows posted regular hours; market days were every Tuesday and Thursday. Only staple crops and necessities were available. Although it was nothing to brag about, we appreciated everything, having come from Warsaw. Whenever we could, we would send some of our food to Dad, almost always to an Aryan address from where Aunt Naomi would sneak it into the ghetto.

In late fall, Mama, too, quit her job. She started her old jam business. It wasn't very profitable since the expenses were high; but it was better than standing in line for free soup. Twice a week, we went to the market and traded with farmers. Then winter set in, and the apply supply was gone. We were out of business.

Chanukah we celebrated at "The Club." My birthday went by without any fanfare. Mama got me a pair of used shoes that she had traded for the last pot of jam. I also got a postcard from Warsaw; it came late. It was signed by Dad, Sis, and Aunt Naomi. They wished me well and conveyed greetings from all.

As the winter dragged on, Mama and I volunteered for work at "The Club." I chopped firewood and cleaned off the snow. Mama helped in the kitchen and did some paperwork for the city clinic.

When curfew hours got longer, I spent the evenings at neighbor Heniek's apartment. Among the guys and girls who gathered there a couple of times a week, only two girls were my age; all others were older. Leon was in the Jewish Police Force, and he would bring us news and rumors from the streets. There I learned stories about broken hearts and sex and crimes, and songs about love and flame and cocaine. I wondered why Mama didn't like me going there. This place was a great source for my diary.

From the coded postcards that we were receiving from Dad, we made out that the situation in Warsaw had worsened. Naomi's travel arrangements for getting out of the ghetto seemed to be stalled.

In Sandomierz, more goods were being confiscated from the Poles and going to the advancing Eastern Front.[52] Whenever things for the Poles worsened, the Jews suffered even more.

Finally the winter came to an end. The masses of snow began to thaw, and the sun started peeking from behind the clouds. Mama started her trading again, and I helped out. With the beginning of spring, Jews started preparing for Passover. I found a temporary job in a matzo bakery. Besides learning a new trade, I got free matzo for the holidays, some money, and good stories for my diary.

For the Seder, we went to "The Club." Everyone helped with the preparations. Most of the food had been donated. Older refugee men conducted the services and prayed that the Lord, God of Mercy and Salvation, would hear us and spare us. Some older women cried. We all left with new hope.

On Easter Sunday, Sheyndele took me for a walk around town. Despite German patrols guarding every corner, the streets were lined with horse-drawn wagons, all the parishes were full of worshippers. We watched Christian families going to and from church. They, too, were praying for a miracle to happen—for the end of this terrible war and this brutal occupation.

We passed by the German headquarters. SS soldiers were walking in front of the main entrance, parading their *"Gott mit Uns"* ("God [is] with us") belt buckles. As we were passing them, Sheyndele pointed to the yard behind the iron bars. There, under a tree, stood a slim young girl with her arms laced around a soldier's neck, her long blond hair blowing in the April breeze; his arms were planted firmly below her waist. Next to them another soldier's body was being partly covered by a girl facing him, her right leg wrapped around his upper thighs.

"Who is that?" I asked.

"Don't ask stupid question," she said. "Just look!"

Farther down, behind a church, two more cuddling couples were paying no attention to the passersby, nor to the church crowd. We kept walking. I asked no more.

Right after the Holidays, Aunt Naomi and Sis arrived in Sandomierz. It had taken them much longer than they expected, but they had made it safely. Aunt Naomi said that the Warsaw *Judenrat* was now being compelled to provide the Germans with certain quotas of Jews, some for work, others for deportation. Everyone was confused. The few with money were buying up ID cards identifying them as employees of German workshops who, like employees of the *Judenrat* and the Police, had thus far been exempt from deportation. Some of the poor and starving masses were "voluntarily" signing up for labor camps just to be eligible for bread and soup. She told us in detail about friends and relatives who had died since we left the ghetto; the list was long and depressing. She said that Pinkert's three-wheelers were now no longer able to keep up with the dead. Corpses and the dying were lining the streets. She also said that Aunt Polla had married a widower with a little girl. There was a card from Cousin Sruel and his wife, Mollie; they were in one of the Asian republics of the USSR. Cousin Zalmen had changed his name to Zbyszek and moved, supposedly to live with a Gentile girl. He might even have converted.

Aunt Naomi had changed. She had some gray hair, and wrinkles were showing around her eyes. Sis had changed, too. She had grown and slimmed down a lot. I noticed that she was wearing a bra now.

Mama showed Aunt Naomi the bed in which she and Sis would be sleeping. It was the one in the kitchen where our landlady's mother-in-law, who had died two months before, used to sleep.

We spent a few days and nights talking and getting each other up-to-date.

After the initial excitement, our lives normalized. For a while, Sis helped Mama in the trading business, then she found a babysitting job. Aunt Naomi returned to Warsaw against Mama's pleading. It was her boyfriend, more than the smuggling business, that had made her want to go back. Plus, she had good ID papers, and she was spending most of her time now outside the ghetto.

Mama was happy that both her daughters were with her, that stomachs were being filled, that everyone had a place to sleep. As long as there were no new decrees, we could survive. We knew that one day the War would end. "Nothing lasts forever." Meanwhile, newspapers were full of German victories, of how they were advancing deep into the USSR. More workers and supplies were needed to support the war effort.

Every evening people would sit outside their homes, discussing politics and the news of the Front.

One of these nights when I came home from work, I stopped and listened to the conversation that was going on outside of our building. "Don't you want to go to bed?" asked Mama, when it was getting late. "You need some sleep; you have to get up for work early in the morning." I went in and washed my face and feet, then lay down and fell asleep. I was in a deep sleep when I felt a hand on my shoulder and heard Mama's voice: "Wake up."

"What's going on?" I said, half-asleep. "Is it time for work already?"

"Someone wants to see you," Mama said in a shaky, half-crying voice. I rubbed my eyes to see what was going on. "Didn't you hear the knocking on the door?"

I opened my eyes and saw Mama and Sis standing by my bed. Behind them stood a uniformed Jewish policeman. I recognized Leon, the young, nice guy I kept meeting at Heniek's house. Next to him stood a tall, blond guy in civilian clothes.

I quickly learned that they were rounding up Jews for work. The Sandomierz *Judenrat* had gotten an order to supply workers. "We are only obeying orders!" said Leon, kind of apologetically. They were looking for people between sixteen and twenty-four years of age. They had a long list of names with them. I wasn't yet sixteen, but I had no documents to prove it. It probably wouldn't have mattered anyway: they needed to fill their quotas. While I dressed, I heard Mama asking Leon where and for how long he was taking me. I didn't hear his reply. He was watching me put on my dress and looking at his watch. "Hurry up! We don't have all day!"

The two men walked me to the city square. Mama and Sis followed us. We got to the City Hall. Near the gate, like a statue, stood a handsome Polish officer, his eyes like transparent glass, staring into nowhere.

He said nothing. I saw more young people being led into that government building. The inside hall was filling up with young women. The group of rounded-up men was being taken to a nearby building; we could see them walking through the gate.

The sun was now rising. Through the open windows, looking out onto the square, we could see a crowd of friends and relatives gathering outside the building. They were desperately trying to find out what was going on. As news of the roundup spread through town, more people began to come to the square. I saw Mama and Sis standing not far from my window. I waved. They waved back.

Some folks in the crowd were weeping, some were screaming hysterically. "Where are you bandits taking our kids?" yelled a heavyset woman, wiping her eyes with her sleeve.

"Stop it! Stop it! This is not a funeral!" yelled another one standing near her.

Rumor had it that we were being taken to Germany for farm work; someone had heard that we were going to be working in munitions plants in Poland; others said that we were going to be cleaning German quarters and barracks; or else we were being sent to the Front as support crews.

The answer from the police and the guards was, "Don't worry! They'll be okay!"

Many of our friends and relatives were trying to get their loved ones released, claiming that they were in poor health, that they were the only providers in the families, that they had small children at home, and so on. Mama thought that she could get me out on account of my age.

The authorities assured the crowd outside that we would be well-treated. They asked the people to disperse, assuring them that all detainees with special needs would be taken care of. Those in the crowd who had any pleas should line up at a table that had been put next to the front door, and fill out some papers. While a line of relatives and friends was forming at the front door to file claims, we who were inside the hall were being lined up at the backdoor, to be loaded onto open trucks.

My truck drove by the front of the building. I saw Mama and Sis standing in line as others were filling out claims.

XII. Skarzysko

There were thirty girls with me on that uncovered truck as it pulled away onto the open road. The square was still full of people. We drove through paved highways and cobblestone roads. We passed small towns, villages, and fields. Many farmers working in these fields waved to us; we waved back. The heat of the day and the bumpy roads made us tired. Many girls sat down on the dirty floor; some napped.

Late afternoon, one of the girls loudly read a road sign, "Skarzysko-Kamienna." One of the girls sitting on the floor said, "I have an aunt who lives there. I wonder where they are taking us...." I had heard of Skarzysko in geography class. It was known for its railroad track crossings.

In late evening, exhausted and starving, we arrived at a large brick building that could have been a factory, a school, or a government facility. In the semi-darkness, it was hard to tell since only the entrance to the building was lit from inside. In front of us a truck was unloading people. At the large gate, a few guards in Ukrainian uniforms with flashlights and rifles were keeping order.[53] They ordered us to get off the truck and enter the building. We were searched, counted, and moved into a big hall.

Through a wide, open double door, we could see a large auditorium lined with four-tiers-high bunk beds. In the hall where we were assembled were five long tables separated by low wooden partitions. Sitting behind the tables were Polish policewomen. We lined up at the table marked "Station #1." There, every girl was sprayed with some kind of disinfectant, then told to move on to the next station. I stopped at "Station #2."

"Your name," said the woman behind the table, not looking up. She wrote it on a line next to a number, then, pointing to one of the two-by-six centimeter red cloth tags that were lined up on the table, said, "Pick up number 921 and pin it to your dress." The whole time she was speaking in Polish, then she added in German, *"Macht schnell!* Move fast!"

At "Station #3" stood a man with a paint brush in his hand. Next to him, on the floor, was a large bucket filled with red paint. He painted two red stripes the full length of my dress, one on the front, the other down the back. *"Macht schnell!"* he said.

At "Station #4" each girl was given a slice of black bread and a half-liter tin can of beet soup. At "Station #5" we were given gray army-type blankets and shown a place on one of the bunks. I sat down next to a girl with long blond, braided hair. Her new name was "894." While gobbling up my food, I watched the long line of girls still being processed. Everything was proceeding in a very orderly fashion.

Once all the girls were in their places, two Ukrainian guards, accompanied by a civilian-dressed, tall, heavyset woman, came into the auditorium. The woman was talking to us in a Polish that was mixed with German. "You are now part of a labor force that will work in the new addition of the HASSAG munitions plant. If you work *fleißig* [diligently] you will be provided with food and a place to live."[54] She stopped, looked around the room, then added, "This is not a *Konzentrationslager,* but neither is it a scout camp or a recreation center. My advice to you is this: Don't ever think about sabotage or escape! Don't get any funny ideas. If anyone of you disobeys the orders, or if one of you is missing at the *Appell* [roll-call], all of you will pay the consequences. The price for such offenses is high! We'll hang five of you right on the spot for each one that's missing. *Verstanden?* [Understand?] That's how we operate. We just pick at random."

She put away the paper from which she was reading her speech. "Now you may all go to sleep. Someone will talk to you in the morning." She started walking to the door, then turned around and added in a non-nonsense voice: "All of you will have to watch the hanging, so think hard before you make any stupid moves." Happy with her performance, and proud of her superior position, she turned off the lights and left the room.

In morning reveille, we were awakened by a tall, heavyset woman who looked almost like the one who had talked to us the night before; only this one had a funny accent and spoke in a broken Polish, mixed with Ukrainian and faulty German: "*Achtung!* Attention!" she shouted through a bullhorn. "Everyone up, and out *Na dwor* [out into the yard]. *Machen schnell!*" She kept yelling until everyone was outside.

We assembled in the yard. "Stay right where you are!" yelled a short, stout woman in a Polish police uniform, who stood in front of us with hands on her hips. "You are new here, I know. From now on, I want all of you to learn these words by heart. "*Achtung! Appell! Halt! Heraus!* [Attention, roll-call, stop, out of here]. Other useful expressions you'll learn later."

We were told that from now on there would be two *Appells* daily, one in the morning, the other in the evening. We had better be sure never to come late, or to miss one of them. "Today each of you will be assigned a job, and you will be given the rules. And now," she said in a voice of a military commander, "line up in rows of five! I mean five abreast!"

Two Ukrainian guards counted us, writing their findings on a special form. They gave the paper to a German gendarme who signed it and then drove away on his motorcycle.

There must have been two hundred of us girls in the column that formed in the yard. More Ukrainian guards with rifles pointed arrived. "Turn right!" one of them yelled. "Forward, march!" was the next command.

We walked through deserted side roads until we came to a large iron gate shielded by two high watchtowers. We stopped. There were German gendarmes in front of the gate, behind it, and more of them in the watchtowers. As far as the eye could see stretched a high brick wall topped with rows of barbed wire. One of our Ukrainian guards handed some documents to the German gendarmes. They counted us, stamped the papers, and opened the gate. We marched in. The gate was locked behind us. The Ukrainian guards who brought us to this place left.

Scattered about the large area inside the fence were large and small brick buildings. Our group was divided into groups of twenty five. Each of the small groups was assigned a supervisor who then led it into one of the buildings. My group was taken to a building that had a small sign over the main door. It said *"Malarnia"*—paint shop. A line of work stations mounted to the cement floor filled the long, brightly lit hall. Polish men and women and a few Jewish workers (with painted stripes and pinned-on numbers), were minding the stations.

I saw one young Jewish man pushing a cart loaded with what looked like large empty aluminum bottles with wide open necks. He was going to say something, but when he saw the German supervisor, he moved on. The supervisor, talking through a translator, told all us new girls the rules of the game: We weren't to talk, not to ask questions, never to leave the workshop without supervision or a special permit, not even when going to the latrine. *"Verstanden?"* The interpreter stopped without finishing the sentence.

The shop foreman, a middle-aged Pole, assigned jobs to us. He called us by our numbers (I noticed that our names were written out clearly on the paper he was holding). I was assigned to work with a young, good-looking, tall blond Polish guy. "Here, Janek," said the foreman, "she'll be working with you. You tell her what to do, show her how, and make sure she does what you say." The young man introduced himself politely: "Janek Kaczmazrek." (Although I knew it from the name tag on his jacket, I appreciated the courtesy.) "Most people call me Jasiek. Consider yourself lucky. This is a fairly good place to work." He told me that he used to live in Skarzysko, and had been working here for about a year.

I found out that his job was to spray-paint the insides of the aluminum "bottles," which he did with a long-handled spray gun. He would wear a mouth-nose mask during the spraying. My job was to put protective covers over the screw threads in the bottle necks while he did the spraying. He explained my assignment and pointed out a large box of rags. "Make sure always to use clean rags so that no oil or paint is ever left on the threads. These are grenade shells. I am responsible for the work. If they find anything wrong with them during the German inspection, my head will be chopped off." He moved his right hand over his throat.

I asked him about talking on the job. He said that it was okay so long as there were no guards around or squealers to report on us.

At noon, we *Häftlinge* (prisoners) were given a soup made of beet greens, potatoes and groats. It was poured into the tin cans that we had been given the night before, the ones that we were told to mark with our numbers and always to carry with us.

At the first opportunity, I walked over to a Jewish woman and asked her where she was from and how long she had been working here. She said that she was from Ostrowiec, and had been working here a little over six months. She was eating her soup and talking at the same time. "Looks like you just came. How many people arrived on your transport? We are getting new people here almost every day now. Where did they take you from?" I answered all her questions, and then asked if she knew when she and her group were scheduled to return home, because I had heard that we were brought here to replace workers who had finished their assignments and were being sent back home.

The woman gave me a funny look. Turning to a Jewish guy who was delivering work to her, she said, "Did you hear, Archie? That dumb chick thinks the new people were brought here to replace us. Ha! Ha! Ha!" Then, looking me straight in the eye, she said, "Don't be stupid, kid. Here, people only come; no one ever leaves this place alive. The only people who are being replace here are the dead ones."

The rest of the day, I concentrated on learning my job. Before the workday was over, I found out that this plant was working in two ten-hour shifts. I had been assigned to the dayshift. I also learned that there were three separate branches of the plant: Branch A, where I was working, and Branches B and C, which were located within a few kilometers' area. Each had its own camp.

Here, we learned new survival skills, which went as follows: Forget everything you know. Don't complain. Follow all instructions, never argue with your superiors. Don't make your own rules. The sooner you learn these rules, the better are your chances.

One day after work, instead of going back to our by now overcrowded building, we were put into groups of fifty and taken into army barracks located by the railroad tracks. We were told that these were only interim quarters; new barracks were under construction. While going to work we could see brigades of male *Häftlinge* working on construction.

After a few hectic weeks of induction, work assignments and moving, life began to "normalize." Everyone had a number, a job, and a bed. Food rations were allotted: coffee in the morning, soup at noon, bread with margarine or jam in the evening. *Appells* were twice daily. Postal service was established; only postcards were allowed. We were encouraged to write home and tell those who weren't yet here how well we were being treated. After a while, even parcels were allowed into the camp. In my first package, Mama sent me some bread, a couple of cucumbers, a few carrots, and some other ready-to-eat items. I shared the food with a few girls. In a card that arrived later, Mama wrote, "Glad you are okay. We are fine. I sent your address to Dad. Take care of yourself. Regards from everybody. Love, Mama. PS: Write when you can."

Other girls, too, were receiving food from home. Nothing else was allowed into the camp. All parcels were opened and searched. Usually we shared in the feast.

One day, when we returned from our dayshift work, we heard from the nightshift girls that something very unusual had happened in the camp during our absence. The girls were awakened at noon and called to an *Appell.* A commission of German officers did the counting. Then one of them announced that a new ordinance was issued stating that anyone who wanted to leave the camp to return home, for any reason, medical or otherwise, might do so by first registering at the office. Our plant now had enough workers. The authorities wanted only those who were fit for work and who wanted to do a good job. Those who wished to remain would be moved into a new camp.

Many girls registered. Some were accepted; others, for unknown reasons, were rejected. We, the dayshift girls, were sure that the same would happen to us. We waited, but nothing happened. The commission had left the camp. I remember sitting on my bunk that night wondering what Mama would think when some Sandomierz girls returned home and didn't find me among them. All girls in my barracks felt sad and depressed.

In the morning, at *Appell,* we heard new rumors. People were saying that another commission would be visiting the camp shortly. We went to work filled with new hope. When we arrived at work, a few Polish workers told us that the night before they had seen a lot of Jewish girls, with their red-striped clothes, assembled at the railroad station, being loaded into a cargo train. They asked if we knew anything about it. We told them about the registration. I saw a skeptical smile on Jasiek's face, then he bent over and whispered in my ear, "I've never heard of any Jew who went home from here."

When we returned from work to the barracks, some girls told us that around noon a freight train had been passing behind the camp grounds, and they had seen heads peeking through the small windows at the top of the cars. Some hands were waving through the cracks in the walls. Voices were coming from the wagons, but because of the roaring train, there was no way to comprehend what was being said.

Whatever happened to the people during, or after, that train ride is still a mystery. We never heard from or about any of them again.

Autumn winds started blowing; days became shorter, the rains more frequent. We moved to different quarters. The new barracks was set up on a large sandy field surrounded by two rows of tangled barbed wire. At the entrance gate was a check booth where Ukrainian watchmen with clubs and German shepherd dogs kept guard. Outside the gate were two watchtowers from which other Ukrainian guards with rifles and lights kept their eyes on the camp. We were well protected, and quite secure.

There was a section for men and one for women (the rank-and-file folks), and a miscellaneous one for administrative offices, a kitchen, a clinic, and living quarters for the Jewish police, the *kapos* and executives; the so-called camp elite.[55] Each barracks, or block, as we called it, was divided into three large rooms furnished with double-decker bunk beds, a long table in the center, a wood-burning space heater, and a large, lid-covered chamber bucket.

In this new camp the use of loose straw for bunks was discontinued. The beds were outfitted with straw mattresses and gray army blankets. Each bed was used by two girls who were working opposite shifts. One girl in each room was assigned as a *Stubenälteste*, a "room caretaker." She, too, worked at the plant, but after work she was the room boss. For this, she got extra bread and special privileges like reporting to authorities and assigning barracks workers.

Our *Stubenälteste* was pockmarked Wanda, who had been taken away from her husband and small son. She was our protector, judge, and source of entertainment. Always fair with food distribution and chore assignments, she was the most popular girl in our block, and quite well known to the camp guards, who watched us at the gates, the doors, the yard, even accompanied us to the latrine. Our daily life became quite routine: *Appell*, work, food line, sleep. Occasionally, the cycle was broken by the arrival of new people, or a "selection"—a German commission that came to pick out the sick, the weak, and those unable to work. All the "unfits," as they were called, were sent away to some unknown destination. Another variation was frequently watching public beatings and an occasional public hanging, which were punishments for such offenses as pulling a beet from a field on the way to or from work, disrespecting a superior, or for not fulfilling work to exact specifications.

Going to work was for most of us a blessing. The plant was an escape from the camp. It was the only place where we had contact with people from the outside world, where we could occasionally find a page of a newspaper and learn of what was going on behind the barbed wire. There we could also find a few gentle souls—"Righteous Gentiles," we called them, who, occasionally, would help us to mail letters to our families or bring us news from them. Life for the Poles wasn't easy, either. They had to deal with rationed food, killed or abducted relatives, illnesses, and hard work for little pay, among other things. We especially appreciated the few Righteous who were willing to help because most Poles didn't want to mix with Jews or to listen to their predicament.

While in camp, we felt completely helpless, hopeless, and isolated. But as bad as the place was, it didn't compare with the ghetto. Those who hadn't been there couldn't even comprehend. Here, no one slept on the street. Often, while eating my soup, I would think of the dead bodies in the ghetto streets; I could see the children's corpses being hauled on Pinkert's three-wheelers. I wondered how Dad was getting along, and I thought of other friends and relatives who were facing another winter without food or fuel, watching their loved ones starving and dying. I thought of Mama and Sis, who had to worry about their daily existence, for I had heard that conditions in smaller towns were worsening, that there were now critical shortages of everything. Medical supplies were things of the past. The Polish workers at the plant kept saying how lucky they were to have their jobs.

One day I received a card from Aunt Naomi postmarked outside the ghetto. She said that Fredzia and Renia had voluntarily signed up for work in a labor camp so that they could get a loaf of bread. Their parents had died.

News from the Russian front kept changing. The latest tales suggested that things weren't going too well for the Germans. Heavy snows had started covering the Russian roads, preventing German advances. The papers didn't say this; they just stopped reporting victories. Trains that crossed from Russia to Poland and vice-versa were full of soldiers and war equipment. More Polish people were being sent to Germany to replace the German reservists who were being called to active duty. We started working twelve-hour shifts.

Men who were hauling firewood from the forest told us that some strange things were happening out there. They heard shooting and screaming from a distance. Many guards were running around nervously. In the camp, too, unusual phenomena were taking place. Trucks with used winter clothes arrived one day and the cargo was distributed among the inmates. I got a long, beige coat. It was three sizes too big, but it kept me warm.

The days were getting shorter, the curfew hours longer, the rations smaller, the problems larger. Evenings we spent sitting on our bunks, telling each other stories. Our room was a conglomerate of girls from all parts of the country and all walks of life. There were girls from large cities and small villages; there were the rich and the poor, the ultra-Orthodox and the non-believer. We had two high-society girls and a few from the dump, even one from the red-light district. Their ages ranged from eighteen to thirty. I was the youngest in our barracks. Wanda had a word for almost every girl in the room. To all the virgins, it was "You don't know what you've been missing..." She felt sorry for the guys who were spending lonely nights on the other side of the fence. From those evening talks we were finding out a lot about each other. We tried to get along.

In December, around Christmas, we celebrated Hanukkah. My birthday was completely forgotten. We didn't light candles. We just sang Hanukkah songs and talked about latkes and the miracles of the Holy Oil and the triumph of the Maccabees. The religious girls still believed that God would perform another miracle: "Just wait and see. God, blessed be His Holy Name, will never let us down."

Meantime, instead of miracles, bouts of diarrhea, influenza, and typhus were raging in the camp. The winter was cold, snow and ice covered the ground, freezing winds blew through the cracks in the barracks walls. To keep our feet dry and warm, we wrapped them in papers which often could be found in the trashcans at work. I used some of the rags from my work; this was considered stealing German property.

Slowly, the so-called hospital barracks was filling up with the sick and the dying. "Selections" became more frequent. After a while even the word "selection" was enough to cause panic.[56] We hadn't heard from, or about, any of the people who had been "selected" and sent away. One big selection I remember was on a Sunday. That day, quite a few girls were taken away from the camp. When the selection was finally over, we thanked the Almighty for sparing us this time, and we started concentrating on making it through the winter. We still believed that the day would come when we would be sent home.

Our camp—the place behind the barbed wire and the watchtowers—was a separate world. Germans and Ukrainian guards were watching it on the outside, tending gates and watchtowers. Law and order inside was kept by Jewish police and *kapos* armed with sticks and clubs. The evenings, when humane Jewish cops were on duty, we had occasional visitors in our barracks. Some guys would sneak over the fence to the women's side of the camp. They did it with the knowledge, but not the approval, of the Jewish watchers (who themselves had started the practice with the pretense of visiting a "sister" or a "cousin").

Otherwise, during curfew hours, we just sat on our bunks, waiting our turn to leave the room. We were allowed to go outside the barracks only in groups, only under supervision, and only, once every evening, on a trip to the latrine. When the water in the outside faucets wasn't frozen, we would wash off. Luckily, the latrine was a hut with holes in the ground, so only excrement would freeze.

Distributing food rations was another one of the evening routines. The days we had jam with our bread, I thought of Mama. I wondered how she was getting along. The postcards I used to receive from her quite regularly were now coming rarely. The messages were shorter and vaguer. The last message I got was written on a small piece of squashed paper that I found inside some bread. The paper was in Mama's handwriting but not in her usual style. It simply said, "Dear child, got your card. Take care...." My name wasn't on it, neither were Mama's usual remarks like "write when you can.... Greetings from...."

I saved the note. I had developed the habit some time ago of saving every written message till the next one arrived. Many girls did the same. It made us feel as though we were still part of our families. Talking about our past helped, too. In our room, Wanda usually led the nightly conversations. She had the most interesting stories. Very few girls in our room had even heard firsthand accounts of colorful life in a big city. I thought that I had learned a lot in Heniek's house-meetings in Sandomierz; well, Wanda's classes seemed like a university in comparison.

Fortunately, Wanda didn't hold the concession on all storytelling. We also heard from and about people who used to live on the other side of the spectrum. Regina, a twenty-year-old girl from Lodz who was brought up in a very orthodox home and had a brother who was a rabbi, loved to share with us religious stories. She recited passages from the Bible and talked about Jewish laws, writers, and some philosophical concepts that went above our heads. Since most of us were young and not well educated, Regina's old stories, like Wanda's colorful jokes, were all new to most of us. And like some of Wanda's stories, many of Regina's needed interpretation.

Between these two extremes, most girls talked about the various customs they had observed in different parts of the country, about the friends and relatives they had left behind, and, mostly, about food, about holidays and other things that we were all missing. Sometimes we imagined the end of the War and what we would tell our loved ones about life in the camp. We wondered how they were doing.

We reported to one another rumors we heard at work. Public announcements coming through the public media, to which non-Jews had access, couldn't be believed. Special disinformation bulletins were often issued to mislead the public and the enemy. A lot of news was coming through different underground channels; by the time it reached us, it sounded like a "broken telephone" game.

The latest rumor had it that the Germans were advancing deeper into Russia, had already taken Stalingrad. We also heard that the Germans were losing many battles and retreating. Then we heard that the Jews from the camps and the ghettos would be exchanged for German POWs. Then that all Jews would be sent deep into Russia as soon as the Germans occupied that land. Since no one knew the truth, most people believed what they wanted to believe, and discarded the rest. Everyone, however, was concerned about the rumors that Jews were being massacred in forests, and that entire Jewish settlements were being set on fire.

In our barracks, the most discussed subjects, by far, were the problems facing us daily. We talked about the girls who were sick, dead, or dying, and of those who went missing after each selection. There were more of these each day. It was difficult to get over the pain of losing friends and not knowing anything of their fate. We talked about tragic and urgent situations, like what to do about Rifka, who was spitting blood. We wondered why no one was receiving mail from home any longer, and from where the truckloads of used clothes were coming into the camp, and why, from the time we came to the camp, all of us had stopped menstruating.

As winter progressed, illnesses became our biggest problem; not just the common cold or the flu, but dysentery, diarrhea, typhus, other unknown things. It got so bad that no one ever dreamed of being spared, but rather when and how severely it would hit her.

Winter weather made the situation even worse. One night, new snow piled up on top of the old already on the ground. All night we could hear the wind blowing through the cracks in the barracks walls. In my sleep, I heard a voice yelling from the room behind the wall. I knew that it was the voice of Rachu Suka ("Rachel the Bitch"), the next room's supervisor: "Up, up, up! We need the beds!" (Like Wanda, Rachu had a vocabulary all her own. The morning yelling was an indication that the nightshift had returned, and it was time for the dayshift to prepare for the *Appell*.) I was trying to open my eyes, but they kept falling shut. I heard Wanda's voice above my head: "Get ready! It's late!" I heard the girls jumping down from the upper bunks. I tried to raise my head, but it wouldn't move. I felt someone shaking me; I thought that it was my mother standing by my bed. I opened my eyes again: It was Sura, my bedmate. I felt her hand on my shoulder. "Time to get up!" she said. I rubbed my eyes with my fist, but they wouldn't move. I heard her voice calling from a distance, "Get up quickly! Everyone is out on *Appell!*"

I remember seeing Wanda's silhouette; she was touching my head: "You are awfully hot," she said. "We don't need another sick one here." Then I heard her steps moving toward the door. *"Appell!"* she shouted. I heard the door shut.

I have no idea how much time elapsed, but the next person I remember seeing was the cop who was doing his daily routine inspection of the barracks. Next, two skeletons, one on each end, were carrying me away on a stretcher. When I woke again, I was sitting on the icy ground near a long wooden board supporting my body against a barracks wall. A few girls were sitting in front of me and at my sides. I was trembling inside, my teeth chattering. Cold sweat covered my body under the thin dress and long coat. I heard the door to the barracks open and a voice yelling, "Get in, all of you, before you freeze to death!" Holding on to one other, a couple of us girls got off the ground and tumbled in through the open door. A tall skinny woman was walking toward the door, a girl's body dragging behind her on the ground.

What happened after that I remember only in sketchy bits and pieces. A hand grabbed me from behind. My knees bent, and I felt someone dragging me over the icy ground. Then the ground under me changed into a relatively warm wooden floor. The hand let me go, and my body fell to the floor. I don't know how long I lay there. I had no control over my eyes or over any other parts of my body. I remember the abominable stink that, mixed with the warmth of the wood-burning heater, made me nauseous. As I was tried to vomit, some greenish yellow discharge came out of my mouth. It was falling onto my coat. A bitter taste filled my mouth. I fell asleep on the floor, then woke feeling somewhat better.

I looked around. A couple of male inmates were dragging something on the floor. "A former patient," I heard one of them say. "Yes," said the other one, "a corpse."

A woman's voice was saying, "There will be room for you in just a little bit." I don't know whom she was talking to; she was behind the heater, and there were a few of us newcomers on the floor. Her voice said, "This is your hospital. It's the Special Care Unit. I am your nurse today."

Two men kept pulling corpses off the planks and dragging them right by me. I could touch them with my frozen feet. Then I felt someone touch my shoulder. "Get up," a woman's voice said. "Climb up on the top bunk."

"I can't," I remember saying.

"Then go down here." She was pointing to a place between two still breathing bodies from where a corpse had just been pulled. Holding on to a post I pulled myself up and crawled onto a bunk. The nurse pulled a part of a shredded blanket from under one of the bodies and said, "This will be for both of you." The body didn't move. I put my head onto the straw. Colored bubbles appeared in front of my eyes, circling around, dancing by the bunk, touching the ceiling. The ceiling tilted to the floor. Then my mother appeared from nowhere. I was in the ghetto, in my bed. I had dysentery. Mama was crying....

A smell of soup and the clinking of cans woke me up. Through a crack in the wall I could see that it was dark outside. Inside, the "nurse" stood by a soup caldron dishing up soup to those who could walk over to get it. Then I saw her standing in front of me. "Hey, you!" she said. "Want some soup?"

I lifted my head. She handed me some liquid in a can. I tried to put it to my mouth. The contents spilled into the straw. The smell of the warm liquid mixed with the smell of urine and other excrement made my stomach turn inside out. I pulled a handful of straw from under me, put it over the spilled soup, then I put my head over it, and, I think, I fell asleep again.

As if in a fog, I woke up sporadically. I think, one time, that I even drank some soup or water, or maybe I just dreamed I did. Maybe it was an hallucination. Another time, a woman trying to get off the top bunk stepped on my head and nearly killed me. Yet another time, I tried to get up and my legs folded under me; I fell. I don't remember anyone picking me up. When I awoke, I was on the plank.

I have no idea how long I slept between those half-conscious moments, but the next time I remember waking up was when two women were pulling at a corpse that lay next to me. I tried to turn away but my back was sore, my legs wouldn't move, my arms were dead, and my eyes kept falling shut. In the dream, I saw the ghetto streets lined with dead bodies, bodies of children, and I saw my father walking over to me. Then he changed: His figure turned into my aunt.... Then more corpses, barbed wire, and I was flying over the wire and the ghetto wall.... I don't know how long I was in and out of the delirious fancy. Then one day I woke up with an excruciating headache. I think that this was the first time since I got sick that I felt any pain at all. Next time, I woke up with terrible hunger pangs. My body was itching. I tried to scratch my leg. It became obvious to me that it had been scratched before because my fingertips were bloody and there were scabs underneath my fingernails. My eyes were now opening wider. I knew where I was and why I was in this place.

The straw on the plank was full of discharges that could have been bloody diarrhea or revived periods. That terrible stink that almost killed me when I first came into this place no longer seemed to bother me. For the first time, I could hear voices asking for water and people screaming for help.

Around me were lice. Visible lice marching in the straw passing over the still living and over the already dead bodies. Lice weren't new to me. I still remembered them from the ghetto, and there had been no shortage of them in Sandomierz. Here they were thriving, multiplying, feasting. Here we could pick them up by the handful. It was no use trying to kill them. Killing each separate louse would have been an endless process. The little beasts were hard to crack; they slipped from the nails. I had no idea how long they had been my companions, nor did I know how long I had been in this Special Care Unit. I only remember that I started feeling thirsty, very thirsty. My mouth was dry, my lips cracked. All I wanted was water. I was still falling asleep and waking up, but I knew what I was doing. I heard people around me talking.

My mind kept wandering back to the time I had come to this hall, and to the time I first came to Skarzysko. I thought of my mother, and, in a way, I was glad that she wasn't here with me. I remembered how worried she was the time I got sick in the ghetto. Occasionally I recalled happy times, my childhood, my school days. Sometimes I thought of my work in the paint shop and wondered if Jasiek would still need me when I got back. I thought of the girls in my barracks and those at work. I remember asking for water.

The "nurse" brought me some in a can. "Drink slowly, slowly," she kept saying, while holding the can to my mouth. After two or three sips she pulled the can away. "Let's see if the water stays down. If it does, I'll give you more," she said.

I look in the direction where the daylight is coming through the open door. I notice the thin blades of green vegetation that have sprung up in the soil outside the barracks. There is no trace of the snow that once thickly covered the ground the day I came into this hospital.

I feel better now. For the first time, I can see clearly the room I am in. A woman across from me is reaching for a can. She pulls it over to her mouth. I see her choking, but no one pays any attention. I am looking. She catches her breath. Suddenly a half-dead body lying not far from me revives. I see it move. From a top bunk comes a voice: "Water!" No one answers. Beside the door two men are carrying a skeleton. They throw it out the door. A scream. "Help! Help!" comes from the corner of the room. The voice stops.

I watch the "nurse" dishing out soup. "Want some?" she asks, looking at me. I nod. She gives me a can. I get a sip. I wait to see what will happen. It stays down, down in my stomach. "Well," says the "nurse." "Looks like you made it through the crisis." She walks to another bunk.

I pull back the hair that has fallen into my eyes. A bunch of it stays in my hand. I touch my head; the hair starts falling onto the straw. I stop touching it.

Every day, more sick girls are being brought into this place, and more dead ones are taken out. This Special Care Unit is constantly filled to capacity. The dead, the living, and all those in-between, which include the ones who are dead but still breathing and those who are alive but unable to move or act, all are squeezed together. Most of the people here die, but not all. A few do get out. Here, everything depends on luck.

Rumors about an upcoming selection are circulating. There has not been one in the camp since the cold weather set in and we became snow-bound. The people who are removing the corpses and delivering the soup and water are also rumor-carriers. They are our news media. From them I had learned that the word, "selection" didn't apply to the people in the hospital. Everyone caught in this place during an inspection is, without selecting, loaded onto waiting trucks and taken to another place for Treatment and Rest.

Knowing nothing about the fate of those previously Treated and Rested, anyone who is able to breathe and move would rather thank the commission for its generosity and skip the offer.

Hearing rumors that a commission was due any day, everyone who wasn't in a delirious state was trying to get out of the Special Care Unit. I knew that I had to leave this place, but there was no connection between my brain and my body. Every time I tried to stand up, my body folded. It became limp, it kept collapsing. I was still sick and weak, and my hair was falling out in clumps.

A few days after the selection rumors started circulating, I asked the "nurse" on duty if she would let me go back to work. "Try," she said, "but go after the morning count." Yes, even in this unspeakable place, everybody, dead or alive, had to be accounted for. Under German law, everything is done with precision.

Holding on to the bedpost with one hand, I brushed the straw off my coat with the other, and, my knees buckling and shaking, I started for the door. The "nurse" straightened out the number on my coat so that she could read it. She marked something in her notebook, then she said goodbye and good luck and "I hope you'll make it." A Jewish policeman who was guarding the door checked the notes and my number and opened the door widely. I walked out.

The fresh air made me dizzy. I held on to the barracks wall and didn't move; everything around me did. The ground, the barracks, the sand, the sky, all were in motion. I was sure that I was seeing the world turn on its axis. I wondered why I had never seen it doing this before. I sat down by the wall and waited for something to happen.

Around noon the two guys who delivered soup to the hospital helped me get to the fence of the women's sections. The nightshift girls were sleeping when I got to my room. I sat down on the floor. One of the girls woke up and noticed me. She cleared her bed and crawled on to a top bunk with another girl. I didn't wake up until the dayshift girls came from work.

I had no mirror, but from the expressions on their faces, I could tell that they were not very pleased with what they were seeing.

Wanda was the first one to take action. She pulled off my lice-covered clothes and handed them to a girl whom she ordered to drop them in the latrine hole. She then collected some clothing from the girls, and put them on me. Luckily, most girls had extras: A new transport of used clothes had arrived only a few days before.

My hair kept falling out until there was hardly any left. Sura made a bandana out of a blouse and wrapped it around my head. Next morning, the girls dragged me to the *Appell*. The ground was moving. The merry-go-round wouldn't stop. My knees bent. I fell. Supported on both sides by my friends, I made it to the plant.

Jasiek looked at me. He didn't say a word. He tried not to look shocked, but it showed. He was swallowing his tears as mine were rolling down my face. Jasiek was nice. He took me back to my job when I couldn't even lift a finger to help him with his work. My back was hurting. The cement floor under me was moving, and the work station was turning. I felt seasick. I began to doubt whether it had been such a smart idea to get back to work. I had no idea how long I had been in that hospital. I hadn't counted the days or the months. I had forgotten that they had names. It had been winter when I went it; it looked like spring now.

Not only was I ignorant of time, I didn't even know what disease I had. Had it not been for the people at work and those in camp who disregarded German rules and helped me get on my feet, there would have been another number added to the millions of dead.

Among the helpers were *Pan* Bukowicz, a Polish department supervisor who, for almost a month, had let me scrape out the leftovers from the Polish soup caldron; and *Pan* Wieczorkowsky, the oldest worker in our shop who, among other things, was in charge of the walking permits, and who had given me additional latrine passes. *Pan* B. was a nice, easygoing, friendly man, so it came as no surprise that he wanted to help. *Pan* W., however, was an unpredictable type. When drunk, he was vicious: he hated everybody, especially the mongoose, the rats, the *Schwabs*, and the Jews. He beat the Jewish boys who worked under him, calling them kikes. On more than one occasion, he "accidentally" sprayed them with the boiling chemical that was for washing grenades. The Polish people who knew him said that he hit his wife, and he had beaten his children when they were younger. Who would imagine that this man would help a Jewish skeleton with a bandana?

Slowly, some of my strength started returning, but boils that had formed on my back were getting worse; also, the dizziness was keeping me constant company. There was nothing that I could do about the dizziness. As for the boils, the suffering that they caused was becoming unbearable. My clothing was soiled with pus from the two cracked ones. The other two wouldn't open. There was no way I could lie down, bend over, or even breathe, without excruciating pain.

One day I asked *Pani* Grarzyna at work if she could bring me a razor blade. I had a dress, I told her, that needed to be cut down. She was very nice about it, suggesting scissors instead. I persuaded her that scissors were too difficult to get through plant security. A day later, she brought a razor blade. On Sunday morning, right after *Appell*, Teresa, a girl from the nightshift who had some nurses' training, performed an operation on my back. She cut open the boils and bandaged them up with one of the old rags I had brought from work.

I was very grateful to *Pani* Grarzyna. I told her how her blade had been used. She said that she wouldn't have brought it had she known. "The wounds could get infected," she said.

Slowly, aside from the dizziness and headaches, my life started returning to "normal." Time was passing. New rumors started reaching the camp. The Germans, it was said, were still deep in Russian territory, but their armies were suffering devastating defeats, and they were short on supplies and equipment. Whatever was still left in Poland was now being taken out and shipped to the retreating Germans.

"The *Schwabs* don't care if we Poles starve; they don't give a damn," said *Pani* Krysia when she arrived at work one morning. "All our important people are being arrested, many sent away to Germany for hard labor. They took my brother yesterday...."

Other news from the outside world was that a Polish guerrilla resistance movement was hiding in the nearby forest. Some of the fighters reported seeing many Jews being shot there. The few who managed to escape joined their movement.

With the War worsening, the retreating Germans blamed all their troubles on the Jews. That of itself wasn't new. Jews had been scapegoats for years; they were a minority and an easy target. But now German persecution of the Jews took another step. Polish workers talked about seeing freight trains full of Jewish men, women, and children bound for deportation. No one knew where they were being taken. It was supposedly for resettlement. We also heard stories about traditionally dressed Jews who had been seen in forests, forced to dig ditches. Some reported seeing Jews being shot and their bodies thrown into ravines. Some of the stories that people were telling were so bizarre that no one believed them, not even the people who were telling them. Besides, we figured that these stories had been traveling so far from mouth to mouth that they were either complete lies or greatly exaggerated.

We knew, however, that something was happening. We hadn't been receiving any mail. Our food rations and all supplies had been cut. We were spending less time eating and cleaning up, and more time working and suffering. There were more frequent inspections, selections, and hair shavings. (By that time, however, I was bald.) There were shortages of everything but slave labor. No matter how many workers were sent away during selections, or how many died, new slave laborers were constantly being brought into the camp. Working hours were getting longer, the camp grounds more crowded.

It was one nice spring day when, on returning from work, we found on the camp premises a large group of new arrivals. The women looked tired, worn, and dirty. Their outer garments were painted, on front and back, with large red letters, "KL." We found out that the letters stood for *Konzentrationslager*.

After further investigation, we learned that the girls were originally from Warsaw, that they had been shipped by freight cars to a terrible camp named Majdanek, a place near the city of Lublin; that most girls had been left there, but this group had been loaded on trucks and shipped to us. They told us that the Warsaw ghetto no longer existed. All that was left of it were ruins and ashes. They told us, little by little, about the conditions and events that had led to a ghetto uprising, and to its destruction. The people who survived the shootings and shellings and burnings were all taken to somewhere...possibly to other camps.

The girls told us how they had been rounded up in Warsaw after a doomed ghetto uprising. They were surprised that we hadn't heard about it, for they were sure that the whole world knew of what had happened to the ghetto. And they talked about the first trains of Jews that had been taken out of Warsaw for "resettlement," supposedly for work in some labor camps, promised with good jobs and good food.

All the stories that were told to us were in bits and pieces and out of context. They were especially difficult to comprehend for Skarzysko girls from small towns who had never been to a large city nor had experienced life in a ghetto. They, like most people, tried to believe that these stories were highly exaggerated. It seemed that, on the subject of rumors, many by now considered themselves experts. For example, they knew that the rumors regarding the "Final Solution"—one that called for the destruction of all Jews, men, women, and children, as well as the outlandish one suggesting that people were being led into gas chambers disguised as bath houses, there to be poisoned and their bodies burned in crematories—should be completely disregarded.[57]

But what the girls said they had witnessed themselves was that more people were being deported to unknown destinations and more bodies were being picked off the streets by Pinkert's three-wheelers. Not even the *Judenrat*, the police, or the cemetery workers, were immune from deportations. The matter was no longer whether to live or to die, but whether to die fighting, or to be murdered. While some ghetto residents, especially the Orthodox, were still waiting for God's miracle, for the coming of the Messiah, others were beginning to organize weapons and prepare for resistance.

It was during Passover Holidays that SS guards came to round up people for another deportation, and the shooting and throwing of Molotov cocktails started. It ended with the whole ghetto being set afire. The KL girls told us that from Umschlak Platz—the central deportation site near the railroad tracks—they could see the ghetto engulfed in flames....

Among the KL girls, I recognized one of my cousin's best friends. She knew a few of my relatives, and told me about a couple who had died in the ghetto and about some who had been deported. Many, however, were still there when she was taken away.

With all the new people, the camp became more crowded, the lines for soup longer, the bread portions smaller. We slept cramped four to a bunk—two nightshift, two dayshift. But life also became more interesting: If we didn't gossip, we talked about political rumors that had been spreading at the camp and at work. The latest one circulating at work was about the War. We heard that the city of Hamburg had been bombed and that a lot of damage had been done to the port. Filled with new hope, we discussed the event. We were glad to hear that there might still be an end to this horror, that everything wasn't yet lost, that we weren't completely alone. That night we rejoiced. We laughed and talked and cheered until Regina spoiled the party. She was sitting quietly on her bunk, her face sad, not saying a word.

"Hey! What's wrong with you? Come on, holy virgin, say something," said Wanda, looking at Regina's sorrowful face.

Regina didn't answer. She was my good friend, so I climbed onto her bunk and asked, "What's wrong, dear? Don't you feel well?"

"Don't you know," she finally said, "doesn't anyone here know that rejoicing at someone else's misfortunes isn't Jewish?"

Yes, I actually knew that. I remembered Grandpa telling me that; I must have been about eight or nine. I also remember hearing it from one of the KL girls as she recited an ancient Greek poem.

Nevertheless, the tragic bombing of Hamburg gave us new hope. All summer long rumors of German defeats were circulating. The official media, even though not reporting direct setbacks, showed obvious signs that news for the Germans wasn't good. News coming from underground channels also indicated cause for optimism, even though the situation in Poland was becoming unbearable. Rations for the Polish population were being cut and the supplies shipped to the Front. Many Poles who had never done anything illegal had resorted to smuggling and stealing. Even very patriotic Poles, and very religious ones, felt that patriotism and religion worked better on a full stomach.

In our camp, the soup began to consist more of water than substance. Other rations were cut to starvation levels. What did increase were shipments of used clothing. These clothes were greatly appreciated, especially with another winter not too far away. Some of the items were quite old, others in fairly good condition. The truck drivers who delivered these shipments said that they were picking up the stuff from a city named Oswiecim; they weren't sure how and where their cargo was loaded into these trucks. All of this became even more suspicious when recipients of these clothes began finding notes inside some of them. One note found in a coat pocket read, "We don't know what's going to happen to us." Other notes said, "Death to the murderers—avenge our fate," and, in Hebrew, "Don't forget what your enemy has done to you." We didn't know what these notes meant, but we knew that something wasn't right.

I hadn't received any news from home, and neither had anyone else. I hoped that someone would come from Sandomierz and let me know what was going on there. That little note that I found in the last package was the only thing that connected me with my home. I still kept it in the foot-wrapping rags.

All people who were arriving at our camp had been transferred to us from other camps. The next big shipment of workers were girls from Krakow and the neighboring towns. They came from a camp named Plaszow, where they had toiled for the Germans. They told us that many Jews from small towns in southern Poland were being deported, that some had been brought to the Plaszow camp, but the majority had been shipped to some other places. They didn't know why different people had been transferred to different camps.

Besides all the problems of the world, at work and in the camp I encountered a few of my own. The dizzy spells and headaches that had been bothering me since my illness now became more frequent and more aggravating. I also developed frozen toes and an abscessed tooth. There was little that I could do about the spells and the toes. The tooth was taken care of in the "hospital barracks" by a fellow whose knowledge of dentistry consisted of having once washed instruments in a dental lab. He performed the surgery with a pair of carpenter's pliers. The wound bled for days, my face was swollen for weeks. Finally, the operation was declared a success.

Slowly another winter was upon us. It was bad. Even during peaceful times, winters in this part of the country were feared. They were long and often severe. Since the War started, each consecutive winter seemed worse than the preceding one. During this winter, not even Wanda could get wood to heat our room. Icicles were hanging inside the barracks walls; the chamber bucket was frozen. The latrine grounds and holes were no better. The long lines that would form around the shed weren't due to overeating, nor even to the overcrowding, but to the diarrhea and dysentery that were infesting the camp. I missed out on it, but many others didn't. Standing in the endless latrine lines, I watched girls crossing their legs, trotting in place and cursing, while greenish liquid, often mixed with blood, soaking through their dresses or running down their legs. Entering the latrine, we would slip and slide on the frozen excretions. When we finally got ourselves positioned over the open hole, we had to make it fast, not only because the uncovered parts of our bodies were freezing but also because the girls outside were constantly shouting for us to hurry up.

It was a terrible winter. We lost many girls to selections and death.

With the coming of spring, many winter-related problems disappeared, but that didn't mean that we were left trouble-free. As soon as the weather warmed up, the rats and flies returned to the latrine, to the yard, and to our barracks. Rats as large as rabbits, fat with shiny hides, reminded me of those that I had left behind in the ghetto. Sometimes, during the night, they would wake up from their gloomy sleep and run through the room, or sit on our beds to keep us company. Wanda was the only one in our barracks who wasn't afraid of them. She would get up in the middle of the night and chase them around, cursing. "Go to the shit-house," she would yell. "You can eat yourselves to death out there! The swarming flies will keep you company!"

Soon these adventures became part of our lives. And again, like so many times before, we redefined the word "normal," learning to live with the situation.

In the evenings, we were continuing our discussions, singing, reciting poetry, just talking. The news from the Front was that the Red Army was advancing westward. Russian planes were supposedly bombing German positions. Previously victorious Germans were being captured, many killed. Transports with wounded Germans were seen traveling through Poland.

At work, we heard that the Front was nearing the Polish-Russian border, that there were reports that some people heard artillery shots and others saw fire coming from afar. If we could only hold out a bit longer, the Russians, our liberators, would be here. Filled with new hope, our nightly discussions turned to new topics: What will we do after the War ends? Of course, we'll all be going to our respective homes.... We promised each other to keep in touch.

Our rejoicing was short-lived. Now that the Germans were losing battle after battle, they were taking all their anger out on the Jews even worse than before. Along with the rumors of German defeats, we heard that there were more talks about this "Final Solution." There were also new rumors circulating, supposedly coming from the authorities, that our camp was to be evacuated. We became very apprehensive. At the plant, the Polish workers, too, had heard that the whole plant was to be shut down, the workers laid off, all the slave laborers deported. There was no way to tell if this was just another rumor, an intended spreading of misinformation by the Nazis, or a real fact—that we would be shipped to a place named Oswiecim, better known by its German name, Auschwitz, the place our clothes where coming from. The place, rumor had it, that was an extermination camp, the place where Jews, Gypsies, and other "undesirables" were taken for the "Final Solution." A place that we didn't think existed (besides in vicious rumors). We tried not to believe the rumors of our deportation, but we couldn't completely disregard them, either, not after what we had heard from the KL girls and from the accounts of the Polish workers.

Anyway, the people in our camp were getting very nervous about the whole thing. The closer the time of the alleged evacuation came, the less we chose to believe that what had already happened to millions of people could now happen to us.

Many Polish people were getting nervous, too. Those who had joined the guerrilla movements in the forests were getting nervous out of happiness and anticipation, knowing that their struggle would soon be over; that their luck would hold out till the end. And nervous, of course, were those Poles who had cooperated with the Germans, for their luck was now running out. And nervous were the people at our plant, for they were to lose their jobs. Nervousness was also getting to *Pan* W., who was taking to drinking more, and who was beating the Jews more. One morning, in a vicious temper, he beat up two of the three Jewish men who were working for him. He broke the nose and jaw of one man and kicked another one in the groin until he fainted. The third man managed to escape into the hall, from where he yelled, "You old bastard! Just wait till we get even!" Whether this warning got to *Pan* W.'s head, or for whatever other reason I don't know, the next morning the old man came to work transformed. He told us that during the night he had come up with a plan for how he could help the Jews. He said that he, too, had heard the rumors about deportation, about death camps, and he suggested that we defy the German orders and try to escape.[58] When the evacuation day came, he said, we should run away and hide in the nearby fields and forests. "These guards can't shoot all of you. There aren't enough of those rotten *Schwabs* here to do the job. Try to run in different directions." He gave us a detailed plan of how he and a group of his friends, friends he could trust, would patrol the area, bring us unmarked clothes, pick us up, and hide us until the Russians arrived.

It was hard to tell what his motives were: Did he mean what he was saying, or was he planning some harm? Maybe his conscience was bothering him. He was a good Catholic, after all.

We seriously thought about some kind of escape, a rebellion, or some other form of defiance, of not letting ourselves be shipped to some kind of an unknown destination. His talk just prompted us more into considering such measures.

The escape itself was never our biggest problem. As difficult as it might have been, it was not impossible. The reason that prevented many of us from doing it was twofold: One was the punishment that awaited those in camp; we knew that many innocent lives would be lost, and many others would suffer for our actions; the second problem was—a sad fact of life—that there was no place for us to go once we did escape. The majority of the Polish population wasn't only unwilling to shelter Jews; some were even eager to turn them in, sometimes for a reward, sometimes even without one. Those Polish people who would have helped feared for their own lives.

Therefore, we could hardly make sense of the old man's suggestion.

Nevertheless, many of us didn't dismiss his offer; after all, it was to be a deed of last resort.

A few days had passed since the man's proposals. The possibility of evacuation became more real. There were even talks of sending Polish workers to Germany in order to replace the Germans who were being sent to the front. The decision to escape or to take a chance and believe German propaganda—that the Jewish *Häftlinge* would be shipped to Germany for work—became more serious.

We had lived on rumors and false hopes for so long, and we always tried to believe the positive. It was time to do something. If local people would keep quiet and not turn us in, we might survive an escape. It also stood to reason that no one in his right mind would, at this stage of the War, cooperate with the Nazis. Yet life taught us that not all people at all times acted logically, that emotions and logic don't always work together. We heard of Polish guerrillas who wholeheartedly fought the Germans and at the same time helped to kill Jews.

We, the potential escapees, knew well that our chances of not being shot by the guards, not being turned in by some local people, not breaking a bone by jumping and running, weren't in our favor. The question to consider was whether the risk of being deported to an unknown destination was greater than the escape. This decision, of course, had to be made by each of us individually.

One evening after work, a group of us girls from different barracks gathered outside in the yard to discuss this dilemma. It was well past curfew hours, but no one was patrolling the grounds. We stood talking and listening to a distant rumbling that sounded like thunder. Far out on the eastern horizon, the sky was lit up; it looked like lightning, but the flashes were lasting much longer; they didn't disappear. I heard a voice in our group say, "I wouldn't doubt it if the fire was coming from the front." Another voice added, "Those *Schwabs* will never have time to get us out of here. The Russians are only twenty, maybe thirty kilometers from here." Other voices kept coming in. One male voice yelled, "Those stinkin' Ukrainians better start running from here before we get even."

While this conversation was going on around the yard, the pounding on the horizon continued. We talked abut the Russians. We knew from previous stories that the Russians were no angels, that soldiers on a frontline don't behave like knights. But now they were to be our liberators. We could hardly wait to greet them.

155

160

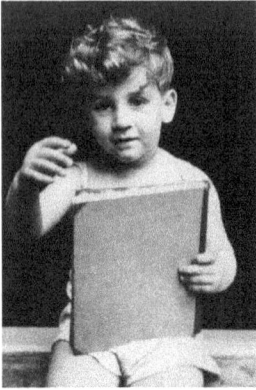

MS „GENERAL HARRY TAYLOR" in Bremerhaven vor dem Auslaufen nach Amerika

163

XIII. The Train

We were still talking about our approaching freedom when Ukrainian guards with rifles pointed encircled the field. We heard *Kapo* Potbone's voice yelling through a bullhorn, "Everybody out of the barracks! Run to the gate! Get into formation!" From across the field, we heard another *kapo* echoing the order: "You have five minutes to assemble at the gate. Run! Run! Run faster!"

A panic struck everyone in the camp. The rumors of evacuation suddenly became reality. We were gong to be deported. Where to...?

Before we could grasp what was going on, Jewish police with their whips and clubs, Ukrainian guards with their rifles pointed, and German gendarmes with their dogs, all were rounding up the *Häftlinge*. Attempting to avoid the whips, the clubs, the rifles, trying to prevent our bones from being crushed and our heads shot off, we did as we were told.

We were counted and loaded onto waiting trucks. In the darkness of the night, I heard someone ask a guard what he knew about the destination of our journey. He didn't answer. He only laughed. Other guards joined in. They seemed to enjoy watching panic-stricken people.

"Macht schnell!" the guards yelled. "Onto the trucks! Up! Up!" A few guards stepped up to the outside platform. The truck caravan proceeded forward.

On our truck, most girls were wondering why we had obeyed the order, why we hadn't reacted differently. Why we hadn't run, resisted, or jumped the armed guards? Ever since we heard the horrors of deportations, we kept discussing how we would react if put into such a predicament. Sometimes we even wondered about people who, we heard, would go into freight trains without resisting, even though rumors of death camps circulated.

We had talked about escaping, about resisting, about revolting, about trying to develop a workable plan. We had no support, no connections, no place to go. We also feared that the guards would kill many innocent girls for each one who escaped. We had reason to believe it. We knew for a fact that in cases of killing prisoners, the Nazis always kept their promises. Nevertheless, the idea of running away was constantly with us.

Our trucks drove through dark roads lined on both sides with thick brush and tall trees. I heard girls whispering to each other. One of them said that if we were ordered on a train, then, no matter what the consequences, she would escape; she would never get on a train; she would rather run under the wheels of the train. Talk of suicide wasn't new. It had been going on for quite some time. Suicide was committed by people who just could no longer take it, for whom the stress, humiliation, and loss of loved ones were more than they could bear. But to most people, life was too precious even to consider such an absurd act. Besides, suicide wasn't a Jewish answer to problems.

Now being taken to an "unknown destination," some girls reasoned that they would rather jump off the truck and take a chance on a dangerous act than be burned in a crematorium. (By now, everything that previously had sounded absurd and crazy was believable, even probable.) I sat in a corner of the truck, listening to the girls talk and to the truck rumbling over a gravel road and to the noises of its motor. The truck hit a couple of bumps in the road, turned a corner, and stopped.

A silhouette of a freight train car appeared in the darkness. Far on the eastern horizon, fire lit the sky. We could hear the distant pounding of artillery. By the short distance we rode, we knew that we weren't very far from our camp. It was almost obvious that we were only a few kilometers from the Russian front. Amid the pounding of artillery, we could hear the creaking sounds of opening boxcar doors. A few of us held hands; we sighed helplessly. Some girls flung their arms around one another. Others sobbed. A few prayed.

Our truck pulled over and stopped in front of an open cattle-car door. One of the guards unlocked the back flap of the truck. He ordered us to jump off. Another guard commanded us to climb into the train car. The first few girls did as directed. The next few started running away from the train. In the darkness, I could only see their silhouettes disappearing behind the trees. An array of bullets followed them. The girls kept running and the guards kept shooting. The stillness of the night vanished in the rifle fire. The girls disappeared in the darkness. How many girls escaped the torrent of bullets, no one could tell. I knew that the sound of the firing guns had prevented me and a few of my friends from escaping. Instead of following the runaway girls, we climbed obediently into the freight car. It was about three-quarters full when I got it, then it filled up to capacity.

One guard climbed on to the car roof, another pulled the sliding door shut. We could hear the door being bolted from the outside. Without food or water, we were locked in and ready for shipment to somewhere. We stood quietly. Not even a whisper could be heard.

After some time, seemingly hours, we heard remote sounds of colliding booms, felt a jerky motion (one that would have made us fall to the floor had we not been so tightly packed), and sensed the movement of the train as it pulled away. We knew that only a miracle could save us now. Even though most of us were past the stage of believing in miracles, we weren't ready to give up on the idea. Slowly, one by one, we tried to arrange some sitting space in a place where there was hardly room to turn around. When we were almost settled, we realized from the stench that we would have to cuddle even closer together in order to designate a corner for an outhouse. Finally, with a lot of manipulation of body parts, with arms and legs overlapping and tangled around each other, most of us found a resting place on the straw-covered floor. Some girls fell asleep to the sound of the iron wheels gliding over the rails and the constant swaying rhythm of the moving train.

At dawn, we greeted the first of the sun's rays that penetrated the tiny barred windows located close to the ceiling. We looked around the car, then at each other; we began to assess our situation. We realized that if this trip wasn't over soon, we would either starve or suffocate. Our train kept moving forward as it had for most of the night. We were curious about our whereabouts. From my position, and through a few slits in the floor, I could only see the ties between the tracks that were passing quickly by. To investigate the outside world, one girl at a time was lifted to look out the windows. The lookout girl reported her findings: We learned that the outside world hadn't changed; there were fields and trees and roads. People walking down the farm roads were paying no attention to the passing train. Later in the day, I managed to pull away a splinter that hung loose at the door. Climbing over one another, we took turns looking through that one-centimeter crack.

As the day dragged on, we started talking about our fate, about the possible destination, and tried to give one another courage in this hopeless situation. By evening and into the next day, most of us were getting too exhausted to worry about such trivial things as the world, the War, or our whereabouts. Our conversations became shorter and quieter, until they almost ceased. Besides, there was nothing good to talk about. Eventually, we not only quit talking; we gradually stopped using our limbs and brains. Conversation, like body movements and thinking, used up too much energy.

The following evening the train pulled into some kind of a large railroad intersection. That night and the whole next day, we stayed in this place. Our lookout girls, who took turns, reported seeing a few unattached locomotives moving back and forth on different tracks. Our locomotiveless train was on a side track. At night, all of a sudden, we heard the by now familiar sound of colliding booms, a jerk, and a forward movement—the train was again on its way to somewhere.

The following days on the train, most of us developed a feeling of exhaustion, suffocation, and abandonment. A couple of girls were lying unconscious in one corner of the car, reminding us of our helplessness. Then came another night. Again we stood stranded for hours on some lonely track. By now it hardly mattered. Most of us were no longer interested in where we were or where we were going. Indifference and a feeling of "let's get it over with" set in. Occasionally, a hand would touch mine. I would touch it back—a sign of reassurance and affirmation: "Don't give up, sister, not yet."

We expected to stay there for hours, but this time something unexpected happened. We heard someone banging on the freight car door. Then, through our secret crack, one of the girls saw an armed, uniformed guard doing something at the door lock. We heard the jingle of chains. The door rolled open.

It was a sunny but chilly morning. The bright light and the fresh air that entered the car made me dizzy. I touched my head. It was still in the same place. Everything around me was whirling and turning. It felt like the day I left the Special Care Unit. I felt that I was falling, but had no place to drop. I was lying on the floor with my legs underneath some people. It took a while to pull out my arms and find the legs that matched my body; it took some maneuvering before I finally managed to untangle all my limbs. I moved to the door to seize a breath of the fresh air.

From the position of our car, no name of a city was visible. We could only see a gray one-story building with two signs on it. One said *Für Männer* (men's), and the other, *Für Damen* (ladies'). The platform in front of the train as well as the surrounding area indicated that it was a train station. The place was remarkably clean, deserted, almost abandoned. The Ukrainian guards who boarded our train near Skarzysko must have undergone a metamorphosis, for the one who opened the car door wasn't a Ukrainian but an SS guard dressed in a *feldgrau* uniform. The two next to him wore black uniforms, bearing skull insignia on their hats. Their rifles were pointed straight at us. A group of boys ranging in ages from eleven to thirteen stood lined up against the gray building wall. They stared curiously at the freight train and its unusual cargo, proudly displaying their red and black swastika bands wrapped around their *Hitlerjugend* uniforms. The boys looked immaculate; the sun rays shone from their polished shoes like cold fire. Their faces, sober and dignified, their uniformly short blond hair, their posture and behavior, all reflected strict discipline and obedience. The boys looked as mystified by us as we by them. As though by a specific command, all of them walked over to the train and politely started handing out cans filled with water. Then they again lined up against the wall. Of the few cans of water we got for our car, two went to revive the fainting girls. While we were still working on them, the door of the car was shut and locked. We heard the puffing of the engine, and black smoke hid the sun. A few soot flakes blew in through the tiny windows. The train started moving.

It moved, it stopped, sometimes halting for hours. Opinions varied about the duration of the journey. Some thought we had been on the train for five days; others insisted that it had been a week; all agreed that it seemed like a month. We still didn't know the destination.

One night the train halted. I closed my eyes, preparing for a long, uneventful stay. Then, the car door pulled open, and a breath of fresh air blew in. Outside was pitch dark, but we could hear strange voices: *"Raus! Alle Raus! Macht schnell!"* Frightened and confused, we started untangling our limbs and, stumbling over each other, began to jump off the train.

"Line up for counting! Line up by fives! *Macht schnell!"*

By the time I was ready to leave the cattle car, my eyes had adjusted to the darkness. I could see silhouettes of dogs and soldiers with rifles pointed. There were many rows of girls in front of me and many lining up behind me. Next to me was one of the barely revived girls. She wasn't able to stand up. With the help of another girl, I was holding her up. A few rows to the front, guards with flashlights and notebooks in hand were walking on both sides of the formation counting the rows and recording their findings.

"Forward, march!"

The column started moving. In the distance, we saw some lights illuminating a road that led to watchtowers and a barbed-wire fence. We marched in the direction of the lights. At the gate we were counted, then one by one led through a door into a large brick building.

XIV. Leipzig

By the time I came in, the large assembly hall inside the building was almost filled with women. All were sitting quietly on the floor waiting for further instructions. A tall, blond woman in a black SS uniform, armed with a whip, stood in the corner of the room, observing each girl who walked through the door; by mechanically pointing her weapon, she would direct her to an available place on the floor. Other SS women were placed throughout the well-lit hall. A short husky one caught my eye. The name tag on her *feldgrau* uniform said, "Anneliese."

"*Ich bin Lagerkommandantin,*" the woman with the whip introduced herself through an interpreter. ("I am the concentration camp commander.") "Everyone undress!" she said. "Leave all your belongings on the spot where you've been sitting. Line up at this shower door when your number is called." She pointed her whip at a closed door on the opposite side of the entrance. "If you cooperate, you'll be processed in no time."

Everyone must have heard what she was saying, but no one moved. I looked around. In the crowd were many unfamiliar faces. Some girls with yellow hair, skin, and fingernails were sitting in one corner of the hall. Another group in their KL-marked clothes were sitting nearby. Not far from them were several girls from our car, still carrying the tin water cans given to us on the train.

I asked one of the girls sitting near me where she came from. She had come on our train, but in a different car. The girls with yellow faces had worked at Branch/Werk C, the finishing plant where the grenade shells were filled with yellow Pikrina—picric acid—powder. Many slave workers died there from this poisonous substance.

"Everybody undress! I mean it!" yelled the *Kommandantin,* cracking her whip in the air. *"Macht schnell!"* "Do it fast!" echoed the interpreter. Suddenly, all the stories that we had heard about potassium cyanide and *Zyklon* showers rang in our ears.[59] The previously disregarded rumors became real. Cold weariness crept into our bones. Girls started crying, pulling their hair, cracking their knuckles; some just froze and turned numb.

The few girls by the shower door, who had started screaming at the initial announcement of the showers, stopped their hysterical outbursts, and sat now speechless and motionless. Whether it was from fear of the *Kommandantin's* whip that kept them quiet, or the realization that their screams were useless, that it was too late to react or worry, I don't know; I only saw how they slowly and hesitantly began taking off their clothes. We all followed.

I took off my shoes and, in one of them, found a small piece of squashed, blackened paper. I straightened it out as much as was possible; I looked at the few barely recognizable words: "D...r ....l., ...T..k. ..re." I was about to put the note back into the foot wrapper so that no one would be able to find it, but I decided to save it. I just held it in my hand and thought of Mama.

Frau Kommandantin stood quietly watching us undress. The look on her face and the manner of her behavior suggested she might have been puzzled over our reaction to the undressing. I saw her carefully listening to the whispering that was going on among some girls. I saw her talking to the interpreter and shaking her head....

The few whispers that I heard from the girls around me sounded more like confessions, like final farewells, like making one's final peace with God. Some girls were telling their personal secrets, not realizing—or perhaps because they were realizing—that the talkers and the listeners were destined for the same fate.

None of my close friends were sitting near me. I didn't feel like talking to strangers. I just sat there, occasionally glancing at my note and listening to other girls talk. I think that I was just glad to be alone, having no one to worry about, having no one to feel sorry for, no one to pity me.

Frau Kommandantin's whip snapped. She cleared her throat and cried out: "Aren't you *Schweinhunde* [pigs] ready yet?" Her whip hit the backs of two girls who were sitting next to her.

The door marked "Shower Room" opened. We could see a small room. In it a few SS women were sitting at a long table.

The first group of fifteen girls entered the room. The door closed behind them. Breathlessly we waited to see what would happen. After all, they had to come back and pick up their clothes....

Time dragged on. Minutes seemed like hours. The longer the girls were gone, the longer seemed each waiting minute. An eternity passed. There was no sign of the girls.

Frau Kommandantin's whip snapped again. She stamped her foot. A second group of fifteen girls was taken behind the shower door. The first group hadn't returned. We waited. There was no way out of here. Nothing could be done. Should we have listened to old *Pan* W.?.... Maybe we should have hidden in Skarzysko.... Did we miss opportunities to escape, to jump off the train?.... It was too late now.

The third group of fifteen girls was called, but still no sight of any girls previously taken. "Fifteen, march!" I heard a voice next to me say. The room was dead quiet. An SS woman counted, *"Eins, zwei, drei...fünfzehn! Schnell, macht schnell!"*

The door opened. My group walked in. In the room there was still no sign of the other girls. An SS woman at the table looked at my face. She eyed my nude body from head to toe. She checked a long list of names and numbers.

"1191. Remember!" she said. It was to be my new name.

After registration, we went through other induction procedures. At one of the processing stations stood SS women equipped with clubs, magnifying glasses, scissors, razors, and flashlights, all waiting for us to pass their inspection. Lice check. Click, click, went the scissors. The hair was on the floor. I was spared the humiliation; my hair hadn't yet grown back. Only stubble covered my otherwise bald head. All underarm and pubic hair was shaved off. All six body cavities were searched for secret documents and/or hidden treasures.

Oh! My piece of paper! It was still in my hand. A hotness pierced my body.... One swallow; it was gone. I closed my eyes, thinking. I saw Mama's face. My sister and all my relatives I had left in Warsaw were marching in front of me.

I heard, "Forward! Move!"

"You must believe that this is not happening," I told the girl in front of me as we followed the girls ahead of us into the shower room. The girls who had gone before us were still nowhere to be seen. Reluctantly we dragged our feet, trying to avoid a last-minute whipping. The door shut behind us. We stood shaking, just waiting for whatever was to come out of the shower heads. Fifteen naked girls waiting, shaking, cursing, praying.

A rumble in the pipes interrupted the tension. To our amazement and relief, streams of precious, warm water started sprinkling over our bodies. "Water!" We embraced, we laughed, we clapped hands; danced like little children in a fountain....

"Hey! We still don't know what happened to the other girls," said one of us. But hardly anyone paid attention. We rejoiced as the refreshing water spurted onto our dirty, stinking, but still young and firm bodies. We could hardly believe that this was truly happening. We even got soap.

"Raus! Alle raus!" we heard someone yelling. One of the SS women ordered us into a room that smelled of disinfecting powder. It was full of shelves stocked with nicely folded garments. There, to our great amazement and joy, we found our lost girls. We finally knew that the "shower stories" had been vicious lies spread by Jew-haters. Tears were rolling down our cheeks and faces onto our naked breasts. With relief, we watched our friends put on their new attire, which consisted of four items: an undershirt, a pair of underpants, a dress—all made of a coarse material conspicuous for its broad prison stripes— and a pair of clogs. The wardrobe came in two sizes: large and larger.

Before we got to join the girls on the benches, we were sprayed with disinfecting powder, counted, given number patches, then led into a large hall full of three-tier bunk beds. We lined up for tea and bread. On the lid of the caldrons, we read "HASAG-

LEIPZIG." For the first time since we left the Skarzysko camp, we knew where we were.

Here was absolute German Law and Order. The SS made the laws; we obeyed the orders. Twice daily were *Appells*. Work a lot, eat a little, sleep. Unlike Skarzysko, where all the inmates were Jewish, Leipzig was an international, all-female camp. When we arrived, there were already Czech, French, German, Greek, Hungarian, Polish, and Russian women here. We were the only Jews. Most of the inmates were there for various "anti-Nazi" activities, such as underground movements, political adversity, smuggling, hiding German enemies, or other, allegedly forbidden acts. Most Russians were POW girls taken from the front. Our crime was that we were born to Jewish parents.

The plant where we were to work was located on the outskirts of Leipzig. Nearby were sites where the slave labor camps were situated. Our block-long brick five-story building had been previously occupied by the German military. It was a great improvement over the Skarzysko barracks. Food here wasn't gourmet fare, nor was there an abundance of it, but we wouldn't starve, either. Like Skarzysko, Leipzig was a labor camp. Aside from a small number of prison women who were assigned to kitchen duties, camp cleaning or field jobs, all girls worked in a munitions plant preparing killing supplies.

I worked on an assembly line making small parts for "something." Of approximately one-hundred-fifty people working in this hall, about three-fourths were prison women. A few were "free workers," people who, because of intolerable conditions at home, had signed up for work in Germany in order to receive room and board and a little pay. All the rest were German employees—almost all women. The few German males were old or disabled. The Germans intermingled with the prisoners and the free workers who inspected the killing gear and guarded against any sabotage. (There was always the temptation on the part of the foreigners to incapacitate war supplies.)

In camp, SS women and tower guards were always watching the prisoners. Even though there were language barriers among the prisoners, unfortunate circumstances had forced us to communicate and get along with one another. Our similarities and our common goals had kept us together. Sometimes we had had to use a few translators from different groups to get something across, but somehow we always managed. And so, now, here in the Leipzig camp, my education continued.

We worked six days a week; on the seventh day we didn't rest. We spent Sundays washing our dresses, checking for lice, standing in lines for food, cleaning the premises, getting acquainted with women from other blocks, and, of course, collecting and spreading rumors about the outside world. Our *Stubenälteste* was a Polish prisoner named Nunia. She despised Germans and Jews alike. I don't remember ever having an argument with her, but many girls did. Nunia was moody, unjust, often vicious. She didn't mind turning in girls to the SS just to show who was boss, knowing full well that her victims would be put into solitary confinement, or starved, or tortured. The complete opposite of Nunia was Analese, our SS *Aufseherin,* or "overseer." She loved girls, especially those with beautiful bodies. Whenever other guards weren't around, she would pay no attention to the rules; she would order extra soup for us, let us use toilets without supervision, and even overlook it if we talked to the other workers.

As in Skarzysko, we spent many evenings talking and discussing rumors we would hear at work. We shared tears, confessed sins, learned from one another. We heard that many Skarzysko girls had been shipped to other places, that the men had been supposedly transferred to a few different places, but no one knew where. From the French girls we learned about the French underground, and about the trains that transported French, Belgian, and Dutch Jews to some "unknown destinations." Luckily, there were in each group girls who spoke another language and so could translate. From the Polish girls with whom we had a common language, we found out that most of those who had been arriving here lately came from Warsaw. They had been rounded up during the 1944 Revolt and charged with revolutionary activities. They told us that some Jewish men and women who miraculously managed to escape to the Aryan side during the 1943 Ghetto Uprising had fought with the Poles in the 1944 revolt.[60] One of the girls explained, "The Germans arrested these Jews just as they did us, but when they recognized a Jew in the crowd of detainees, they shot him or her right on the spot. Some gendarmes beat and tortured their victims before shooting them. The same happened to many Polish prisoners who were mistaken for Jews. We had to watch all of it." Before she finished her story, another girl interrupted, "Don't be surprised if you find some Jewish girls here among us."

This was new information to us. Not even the KL girls knew what had had happened in Warsaw after the Ghetto Uprising, after they were shipped to Majdanek. Some heard of a camp named Treblinka, which was being called an extermination camp, but no one had ever returned from there to tell us for sure.

The girls here weren't only from different countries but also from many different walks of life. Among them were the rich and the poor, and college graduates and the barely literate. We had aristocrats and peasantry. There were also a fair share of anti-Semites, who couldn't, even in the camp, be cured of their prejudices. So, along with friendly and informative discussions, we also had a few heated debates in which the KL girls had to remind our compatriots that very little help had come to the Jews from the Aryan side during the Ghetto Uprising. "We expected at least the Polish Resistance Movement to send us some help as we fought a common enemy." A KL girl added, "We were disappointed."

Other girls praised those individual Poles who had had the conscience and courage to provide food, ammunition, help for the ghetto fighters. Many even commended those Poles who had sold survival items to Jews for large sums of money; any help to the Jews was a risky business—a capital offense.

Our Leipzig news and rumors came through many different channels. Occasionally, some German-speaking girls would manage to eavesdrop on radio programs at work; or someone would find a newspaper article or a discarded letter in the trash. Some stories were being picked up by foreign workers from clandestine radio stations and related to prisoners at work. These stories were usually from intercepted British and French underground radio. One of the rumors had it that there had been an assassination attempt on Hitler himself.[61] We weren't sure if it was only wishful thinking. We didn't find out what really happened, but the next day, Hitler gave a long, patriotic speech. We no longer knew what to believe. A few days later, however, an incident confirmed that Germany was in trouble: The German workers seemed very nervous; they were listening closely to their radios, whispering to one another; some looked scared. Shortly before noon, we were told to stop working, vacate the building, and leave for the bomb shelter that was located on the plant premises. In the concrete shelter, about two stories underground, the German workers told us that this was only a drill.

In the smaller room where the German workers were sitting, we smelled coffee brewing. The radio was playing *"Rosamunde"* (the famous "Beer Barrel Polka"). The hall designated for prisoners was equipped with hardwood benches. The only German person in our room was Analese, who was sitting next to one of her favorite girls, smoking a cigarette.

We sat there till the "All Clear" sirens sounded. Next morning at work, we heard that the "practice drill" had been due to an actual air-raid by American and British bombers; much damage had been done to the city.

No longer could the German workers and the guards disguise their concerns and worries. Their newspapers and radios kept reporting successes on battlefields and were predicting victory. The mail from their loved ones, even after being censored, indicated problems, defeats, misery. The people's disappointed faces were telling us the story. In the evenings "on campus," we would discuss these new developments. As time went on, the raids became even more frequent. We were spending more time in the shelter and less at work. Rations were being cut. Guards were nervous. We got to know more about the German *Frauen* who worked alongside us. Our German-speaking girls started conversing with them more often, and we discovered a terrible dilemma: Whenever we saw the women crying and praying for their men, who were away at the fronts, we started feeling sorry for them. Our morale was like a yo-yo.

One day, we would be delighted that Germans were being killed; then, on another day, we would feel sorry for the ones whom we saw crying for them.

Meanwhile, camp life continued. Sundays we cleaned the premises and stood at *Appell*. Whenever the weather was nice, we could see people strolling along the field outside the wires. We watched old people and young women just out walking and enjoying the day. We saw children running, kicking soccer balls, hugging dolls, just playing in the field, often stopping and pointing their small fingers in our direction as though asking, "What kind of animals are those in that huge cage?" We must have looked like herds of zebras. Many tower guards paid no attention to them; others whistled and motioned for them to get away. Some obeyed; others ignored them. The first Sunday I saw people walking in the field, an electric shock went through my body. There were grandmothers and grandfathers and mothers with their children out walking together in family units. I suddenly realized that for years I hadn't seen a child. Yet, surprisingly enough, it hadn't occurred to me before. I mentioned it to a girl who was standing next to me at the *Appell*. She looked at me astonished. "An interesting observation. I hadn't thought of it, either," she said.

These scenes were especially hard on the women who, by force, had been separated from their children. These sights brought about many sighs and tears. It seemed strange that somewhere behind this barbed wire lay a different world, a world where people had relatives and friends, where they were free to live and to love.

During the evening hours, we often discussed these painful scenes, comforting and reassuring the mothers, truthfully believing that they would eventually be reunited with their offspring. It made us feel good, and it gave the mothers something to dream about, something to hope for. Luda, a girl in her mid-twenties from Kielce, used to become hysterical and frantic whenever the subject of lovers and children came up. Those of us who had left behind no boyfriends, lovers, husbands, or children, had little to add to these conversations. We did have much to learn from the girls who did, however.

Occasional arrivals of new prisoners would bring variety and news to the camp. The latest transport had come from Hungary via other camps. These girls told us of the plight of the Hungarian Jews. The news was frightening: Most of them had been shipped to Auschwitz and other camps. We talked to them about the life in our camp. Here, we told them, you don't worry, you don't plan, you don't think. You do as you're told; follow the rules, don't ask questions. Such lessons come in handy. The sooner you learn them, the better. During air-raids, you're sent to the shelter. The bombs are falling, and you hope they'll miss you. You hope the bombing stops.... Well, maybe not; you have mixed feelings. Deep inside, you really want the bombings to continue. Then, you think again: Maybe you don't really want the people to die. You can't take revenge on dead people. Maybe what you really want is for them to live, to see you succeed, and later to beg for your forgiveness and mercy. And surely, you never want anything bad to happen to those you know. Well, you actually believe, you hope, maybe you can be nice to them. You hope you can.... All these voices are talking to you simultaneously. You really don't know what is going on. Will all this ever end? End for good? Are all hopes and wishes only fantasies?

The door to the German room opens. The radio is playing patriotic music; we hear some announcements. Then the music continues; cheerful music; military marches, victory hymns. The faces of the German women are dreary, sad. Like other prisoners, I am here with strangers. It is just as well; I am spared the grief of seeing loved ones suffer. I hope to see them some day and tell them my stories of Sandomierz, the farm, Skarzysko, the train ride, Leipzig. The Hungarian girls listen. We have heard new rumors: "The Russians have crossed the German border. Poland is now free. It won't be long now.... Families and friends will be reunited. Our relatives are waiting for us. Our dreams are coming through. We have even heard rumors that the Americans are now joining the War, that they are coming to help in the bombing. We disregard it—it's too good to be true." German papers are still bragging about military successes; they predict a final victory. "We will save our beloved *Vaterland*!" yells the radio announcer. "We will fight to the last soldier!" The talk sounds familiar, only this time it's in German. We don't understand what's going on, but time passes. The announcer talks about German soldiers performing miraculous victories on the Front. Luckily, no one talks about the Jews. The raid is over. We leave the shelter. On the stairs we hear a German *Frau* say, "It's not very heroic to drop bombs on defenseless people and then fly away." Other Germans agree with her. Walking through the yard to the work hall, we see thick, black smoke coming from one side of the city.

Another winter is quickly approaching, and the prolonged curfew hours keep us inside the building. Winter evenings we spend talking, singing, crying, composing lyrics to familiar tunes, making up poems. We speak about the camp and the War. We talk abut home and family and freedom. The latter we call "fantasies." We talk about subjects that are happy and sad and forbidden.

Hanukkah we celebrate around Christmas time. We sing old traditional songs. No candles, no latkes, no birthday for me, and no Maccabees miracles. Our Christian friends talk about miracles, too. They talk about the Christ Child, Who is to save the world. Christmas songs and poems come in many languages; every nationality has its own version. Even the girls from godless society sing their interpretation of Christmas carols. Each group in its own way celebrates the holidays by recalling the past and hoping for the future. Many trust God's miracles will come true. They believe that only God can save us. Others have long given up on the idea that God will intercede; they call it a "wishful myth." I couldn't be angry with God, for, after all, when I wanted to see a real war, God granted me my wish.

I even lived through many experiences that I didn't for. Among them was a memorable Sunday when a routine *Appell* turned into a nightmare. That Sunday, the guards couldn't come up with the correct number as we were counted. One girl was missing. *Frau Kommandantin* was called. She checked the count. It was one short.

"Tell those foreign pigs," she yelled to the interpreters, "that I'll have ten of them shot dead on the spot if that bitch doesn't show up!" She walked into the building to warm up. It had snowed the day before and all through the night. The sun had started peeking through the clouds just before the *Appell* was called. It was freezing.

After a while, the *Kommandantin* returned. She expected the problem to have been solved. Nothing had changed. No girl in sight. Shots had been fired into the air, but thus far, no one had been killed.

A few of the guards went into the building to eat and warm up. Additional ones were called to help. They took turns. We kept standing. About noon the sun started going down. The wind subsided a bit. Behind the fence, out in the field, children were throwing snowballs. The tower guards chased them away. We kept standing.

Late afternoon, the snow returned. By then our feet were so frigid that they stopped aching. The three-quarter-length striped prison jackets that we got for the winter now covered only parts of the icy urine stains that had soaked through many dresses. We kept standing.

The girls who moved or sat down were mercilessly kicked and beaten; some who fainted were revived with a snow massage; those who fell were pushed next to the fence and left lying in the snow.

At nightfall, the *Appell* that had started in the morning finally ended. The missing girl was still gone, but we were allowed into the building. Inside we found, lined up in orderly fashion, caldrons with hot soup and tea ready for distribution. Many girls were injured storming the hot food. Some suffered severe burns.

Next morning, all those who survived that terrible Sunday, even those with severe burns, showed up for the morning *Appell*, ready for another day's work. (After all, killing supplies have to be delivered on time, no matter what.) In the semi-darkness, we marched to the plant.

Still no one knew what had happened to the missing girl, nor to the girls who had been left lying in the snow by the fence. We only learned that Luda was taken to the "Special Care Unit," which was located in a room on the top floor. We also found out why she used to react so hysterically whenever we talked about children separated from their parents: Luda was about nine months pregnant. We worried about her because here, as in Skarzysko, we had selections, and people not fit for work were deported to unknown destinations. We had noticed some time ago that Luda was getting larger, but this wasn't as surprising as it seemed: A number of us were becoming quite bloated from irregular or missing menstruations, and from abnormal nutrition. I remembered Luda exchanging her dress for a "larger" size, but neither I nor the girl who traded with her knew the reason.

Later, at work, we also found out the mystery of the missing girl. She was Kasia, a Polish girl from Block 6. Rumor had it that she was taken out in a trash barrel by a crew of foreign workers and hidden in one of their underground burrows. Her bunk mate, as well as a couple of her coworkers, were put into solitary confinement. A few days later, the three girls were released. They had freshly shaved hair and bruises on their faces and bodies. They talked very little.

At the plant, German workers talked little, too. By now the Russians were coming from the east, the Western Allies from the west. Germany was surrounded; the people looked nervous and worried.

The only consolation was the weather. It was getting better. Yet even this didn't improve the situation. As the sky cleared, Allied bombers resumed their air-raids. In the bomb shelter, we heard German *Frauen* talking about their homes, their families, the upcoming two-day Easter holiday. Jewish girls knew that it must be near Passover time. In the camp, inmates started preparing for the two major holidays, making up songs, poems, recalling the Exodus and the Resurrection.[62] It made us feel better. It gave us new hope. We knew things must change soon. We were right.

It wasn't long before our lives changed drastically.

XV. The March

I don't know the date when our established way of life turned around, but I do know that it was after Passover and Easter, because we had already celebrated those holidays in the usual camp manner. It happened after dark, when we were about to settle in for the night. An unscheduled *Appell* was called. We assembled in front of the building and were counted in a very precise manner. All the usual papers were signed. We weren't dismissed.

The guards seemed unusually nervous. We thought that someone was missing again. We still remembered that January Sunday *Appell*. From far off, we heard the pounding of artillery and the already familiar sound of falling bombs. I covered my ears with both hands, but the fearful noise still penetrated this protective shield. Two searchlights were sliding along, from horizon to horizon, lighting up the sky.

"The Front must be moving closer," I heard someone remark. "Allied planes must be bombing the city. It must be German artillery returning the fire," another voice answered. "The Russians are not very far from here, either," remarked someone from the back.

I grabbed the hands of Eva and Regina, the two girls at my sides. Bronia and Sala were on the outside of the row. No one was able to figure out why an *Appell* had been called at such a late hour. Someone mentioned the resemblance of it to the last night in Skarzysko. It wasn't long before we found out:

"Turn left! Forward, march!" we heard a guard's voice yell from the darkness. Walking through the wide-open gate in rows of five, we were counted again. Guards at the gate looked at our prison numbers and checked off each one carefully. More papers were signed. "They are probably taking us to the bomb shelter at the plant. It's dangerous out here," was the common opinion of the girls.

We marched on a dirt road leading to the main highway. An unusually large number of guards were with us: guards on motorcycles, on bicycles, with rifles and dogs surrounding the long column of marching prisoners. Passing the intersection where we always turned around on the way to the plant, we didn't turn but proceeded straight ahead.

It was then that we began to wonder what was going on: "We are going in the wrong direction. Where in the world are they taking us? Why?" we kept asking one another. The night was cloudy, dark, and fairly warm for April. We walked past all the familiar roads, and still we kept walking. Then, a gruesome thought ran through my mind: "Maybe they are taking us to the train...." I don't know why I said it aloud, but I did. Right then, I could feel the tension rise in the girls around me. "You might be right!" Regina said, pressing my hand.

At dawn, the march came to a halt. I looked around. The column of prisoners was endless. We were divided into groups of twenty-five each, and instructed to sit on the ground. Guards surrounded the field. The ground was wet from the morning dew; the cold moisture penetrated our clothes. "No moving around! No standing or walking!" yelled the guard from across the road when he saw some of the girls lifting themselves off the ground. We got some bread and water, then went back into formation. The procession continued down a side road. We tried to figure out where we were; we noticed that most of the road signs were gone. One of the girls remarked, "They must have taken them off to confuse the invading armies. That's the way we did it in Poland when the Germans were coming."

The next couple of days and nights we spent walking. At the infrequent stops, we were instructed to sit in fields and ditches while the guards ate, fed their dogs, and changed work-shifts. The only nourishment we had was the bread and water that we had gotten that first morning. We resorted to eating blades of weeds and pieces of tree bark that we picked from the roadside during our short breaks. We continued walking down clean, well-kept side roads and abandoned highways, far from towns and villages. Only on rare occasions did we walk through some hamlets; when we did, the places were always deserted. Days and nights, we heard artillery fire pounding from far in the East; some nights the horizon was on fire.

After a few more days of no food or water, our walking pace started decreasing. Besides being exhausted, hungry and thirsty, we felt abandoned and helpless. Adding to the problem were our aching feet. Many girls, including myself, had taken off our clogs because they were rubbing against the blisters that had developed on our heels and toes. Walking barefoot on concrete pavement created bloody wounds on our soles.

Soon, however, the pain was overshadowed by hallucination. We no longer cared where we were going or whether we would ever get there. The idea of freedom was forgotten. Our brains no longer responded to reason or logic. We just mechanically kept putting one foot in front of the other.

It was then that the shooting of those who lagged behind started. The girls who couldn't keep pace with the column, those who fell or stepped out of line, were hit with bullets. There were enough guards who thought that it was their patriotic duty to obey the Führer's orders. They had orders to shoot; they told us so. Although some guards overlooked the strict orders and transgressed against their patriotic duty, there were many others who seemed to shoot with pleasure, as though for the sheer lust of killing. Sometimes, as we were slowing down, the sound of a shot would be heard from the back. Then there would be silence. It had been a warning to continue walking. We saw girls on the side roads who looked like skeletons, some with shaved hair and bulging eyes. I hadn't seen anything quite like it since I left the Warsaw Ghetto. We just walked by, looked, didn't even stop, not even to ask a question or to offer a word of hope.

One day we passed a girl whose pathetic look would haunt me for days: her dress pulled behind her waist, her legs bleeding from wounds, her eyes glazed, foam coming from her mouth. Passing by her, Eva poked me in the side. "I feel like vomiting," she whispered.

"There's nothing in your stomach," replied Bronia, overhearing her.

"Keep going," came a voice from behind. "Don't stop!"

Green watery stuff was coming out of Eva's mouth, running down her filthy dress. Her steps weakened, her knees buckled. "Don't stop!" we begged her, and we grabbed her under her arms.

"You'll make it to the next rest stop," we assured her. She did. She was lucky: About an hour later, we came to a stop at a small pond. The water was covered with a yellowish-green moss and shoots of all kinds of underground flora, with all kinds of jumping and crawling creatures. We looked at the water in amazement. To us, it looked like an oasis. Regina was the first one to jump out of line. "May God Almighty be blessed!" she said as she ran to the pond. Several girls followed her. Holding our breath, we waited for the shots. They didn't come. We looked at the guards. Two stood next to me, looking at the girls running to the pond. One had her hands in her pockets, the other, a cigarette in his mouth. We looked at them, wondering what they were going to do.

Soon, we had no more power to resist the sight of water, and, little by little, almost the whole marching column followed the few girls to the pond. Scooping the slimy water into our soiled palms, we began to swallow it, insects, moss, and all.

I couldn't remember anything ever tasting so good. I took one scoop after another, and was still reaching for more. A shot.... Like a herd of deer at the sight of a lion, we started running into formation, still licking the slime from our lips. Regina again blessed the Lord for giving us the water. We blessed our "humane" guards, who held in their power the future of our lives, who had let us live another day.

After the nourishing break, our column moved mechanically forward, always keeping in mind that the angel of death was never far way. Actually, at times, we weren't even afraid of dying. "You die because you have to die." No problem. The brain could no longer perceive fear of danger. I could not even feel the pain that must have been present in my bare, raw, scab-covered feet, nor the bugs and lice that were helping themselves to the juices of my body. Yet, during all that resignation, there was always the spark that kept saying, "Don't give up! Not yet! Not now! Try a little longer; it's close to the end! So near the goal!"

Artillery pounding usually brought new courage, new hope.

During all the days of marching, we never stopped in towns or villages. Whenever we had to pass through a village, the inhabitants were ordered to stay home. The neatly painted houses with flower-decorated balconies looked friendly and peaceful. Sometimes we saw people working in the fields, but they were always kept away from us. Once, however, a startling incident took place due to an oversight by the guards:

Our road led us through a village, and because we had to slow down in such a case, we could see women and children curiously peeking through their nicely draped windows, surely wandering what kind of creatures were hiking through their town. While the guards were busy watching us, an old woman carrying a large, heavy basket in her arms, ran out of a roadside house and, very unexpectedly, started throwing raw, cut-up carrots into the column of starving, exhausted women. The girls started trampling over one other trying to grab a piece of the life-saving commodity.

I was lucky. I had been walking only a few rows from that woman when she first came out of her house. Other girls were running out of line to take part in the action, paying no attention to the guards, who, at this moment, were preoccupied, arguing with the old lady who was refusing to get back into her house. As my row was passing in front of that lady, Bronia heard her yelling something to the guards. She translated: "You guys leave me alone! I hope someone would give food to my son who might now be walking somewhere in Siberia. God only knows where the Ruskies have taken him!"

The old woman was still yelling when our row moved on. We walked with pieces of carrots in our hands, biting off bits, sharing with those less fortunate who had had no chance to get some of their own. We had passed by this lovely lady, and didn't even have a chance to thank her for the generosity. The girls walking farther back saw the guards stepping on some carrots and two of them pushing the old lady into her house. Before she went inside, she threw the rest of the carrots into the marching column.

We kept on walking. Occasionally, we heard shots fired. We kept walking.

One time, I passed by the body of a girl who had been shot. A female guard was scrupulously entering the girl's prison number into the roster. Everybody had to be accounted for, dead or alive. The corpse was then piled, by other prisoners, on top of corpses that were already on the motorcycle sidecars.

It was the next evening, or maybe the one after, that we halted for one of our rests. The rain that had been coming down all day subsided. The raincoat-covered guards mounted on their vehicles herded us into a fenced-in field, where we were to stay overnight. Only about half of the original number of girls were there, the others having been rerouted to another highway the day before as we passed through an intersection. We were instructed to lie on the ground and not move.

The Eastern sky was lit by artillery fire. In the west and the north the pounding went on for hours— way late into the night. Then the shooting stopped.

We were allowed to get up, but had to remain in the pen. Those of us who were still able to move got off the soaked ground. The water that had penetrated my dress made me shudder—but made my blistered feet feel much better.

Soon, word got around that someone had spotted piles of red and sugar beets stacked in the field outside the pen. "Maybe for planting?" one girl asked. Whoever could move stormed through the wires and, disregarding the consequences, started running for the beets. We were expecting someone to stop us, or for the shooting to start, but neither happened. To our amazement, we found some guards wrapped in their coats and blankets, asleep on the ground. Those who were on duty seemed to pay no attention to our looting spree. "They won't dare shoot now," said a girl's voice from the darkness. "They'd disclose our whereabouts to the enemy if they did."

At dawn, there were fewer guards than before. Many dogs were gone, too. The guards who were left were dirty, unshaven, and tired. They dragged their feet the way we did ours. The road in front of us was lined with an endless crowd of *Frauen* dragging their children and pulling their belongings on carts. It reminded me of the Polish refugees fleeing the German invaders.

"Over the bridge!" we heard one guard shout to another as they passed us on their bikes.

Far on the western horizon, we recognized a silhouette of a bridge. "Yes! Over the bridge, and we have it made!" said a girl. We figured that the aim of the fleeing masses was to run from the oncoming Russian Front. They were hoping that the enemy across the river, the Western Allies, would be more merciful than the Russians. We, the marching prisoners, were being kept as hostages, as shields, maybe even as barter material.

The sun was setting by the time the few remaining loyal guards led us to the river bank. What used to be an orderly column of prisoners was now a disarranged bunch of dragging women. We were told to sit on the ground where the sandy beach met the paved street. We had a great view from that hill. The end of the fleeing crowd was nowhere to be seen. Closer to the river were many abandoned military vehicles and heaps of discarded gear. We saw many soldiers changing to civilian clothes, which they were pulling from the deserted hand carts, not realizing that the military police guarding the bridge and regulating the traffic were giving priority to uniformed soldiers.

From the bewildered looks in the guards' eyes, it was obvious that no one was sure what to do. Their fearful faces revealed pain and cowardice, some human qualities that we never thought these people could possess. How differently they looked from those powerful, decorated heroes who only a few years ago had proudly marched the streets of Warsaw in victory parades....

While we sat, observing the confused, fleeing Germans, the darkened eastern horizon lit up with fire; it looked as bright as day. The pounding of artillery that had been going on the whole evening was replaced now by the roar of planes. We couldn't see them, but we could hear them coming from the north and the east.

A cool wind was blowing from the river; the weather turned chilly. We moved closer together to keep warm.

Explosions and shelling were coming from all sides, followed by periods of silence.

I was tired enough to die, but I forced myself not to fall asleep. From nowhere a ball of fire appeared in the sky. A thunder of guns and rockets broke the silence, followed by machine gun fire that started from very close by. I lay quietly, with my arms wrapped around my ears.... The next thing I remember was somebody shaking me. "Wake up!" I heard Sala's voice yelling. I opened my eyes. It was dawn, but the nightly fog hadn't yet lifted. Sala was kneeling over me. Many girls who had been with us the night before were gone. A few remained. Another group of Leipzig girls moved close to us. We welcomed the new girls, and decided to stick together.

The air around us was filled with smoke. Shelling could be heard near by. "Up! Up!" the girls around me were screaming. Then I heard a male voice and saw a young soldier with a rifle pointed. He wasn't one of the guards. He wasn't even German.

Our guards were all gone.

XVI. Liberation

"*Davai nazad!*" the young soldier yelled in a foreign language, pointing his rifle in the direction that he wanted us to go. "Keep moving to the rear!"

"He is Russian," said Sala. "Get up and let's run from this shooting!" Other Russian soldiers soon arrived, screaming and shooting. All of a sudden, shells and bullets started coming from the direction of the riverboats. All the Russian soldiers dropped to the ground. They yelled some more. "Down to the ground! Down to the ground, you stupid bunch of women!" An older lady, around thirty, who must have come with the new group of girls, remembered a few words of Russian that she had learned from her mother. She translated.

Seeing the Russian uniforms now in front of them, a few of the new girls, who the night before had been too tired even to crawl, were so overjoyed that they started jumping and dancing around the young, confused soldiers. They were grabbing the poor guys by their hands, hanging from their necks, kissing and hugging them, screaming and crying. The poor fighters, with rifles pointed, who were expecting enemies on the battlefield, didn't know what to make of such an unexpected reception. Renewed cannon fire coming from the river made the decision easy; they started running and shooting and shouting, telling us to get down on our bellies again.

By this time, more Russian soldiers had come around us. Like the first few, they seemed to wonder who we were, what we were doing in the middle of the frontlines, what they were supposed to do with us, or to us. Some thought that we were German *Frauen* disguised in prison clothes. Our translator told them that we were Polish—Polish Jews.

One of the soldiers looked at us suspiciously and said, "German spies!"

At the bridge, the scene had changed a lot from the night before. There were still a lot of people, but the crowds at the bank had dispersed. Sporadic shooting was coming from a few riverboats. We found many German military uniforms on the ground. Russian boots were now trampling over the glorious, swastika-marked sleeves and collars, over the *"Gott mit Uns"*-engraved belt buckles.

"Keep on running back if you don't want to get killed here! Run as far from here as you can! The Front is coming through here!" yelled the soldiers as they passed by us.

All roads leading from the riverbank were full of loaded handcarts, German tanks, combat gear, and military vehicles that had been abandoned during the night. A few *Frauen* with children waving white handkerchiefs were running in the direction of the fields, away from the riverbank (which was now full of Russian soldiers and flying bullets).[63] Assuming that these *Frauen* knew the area, and a way to some safe place, we followed them.

All around us, the shooting continued. Planes roared low over our heads; German planes, Russian planes, all kinds of planes, chasing one other, diving and climbing. The air was full of smoke and the smell of acid, saltpeter, and blood. Corpses were scattered among the wounded. All through the fields, limbs separated from bodies were soaking in blood. German and Russian soldiers still alive but unable to move, covered the ground. Leaping over the dead and wounded, we kept running away from the shooting. A woman's body, partly uncovered, lay amid the dead and wounded fighters. A soldier turned her over with his rifle butt, exposing her bare breasts from under the torn dress. Whether she was dead or alive was impossible to tell. The soldier left her where he found her. We were going to stop, but he started yelling, "What the hell are you idiots doing here?"

He didn't wait for an answer. He just ordered us to run.

Farther down the road, we halted and looked into some abandoned carts. "There might be some food in them, and maybe even some cloth to wrap our blistered feet with," suggested one of our girls. But before she had finished speaking, more shooting came our way, and we resumed running.

When the shelling stopped temporarily, trucks marked with red crosses drove into the field. Uniformed men and women with Red Cross armbands ran with stretchers to pick up the dead and help with the wounded. One soldier on the ground was groaning so loudly that we stopped to see if we could help. He was German. His left leg was almost disconnected from his body; blood was streaming through his shattered pants. Two medics ran over to him and laid him on a stretcher. While one of them was cutting his pants with a knife, the other ordered us to move on.

It was midday. By the sun, it was about two or three o'clock when we finally got out of the main area of shooting. But here, too, the roads were full of abandoned German refugee cars and deserted military vehicles. Supply wagons and Red Cross trucks were blocking the main roads. Russian guards and other non-combat personnel were keeping order.

Finally, paying no attention to the Russians who were urging us to go on, we stormed over the loaded carts and started searching for food. We dismantled the first few, but found nothing to eat. Someone must have looted them before, for everything was turned topsy-turvy. We persisted and searched other carts. Finally, in one of them, we found some bread, lard, and sugar. One of the new girls found a cake and some cookies. We sat down under a tree and feasted. While resting, we got acquainted with the girls who had joined us at the riverbank. Our new group consisted of sixteen girls: My five long-time friends, six girls we had met at the river, three Hungarian girls we had met in the field, and the older lady, *Pani* Konova, who had become our official translator, as well as the mother of our "pack." It was a union of girls who during the long march had gotten separated from their friends. Being in a large group, especially in a strange territory, made us feel better. Aside from *Pani* Konova, who was older, the girls in our group ranged in age from sixteen to twenty-two.

After the feast, those of us who didn't get sick from gorging on the looted food, got back to the abandoned carts and started searching for clothes. It turned out to be easier than looking for food. We shed our zebra clothes, dumping them right there on the field, and got dressed in our new civilian attire. We talked about saving the striped dresses as souvenirs, but decided to leave them to the lice. Many of us, however, did rip off the numbers for souvenirs.

The dress I found was light brown, made of a jersey-like fabric. It was embroidered with tiny pink-reddish flowers with pin-head-sized holes for pistils—quite elegant. The other girls, too, were dressed quite elegantly. Hairless and barefooted, we stared at each other and delightfully admired our new looks. The shoes that we had pulled from the wagons we carried in our hands. Our cut, blistered feet weren't yet ready for them.

During our extended break, the *Frauen* whom we had followed from the river, disappeared. Yet all of us seemed quite sure that we would reach our destination without guides, especially since none of us had the slightest idea where we wanted to go.

Farther down the road, where the Russian troops were regrouping, we had to detour to make room for emergency vehicles. Passing the rows of dead bodies, one of our new girls, Zofy, ran over to where the corpses lay and, bending over one of them, began to do something. We thought that she noticed a moving body, so a few of us rushed to see if we, too, could help. As we got closer, we were absolutely stunned when we saw her removing a ring from the corpse's finger.

"No one buries people with rings on," she said, somewhat embarrassed. "Someone will take it if I don't."

From a road behind the crossing, we saw a line of German POWs. They looked distressed and disappointed. Disarmed, with hands over their heads and surrounded by victorious soldiers with rifles pointed, they were following Russian tanks. We watched the solemn, gloomy, unshaven faces of the once mighty "Master Race" dragging their bound-up legs, legs which not long ago had been marching in goosestep, seeming to have the whole world under their feet.[64] Surprisingly, I didn't rejoice in their fate; it just made me sick. Like a flash of lightning, my father's old saying came to mind: "Remember, nothing lasts forever."

Actually, we were already liberated from the Nazis, but we were still on German soil, not knowing what to expect either from the German population or from our Russian liberators. The War wasn't yet over; shooting, shelling and bombing were all around us, and there were still many pockets of German resistance scattered in the woods and villages. Our liberators were still fighting, and were themselves not sure of their fate.

Running in the direction of houses that were now visible a few kilometers up the road, we encountered remnants of the battle and more dead bodies. Some must have been killed not too long ago: The blood under them was still fresh and red. Not one of us could figure out how it happened that they hadn't yet been picked up; this place was at the far end of the battlefield. The mystery was solved when we saw a huge crater nearby. It must have been a bomb or mine that killed them after the Front had already passed. Next to the crater, under a shattered tree, sat a group of Russian soldiers guarded by a tank. We could see only a few of them, but we heard many of them singing. A security guy commanded us to keep moving.

It was almost dark as we neared a village. Black smoke coming from that direction hindered much of the view. The closer we came to the village, the more apprehensive we became. We had no idea whether this place was abandoned or still inhabited by Germans. Now that we were, supposedly, free, we had to figure out on our own where to go and what to do, who was our enemy and who was our friend.

Far out in the field, we saw other groups of girls, still in striped dresses, who were also heading for the village. Just up the street was a skeleton of a house from which fire had burned out, but the smoke of which was still rising and darkening the air.

Entering the village, we spotted an open stable behind a house. We stood for a while listening for suspicious sounds or movements, but the only noises we could hear were those of shelling and explosions coming from nearby.

We stopped for the night. Half of us girls lay down on the manure-filled straw to sleep, leaving the others on guard. When the sun rose, my friends and I were on duty. A loud explosion shook the ground and awoke the girls in the stable. We decided to move on when we discovered two of our new girls missing. Searching the stable, we found Masha and Roza still asleep. They were sick and unable to get up. Most of us had recovered from the vomiting and stomach cramps that we had encountered after our luxurious meal, but these two were getting worse. We had no idea what to do. It was the first time in years that any of us had to make a decision. We found a small, four-wheeled hand-pulled wagon and put the two sick girls in it and started wandering through town.

Roaming the streets, we found many burned-out houses; those still intact had been either taken over by Russian soldiers, occupied by German refugees, or filled by other freed prisoners. At the town square, we came across the Russian temporary headquarters that was set up in the city hall. *Pani* Konova and two of us walked inside and asked for help. We found out that there was no assistance available. No one knew anything about the town, nor the people who lived there. The Russians themselves had been here only for a few days. They suggested that we find a vacant house and stay in it. *Komrad Kommandant* warned us not to venture out of town until the battle moved farther out and the roads around were cleared of mines and other explosives. He also advised that we put on white armbands or else carry white flags for protection, because the Russians were instructed to arrest anyone who didn't comply with that ordinance.

Pani Konova told him that we weren't Germans, that we were coming from camps, but *Komrad Kommandant* said that that didn't matter. Some soldiers, when drunk, might shoot anyone who didn't carry the surrender sign.

Late in the day, we found a small, one-family house. A large white flag made out of a bed-sheet was flying over the entrance gate. A shed door was open, and we could see shelves stocked with cans and bottles. We stopped and asked the old lady who was looking out the door if she would give us some water. She looked scared. She said nothing. She moved away from the door, leaving it open. A few of us walked in, and the others followed.

The calendar on the wall showed "April 30, 1945." We must have been underway ten or twelve days.

Next to the calendar hung a few pictures of German military men. On the buffet were two photos of soldiers, both ornamented with black bands and rosary beads. When the old woman saw us looking at the photos, she pointed to the two in black and, with tears in her eyes, said, "I lost both of them in this ugly war. My husband, well, I don't know where he is." Then, realizing that she was lamenting to the wrong people, she wiped her tears with her hands and left the room.

We spent almost two adventurous weeks in this house, sleeping on sofas, on floors, and in beds. During the first few days, we were busy organizing food, soap, and fuel. Almost anything edible had been taken by the Russians as soon as they entered the town. However, we did find some leftovers that kept us from starvation. I remember the first Friday morning, for it was the day a few of our new girls went food hunting. Soon, Lora came home holding a fabulous fresh fish. "I saw a Russian soldier walking from the river carrying a bucket of fish. This large one was hanging over his shoulder. I just pulled it off and ran." She laughed, proudly displaying her catch. "Yes, he saw me, but said nothing."

Pani Konova, who besides her other duties was also our official cook, prepared the fish, and we all shared in the feast. We even lit the customary candle in honor of the Sabbath.

Our lives began to get somewhat organized.

The day when I found some paper and a pen, I spent most of my time in the outside shed writing notes, recollecting my memories. Of course, I still had my diaries, one in Warsaw, the other in Sandomierz. Nevertheless, I scribbled down everything that I could remember about my life, knowing that soon I would read it to my family and friends. I was making entries of the past and of daily events. There was no shortage of adventures to write about. The girls I was with kept suggesting important events that they thought should be included.

One evening, as we sat in the yard talking, three Russian soldiers came to the fence. "I saw the little German girl with my fish run into this house," one of them said in a broken German mixed with Russian. "I thought I'd come and visit and see how she liked my fish. I brought my comrades to show them the place."

"We are not German," said *Pani* Konova in her broken Russian, and she told the guys our story.

"Well," said the first soldier, "we just came to visit, not to get the fish back." The other one added, "Don't be afraid." They talked with us for a while, then left.

Masha and Roza, the two sick girls, didn't join in our conversation. Masha, who had been sick for quite some time, was spitting a secretion mixed with blood every time she coughed. Her skinny body was lost in her new dress. A dark brown mossy fuzz covered her otherwise bald head. Roza got ill after devouring her first meal. She was still vomiting, but otherwise she did start to feel better. Before the soldiers left, Masha's cousin, Hayka, told them about our sick girls and asked for help.

"Okay," one of them said, "let's see what we can do."

The next morning, five Russian soldiers came to our house. Two of them we recognized from the day before. Among the three new ones was a fellow from the tank division who spoke some Yiddish and a few Polish words that he had learned during his stay in Poland. His name was Boris. He was from the Ukraine. He told us how had he watched his father and little brother being shot by the Nazis. Boris himself had escaped the shooting and, at the age of eighteen, joined the armed forces.

We embraced him and thanked him for coming. We were thrilled not only to see a Jew but to know that some of them were in uniform, fighting the Nazis. Boris came equipped with a military leave and an old bicycle. He was prepared to take our two girls to a field hospital on the other side of the forest.

Roza didn't go. Since Masha's condition had worsened, we wrapped her in a blanket given to us by our "landlady," put her on the bike frame, and, accompanied by her cousin Hayka, Sala, and myself, Boris started pushing the vehicle through the forest. During the three-hour-long walk, he told us about how the Russian Jews who weren't evacuated deep into Soviet territory had been killed by the Nazis, how the Russian armed forces had fought the Germans all the way from Stalingrad.[65] The Russians were hoping to meet with the Allies at the Elbe River very soon and finally finish the War. He told us, proudly, about the liberation of the Auschwitz death camp, about the horrors he saw there and the shocking stories that he heard from the survivors. He asked us how we had survived the War. He was surprised to find some Jews still alive. We had to stop frequently to let Masha rest. She didn't talk much, but at one of the stops, she did tell Boris that her older brother and a cousin had escaped to Russia when the Germans invaded her town. The last she had heard from them was in 1942. Both of them had joined the Soviet military.

Sporadic shots were heard throughout the forest. We were scared that the Germans might be hiding behind trees or in trenches. Boris told us that he had to go back to the front after his few days of leave were up. As we neared the hospital, we saw Russian trucks full of wounded soldiers. We stopped at the fence. Boris showed his documents and explained the problem. After we finished filling out all the required papers, an army nurse tended to Mash. She suggested that we leave her in the hospital until she could be checked by one of the doctors who were all busy with the severely wounded. "I'll see to it that someone sees her as soon as possible." Masha and Hayka signed some papers. The nurse took Masha away after telling us to leave the premises.

From that day on, we had visitors every day. Russians started dropping in at will, "just to see how the Polish girls are doing." At the beginning we enjoyed the visits of our liberators. We talked, sang, and laughed. Soon, however, the visits became a nuisance. Some of our visitors came intoxicated, looking for more to drink. They drank perfume, cologne, rubbing alcohol, whatever would pass their scientific test (namely, setting a match to the liquid: if it lit up, it was good for drinking). Gasoline was rationed and hard to find.

We grew scared of these frequent visitors as the situation began to get out of hand. Our liberators had started looking for more than just drinks. We found out from other liberated girls in town that one of their friends was raped. Some of them thought we owed them favors for freeing us. We didn't deny their merits; their claims were legitimate; we simply didn't agree on the price. When we refused to consider their method of payment, some had become angry and called us vulgar names. *Pani* Konova understood the problem better than any of us younger girls and gave us long lectures. She also begged the guys to leave us alone. Actually many didn't have to be told; they were nice fellows who would drop in just for conversation, to tell us about their experiences in Poland, how courageously they had fought. Occasionally, they talked about their families, or listened to our stories. But the drunkards and vulgar ones were making it bad for everyone. One of them reasoned with *Pani* Konova: "We are going to the Front. Tomorrow we may be dead; yet these 'holy virgins' are worried about a little fun." We did feel sorry for these poor men. A few of us even suggested, quite in earnest, that we would gladly join their army and help them bring this war to an end. They didn't want to hear what we were saying.

Finally, we had to resort to a measure that we had been trying to avoid. Without identifying the offenders, a few of us reported our problem to the Russian authorities. *Pani* Konova spoke to *Komrad Kommandant,* who wrote down our complaints and our correct address. Then he politely told us not to worry; he would take care of it. He apologized for the soldiers' improper behavior and explained that military personnel were prohibited from entering private homes, that the boys were violating the rules. He promised that no soldier would bother us again.

We thanked him nicely and restated the offer that we had made to the soldiers: We knew that there were many women in the Russian armed forces, and we wanted to join them. This idea didn't appeal to him. His answer was *"nyet."*

Well, *Komrad Kommandant* kept his promise. For the next couple of nights, not one soldier came to our house. On the third day, as we were getting ready for supper, *Komrad Kommandant*, accompanied by two high-ranking officers, appeared at the door. The three were older men. *Komrad Kommandant* asked if we had had any problems with the soldiers. We said no, and thanked him for his prompt and helpful action. He then asked if he and his companions could come in. Well, we said, "Yes." They looked so dignified in their classy uniforms, with epaulets and chests full of medals, that we welcomed them with pleasure. They were very polite. They talked about the battles being fought not far from the village, and assured us that the War would be over very soon. After a nice little talk, they left.

A couple of days later, *Komrad Kommandant* returned with a few friends. He then started visiting us almost daily. Like the soldiers before them, these gentlemen enjoyed talking about their great war accomplishments, about their achievements on the battlefield and their lives in the military. They tried to avoid any conversations about their families. Such subjects were too painful even for "macho" guys; brave courageous heroes didn't show vulnerability to emotions.

Nevertheless, embarrassing situations sometimes happened. One time our conversation turned from war heroism to family ties. Colonel Youra started talking about his wife and children. "It has been about two years since I saw them. Even longer since I've seen my parents," he said. He took out a family picture from his wallet and sighed deeply. "I was scheduled for a leave, but I got wounded and spent the time in a hospital." He pulled up his pant leg and showed us a scar just below his left knee. "After my hospital stay came the big German offensive and I was sent back to the front." As he looked at the pictures of his children, we saw tears running down his face. Our brave colonel turned his head and bashfully wiped his eyes. When it became obvious to him that we were watching, he just wept openly. He said that he hadn't heard from his family for a long time, but liked to believe that it was the fault of the mail delivery. "There was a time that I didn't even think about them," he admitted, with downcast eyes. "We were losing many battles and great numbers of our best soldiers. I didn't think I'd make it. With death chasing you day and night, your mind is not in working condition...." He hadn't finished the sentence when *Komrad Kommandant* interrupted.

"Stop whining," he said. "I thought we came here to have a good time with the girls." Saying that, *Komrad Kommandant* then grabbed my friend Tolla, who just happened to be standing next to him, and started hugging and kissing her. As we watched in disbelief, he threw her on the bed. She begged him to leave her alone. We started screaming and pushing him away, but he threw himself on top of her and, holding her down, murmured something in Russian, either to her or to himself, something unintelligible. Before we could pull him off, he got himself up, took a look at the crotch of his pants, and quickly sat down on a nearby chair, putting his hat over the spot on his pants. To Tolla, who was still lying on the bed, shaking in disbelief, he said, "I am sorry, my dear."

Colonel Youra and the other officer took him by his arms pulled him off the chair, and, while walking him to the door, said, "We all had one too many." He didn't need to say it; we had smelled it when these good-looking officers first came through the door.

I went back to my corner in the shed and, by candlelight, put another entry into my diary. As the candle flickered in the bottle, I thought of the ghetto and how I used to do my homework by candlelight; I wondered if I would ever get back to school, and about all the education I had been receiving away from formal schooling. Since I was preparing a diary to be read by my family and friends, I wanted to make sure not to forget any important events that had happened in Skarzysko, on the train ride, in Leipzig, on the march, and afterwards. I was sure that I would find at least one of my two diaries (Warsaw and Sandomierz) intact when I returned home.

Since I had left the riverbank by the bridge, I had seen military men of the "Master Race," those once powerful soldiers, walking disarmed, discouraged, disappointed, with their arms up, hands over heads, following instructions of a few young, armed and uniformed Russian boys. I watched their frightened eyes and bearded faces, and I wondered what the once dynamic heroes were thinking now. I saw once mighty warriors overcome with affection, crying like babies; I saw weak old ladies gaining unbelievable strength and self-reliance. I saw bloodshed, bravery, laughter, tears; love and hate; integrity and viciousness. I began to suffer from headaches as I struggled to sort out all of my experiences; I was running out of paper trying to write it all down. I still kept having the dizzy spells that had been haunting me since my typhus.

For a few days we had no visitors. It was quiet in the house, and we were relaxed.

Then, one day about noon our distinguished guests showed up in the yard bringing a whole group of other Russian officers and soldiers with them. We were surprised to see them at this unusual hour, and in such a festive mood: They were singing, laughing, cheering, and jumping for joy. We got scared. We had never seen so many of them together, or behaving so strangely, not even in their drunken states.

Seeing our frightened faces, one of the officers yelled, "Let's celebrate! Hurrah, girls! Be happy! Let's drink and be merry!"

This talk scared us even more. Finally, we heard one of them yell, "Hurrah! The War is over!" Then all the guys joined in: "It's over! Over! Over! The Germans surrendered yesterday! This is the day we all have been waiting for!" our visitors screamed, almost simultaneously.

The wall calendar showed "May 9, 1945."

Six terrible years of killing, burning, shooting, bombing, shelling, epidemics, starvation, freezing, and torture had finally come to an end. We celebrated.

Besides the drinks, our visitors had brought with them bread and crackers, sugar and jam, dried herring and fresh fish. We ate, sang, kissed, and hugged. After the meal, three girls walked off with a few soldiers to the shed outside, hugging and kissing. Two might have even celebrated this joyous occasion by ending their years of celibacy. Who knows? The third one chickened out at the last minute and, running from the shed, said, "I thought they were joking."

In the next few days many of our visitors were transferred from this village. They were replaced by officers and soldiers who were coming from the already disbanded Front. It didn't take the new guys long to find our address.

We knew that our stay in this village would come to an end. Besides the problems with visitors, we were running out of food. Everything in this village, from the fish in the lake to the last can of preserves, was being looted. Some German escapees were returning to their homes. We, too, started planning for a trip home.

"Planning" was all new to us. Decision making was frightening. We asked our visitors for advice. One of them suggested that we get a travel permit from the Russian authorities if we didn't want to be stopped on the way. We also found out that there was no public transportation anyplace close: All German vehicles had been either destroyed or confiscated. Military vehicles were prohibited from taking civilian passengers. However, some railroad tracks had been restored farther east.

Before starting our trip we had a visit from our soldier friend, Boris. He had returned unharmed, and came to say goodbye. He told us about his last days on the battlefield and took a few of us to see Masha in the hospital.

She was still very sick and couldn't be released, but she was glad to see us. She asked us to tell her folks at home that the Russians had promised to drive her to Poland as soon as her condition improved.

After checking all possibilities for transportation and finding none, we took off on foot. Into the hand wagon in which we had transported Masha and Roza from the stable, we placed the few belongings that we had picked up in the village, and we started on our way.

It was a few days journey to the place where the train station used to be. We walked through farms and villages hunting for food and resting in abandoned stables or barns. Some Russian soldiers, in trucks, on motorcycles and bicycles, passed us by. Some whistled, some laughed, or stopped and asked questions. Without our prison uniforms we were often taken for German *Frauen.*

One morning a canvas-covered truck half-full of soldiers stopped. The driver offered us a ride. He hopped off the driver's seat and was ready to open the back flap of the truck when *Pani* Konova asked him if it was against the law. He said that it was, "But, you know, rules were made to be broken, and who wouldn't break the law for a bunch of girls?"

"We'd better not go," said *Pani* Konova. We skipped the offer and continued walking.

A day later we did accept a ride. The back of the truck was vacant; the driver and co-driver were sitting in the front. They drove us for about thirty kilometers, then let us off, before turning another way. After a few more days on foot, we arrived at a place that once had been a railroad station. Hundreds of people were lining the platform and the field around it. A Red Cross truck was parked at the bombed-out building. A few volunteers were giving out train information and hot coffee. No one knew when the next train was coming, or if it would be filled up. Only freight trains could take us. The few passenger trains that were in service were reserved for special people and military personnel. "Closer to the Polish border," a Red Cross worker told us, "the tracks are restored, and the trains run somewhat better."

We sat on the ground and talked to other prospective passengers. We were still full of uncertainties, mistrust, fear. We had no idea what to do with our freedom. Inside, we were still slaves. The people around us were of many different nationalities and were in Germany for many different reasons. All were heading for their homes, all hoping to reunite with their families and start new lives.

Finally, after two days, the long-awaited train crept to a stop, its freight cars stretching far into the field. It was bound for Lignica. This previously

German city, Liegnitz, was now Polish. Everything east of the Oder River was now Polish territory. The Poles called it *"Ziemie Odzyskane"*—"Recovered Territories"; the Germans called it *"Besetzte Gebiete,"* "occupied regions."

Lignica wasn't the place we wanted to go, but most of us were headed east, and that was the direction the train was going. It was a nice sunny day, and all the wagon doors were wide open. In one of them we saw a group of former male prisoners still dressed in their striped clothes. We were almost shocked when, among them, we recognized a few men who had been with us in Skarzysko. We started inquiring about their experiences in Germany and about some other men who had been taken away with them. I tried to say something to one of them, but over a bullhorn came an announcement: "All Aboard!"

The ride was free of charge, but because room was limited, we were allowed only one small bag per person. The first things that I took were my notes and a pencil. I was wearing a dress that *Pani* Konova had given to me. It was too large for her since she was skin and bones and nails. By comparison, I looked like a stuffed pig with a swollen head and belly. But I looked stylish, and ready for a homecoming.

Before boarding the train, our group had to split up. I got into a car with four of my friends—Regina, Sala, Hanka, and Bella. A girl named Halinka, age nineteen, from Warsaw, joined us on the train. She told us about her experiences, about how her mother was killed during the bombing of Warsaw, about how her bricklayer father arranged for the escape of her and a sister, about how the two girls were hidden by a Gentile family (later sent to Germany to work on a farm). Her sister didn't survive.

In this car full of returning refugees, it didn't take long to engage in conversations, even with those who didn't speak the same language. "Where are you from? Where are you going to? What were you doing in Germany?" Any of these questions would start a nice chat. One man, however, drew special attention with a blackish blue number tattooed on his left forearm, so the conversation turned to him.

"What is that number on your arm?" asked a man who had entered the train with us. The numbered man looked at him in disbelief. "Where in the world could you have been that you didn't hear about the hell of Auschwitz?" he asked. Then, looking at us, he added, "Don't tell me that you girls didn't hear about it either." Only a few days before the Russians liberated that death camp, the Germans had transported thousand of prisoners westward. "Those Nazi *Schweine* starved and killed many inmates, but they especially targeted the Jews and the Gypsies." He told us about his trip in the locked-up freight cars, about all those who froze and died on the way. Then, to prove his statement, he took off a shoe and the large bandage that was wrapped around his foot. He showed us his frostbitten, black-and-blue toes. "They have to come off," he said. "All of them. The doctor in the Russian hospital told me. If I am lucky, my foot can be saved."

After two days, the train ride came to an end. During that time we were told stories that we really didn't want to hear. Then we exchanged little notes with our names and cities of origin. My writing supplies came in very handy; no one else in that car carried either pencil or paper. This train ride marked the end of our enslavement and the beginning of the aftermath. I thought that I had learned everything. Until now, the scholarly curriculum had consisted of physical education, medical miracles, hate vocabulary, endurance, and survival skills. There were only two grades: Pass or Fail. I had learned all these subjects well—but I hadn't learned to hate. My grandfather's words had kept coming to mind: Hatred, he told us kids, is bad for your health, and also for your complexion. Hate is contagious. It harms the hater.

Now I only yearned for home.

XVII. Lodz

Lignica hadn't been damaged very much by the War. Besides, a few months had already passed since the fighting ceased there. Poland and East Germany were now under Russian control. In any case, Legnica, the once German city, Liegnitz, was now Polish. By the time we arrived, law and order had been restored. Shops and markets had reopened, Russian soldiers were no longer drinking perfume and cologne. Bars were officially open; vodka was available for purchase.

Representatives from the Red Cross and other charitable organizations helped thousands of returnees who were clogging into this transit city to find food and temporary shelter. They also provided registration books for those who were looking for relatives and friends. We now ate in soup kitchens, slept in homeless shelters, and had our own names instead of numbers. We all signed big fat journals, and looked through the previously registered names. I found no one. Regina found the name of an aunt who was now living in Lodz. She got the aunt's address and suggested that all ten of us go with her to Lodz, and from there find the ways to our respective cities. All of us Warsaw girls decided to take up Regina's offer. We had heard that the capital was completely destroyed, and none of us knew what else to do.

During the last few years, everything had been arranged for us. We were told what to do and when to do it, when to wash, to eat, to work, to sleep, what to wear; even when to use the toilet. We knew who the bad guys were, who were the good ones, and who was the boss—and it wasn't the one who signed the check but the one with the gun. Now it was up to us to figure all of these things out, and we had no idea how to go about it.

The girls in our group who were from Radom, Czestochowa, and Siedlce, decided to go to their respective cities. We all stayed a few more days in Legnica, then headed for Lodz, which was about two hundred kilometers away. Along the way, we heard more shocking stories about the fate of the Polish Jews. We were more confused, and our hopes of finding our homes and relatives was diminishing. The Polish economy was in a shambles. Many cities were in ruins. Reports about Jewish survivors were discouraging. All these years we had been preoccupied with our own survival. It was positive attitude, the prospect of liberation, and the naïve hope of resuming a normal life, that kept most of us going. Now we began to realize that the dreadful tales we were hearing all along weren't rumors but actual accounts of what had happened to the Polish Jews. Nothing seemed unbelievable any longer. Yet, we were still sure that many of our relatives and friends were looking for us and waiting to be reunited.

Our trip to Lodz was on an open car next to the locomotive. By the time we got off, we looked like chimney sweeps. Otherwise, we reached our destination uneventfully.

Lodz remained almost intact. Many sections had deteriorated due to a lack of maintenance rather than to any destruction. As in Lignica, we were referred to a homeless shelter, where we were registered, fed, and given a place to sleep. Usually, the conversations started with "Where are you from? Where did you survive? Have you seen or heard of?...." Most of the time the answer to the last question was "No." Once in a while it was "Yes." Bella found a friend. He asked her to move in. Regina moved in with her aunt. The rest of us stayed at the shelter.

A few weeks later, Bella invited all of us to her wedding. It was a small ceremony: A *chuppah*, a cake, and a bottle of wine. A provisional rabbi said a prayer and then declared them "husband and wife."

For us girls left in the shelter, things changed, too. The refugee organization found us a one-room attic apartment with a slanted ceiling and a stove for cooking and heating. They also helped us to find part-time jobs. Daily, we visited the shelter and the refugee organization office, but none of us ever found what we were looking for. Another girl from Warsaw, Frida, who had survived in the USSR, joined the four of us in our apartment. Since all five of us were from Warsaw, the first thing on our agenda was to save up enough money for a trip to our hometown. Our free train rides had come to an end, and now we had to pay a fare if we wanted to go somewhere; for that, we were to ride passenger trains.

Luckily, I didn't have to wait for money too long. One day *Pani* Basia came for a visit, heard about my wished-for trip, and offered to lend me a few zlotys for a round-trip ticket to Warsaw. I couldn't believe that anyone would be that nice. Of course, she knew how much I wanted to go, and how much I hoped to find somebody, even a name in the registry.

Well, I went, but what I found wasn't what I was looking for. Warsaw was indeed completely in ruins. Trains stopped in Praga, across the Wisla River. I stayed in my customary accommodation, "The Alms Hotel," and ate in the "Soup Kitchen Restaurant." I had no reservations in either of them. Like others who arrived at the same time, I slept on old newspapers spread out on the filthy floor. Posters on the walls gave the names and addresses of the nearest Missing Persons Offices. Other announcements said that all men of the extended draft age had to register with the Selective Service office.[66]

I went over to the Missing Persons Office, signed up, and looked over all registration books; but I found no familiar names. I met many people, talked with them, asked the customary questions, but the answers were "No." One young man I met there, who had heard that I was looking for my father, said to me, jokingly, "Do you know, young lady, before the War when a father disappeared there were three possibilities: He had run away with a girlfriend, left for America, or his body had been found in a local mortuary. Now, my dear, I am afraid that none of these apply to missing fathers." Then his face became very serious. "Sorry, young lady. Jokes aside, you may just be wasting your time." I said that what he was telling me made absolutely no sense. I had many relatives, aunts and uncles and cousins and friends, and –

"Don't try to make sense out of it. Don't try to use logic. Standard reasoning does not apply in this case. What is rational and what is real are not the same. What happened here cannot be described or imagined in rational terms."

He told me that he had run away from the ghetto just before the Uprising. He lived on the Aryan side, took part in the Polish uprising, got wounded, married a Gentile woman, and they now were living in the Grochow suburbs. He, too, had come looking.

Against his better judgment, and despite what he told me, he was still hoping that some of his relatives would return from Russia, from hiding or from camps. He recited a list of names of his lost people, but I didn't know any of them. He then gave me some advice: "If you want to visit the city, remember that a walk through the ashes, especially through the ghetto, may be very emotional and depressing. Try not to go alone."

Others warned me not to expect miracles; there was nothing left of the Jewish section of town, and the buildings that did remain in the Gentile part— even the occupied ones—were all damaged or burned, or had been shattered by shells. There wasn't a building that survived intact.

A day later, I went anyway. I took with me a girl that I had met at the shelter—Mira, I think, was her name. (She was originally from a small town near Sandomierz. She had stayed in her town until she was transported to Auschwitz. She was freed by the Russians in January. She was reunited with one of her sisters, and was now looking for the sister who lived in Warsaw.) For two days, I walked with Mira through the ruins and ashes of the once thriving city. It was hard to identify the streets. Park Krasinskich gave me a clue that I was on Swietojerska Street. Even the park looked strange. The iron-railing that had once surrounded it was gone, and so were the swans on the lake, and the wooden benches. The German soldiers who used to strike fear into the souls of the people, well, they too were gone. The small lake where I used to go ice-skating in the winter was still there, and so were a few old trees. One of the signs that said, "Don't walk on the grass," had survived the War. Some grass and a few wild flowers were coming back to life. Otherwise, everything around was dead. We walked around talking and looking. My shoes got torn on the broken glass and on the nails that were sticking out of the burned boards. But we kept on walking.

At night, we slept on a bench in a temporary police station. There, a police woman, who worked at the desk, told us about the last days of the Jewish struggle for survival in the ghetto, in which thirty percent of the population lived in two point four percent of the city area. She pointed out how, in 1943, thousands of Jews were deported to the Majdanek and Treblinka camps, and how the ghetto went up in flames. She talked about Jews who had escaped the ghetto through sewers and, with thousands of Poles, were later killed in the 1944 Polish Uprising, and about those who married Gentile women and lived under assumed names.

We asked her about the so-called "Resettlement Program." She said that it had been a hoax. We now knew what had happened to all those who registered for it.

The next day we returned to Swietojerska Street. We stopped at Park Krasinskich and rested on the ground. Mira pulled up her blouse sleeve and showed me her tattoo. Then she talked abut the life in her small town and how she had survived a few months in the Auschwitz-Berkenau camp. "The group of inmates I was with," she said, "was bound for the gas chamber. The crematorium ovens were filled to capacity. Our group was left in the field. We were waiting for our turn to come. The Russians came, and the Germans fled."

I asked Mira if she knew what had happened to the Jews in her town or those from Sandomierz. I told her that my mother and sister were there. The only thing she knew was that all the Jews had been deported. She had gone back to her town after the liberation and found it *Judenrein*. The sister she found after the War had survived in one of the labor camps.

Occasionally, Mira and I passed other young men and women wondering through the ruins of Warsaw. We stopped, exchanged the usual information, and kept going our respective ways through the ghost town.

We stood on the ashes and debris of my home. I didn't cry; not even a tear came to my eyes. I just stood there, numb, looking at the skeleton that was left of our burned-out building. I didn't say a word; I didn't want to talk about the misery, the suffering, and the horror. I didn't want to remember the fight against the ever-present hunger, the food snatchers, the dead and dying kids who had lined the streets. I didn't want to think about their fate.

As we walked the ravaged streets, I told Mira about all the good memories I had of this city, and what it used to look like before the devastation, before the ghetto, before the War, when I was a child happy and carefree. Mira listened curiously. She said that she had always wanted to see the capital, and had planned to visit her sister who was living there. But the War disrupted her plans. I told her about my school, and we sang some songs....

While walking through the now damaged Rynek Starego Miasta—the fourteenth-century Old City Square—I told her some history of those narrow, brightly colored three-story buildings that surrounded the center square, and how, with my friends, we used to race from the basement to the rooftops on the winding iron steps. I showed her the now partly destroyed bulwarks, bastions, and barbicans where I used to play hide-and- seek. Mira and I walked through the narrow streets that led to the Saint John Cathedral, and to Plac Zamkowy, the Castle Square. We stopped at "Kolumna Krola

Zygmunta"—the monument where, on a gigantic pedestal, stood King Sigismund III, holding a cross and saber. This forty-meter-high monument was built in the sixteenth century when the capital was moved from Krakow to Warsaw. We walked by the King's Palace overlooking the Wisla River, then down the famous Krakowske Przedmiscie, where all the foreign embassies and the university used to be. All these places were located within waking distance of where I used to live. Mira listened attentively, then she told me about her life in the small town. We kept talking until we crossed the restored bridge and got back to our shelter in Praga.

A few days later, I returned to Lodz, tired, disappointed, but glad I went. I brought back the list of names that my roommates had asked me to look up. I found only a couple that were on a list of over one hundred names.

The War had been over for a few months, yet the aftermath was just beginning. The full revelation of what had happened to the Jews of Europe had been slowly coming into the open. Details of camp atrocities, gas chambers, and crematories had just begun to be made public. Even those of us who had seen most of it happen couldn't believe the extent of the disaster. We only knew part of the story. What we thought would be a recovery period became a shocking nightmare. During the worst of times, Jews had lived with hope and faith in God. "It is better to depend on God," the Good Book said, "than to trust mortals...." Despite all the information concerning the Nuremberg Laws and Hitler's threats and the knowledge of Jewish history (dating back to the Egyptian Pharaohs, Persian Hamman, and the Spanish Inquisition), Jews didn't believe that such barbarism could happen in "Modern times," in a "Civilized World."[67] Now that belief in miracles had been practically eliminated, what was there to look for? We knew that anti-Semitism flourished in many European countries, and that "Jews to Palestine" wasn't just a slogan; it was a message. Yet we didn't believe that so many of our compatriots, who had been themselves mistreated by the German invaders, would collaborate with their own enemy.

The Polish Jews who survived the War in Russia and were now returning with most of their families, had their own stories to tell. They were prepared to tell their relatives who had remained in Poland how they had suffered from hunger, disease, cold, and filth; how they had been evacuated when the Germans invaded the European part of Russia, how their children were now getting sick during the freezing Siberian winters or scorched by the Central Asian heat. They wanted to tell us in detail of the malicious venom that the Germans had released on the Russian population, especially on the Jews, and about their men who had been wounded or killed while fighting the Germans on the frontlines, in guerrilla groups or in resistance movements. They thought that their lives in Russia were terrible until they started finding out what ours had been like. They had heard many tales about the atrocities being committed by the Nazis in the occupied territories. Some had seen Jews being burned inside synagogues, or tortured and murdered, even being made to dig their own graves. Yet, like the rest of us, they couldn't believe the extent of this disaster. Finding all of their relatives dead, their towns destroyed, their synagogues burned, they began to realize, just like the survivors of the camps, that, despite all of their problems and suffering, they were the lucky ones. Among those returnees from Russia were the first Jewish children and old people we had seen in years.

By Pure Luck

The world was shocked by the reports of the exterminations and the carefully planned genocide. We, the camp survivors, were still waiting for a miracle to find someone alive.

Which, once in a great while, did happen. Someone met a brother or a sister, an uncle or a cousin. One day, I saw a woman at the market pressing a little girl to her chest; she was telling the peasant woman who was selling beets and turnips how that child had been hidden by a Gentile family and how those righteous people had saved the little girl's life. Another time, we met with a young man with one leg, who had just arrived from Russia. He found his sister's name on a list of survivors. He hoped to meet with her soon. After a long talk with this man, we found out that his sister had been in a German labor camp, and her description matched that of Masha. We told him to check with the Russian authorities and the hospital in Germany. We told him that we had registered Masha's name in the Red Cross files. We told him about his cousin Hayka who had gone back to her hometown. A few weeks later, we learned that he went with Hayka to the Russian hospital. Masha was still there, still very sick.

We knew of a few other reunions. They were mostly people from large families who lived in small towns that were taken over by the Russians.

As sad as the situation was, nothing could be done to change it. Life does not stay still. One cannot look to the future with an unfortunate past constantly disturbing the present. So we had to learn to make the most of what we had and the least of what was gone.

Slowly people, especially the young, started adjusting, finding work, getting married. Almost every week, I was invited to a wedding or two. Courtships were short: Boy meets girl; they date a week or two;

they go steady for a month; a few days later, they marry. Three months is considered a long love affair. The wedding ceremony takes place in someone's apartment. It is unpretentious, attended by a few friends. It is performed by a provisional rabbi, or someone claiming to be one, or a student of a rabbinical school, or one who has said that his father was a rabbi. The "clergyman" gives the couple a homemade *ketubah*—a Hebrew marriage contract— and pronounces them "husband and wife" in the presence of a few witnesses and God. The couple is now married. Everyone is crying.

Since I had only attended two weddings before the War, I had little experience in such matters. One of the weddings was that of our candy woman, Gucia. It was a quiet ceremony in my aunt's house. The other one was that of Uncle Sruel and Aunt Hanna's daughter, Regina. It was an elaborate wedding. It was on a "lucky Tuesday" night, in a huge ball room in which there was a catered dinner, an orchestra, a *badchen*. Everyone was dressed in formal clothes, and a special coach drove the bride and the groom home.

Here in Lodz, neither the weddings nor the couples resembled any of the ones that I had seen. The guests were strangers or, at best, camp acquaintances. And the ceremony always ended in crying.

There was an acute housing shortage. Very few of us had marketable skills, and even fewer had an education past junior high-school. Survivors my age didn't even finish primary school.

It had been a long time since I had thought about school. My education continued quite well without it. I was still keeping a diary. I remember that when I initially started writing it, it was to be for the kids in my class. Then I wrote a collection of my camp memories, which was to be read by my friends and relatives. Now I was keeping a combined journal of all my memories that was for myself—and for anyone who would want to read it. I hadn't yet completely given up looking for survivors.

Now that I was free to do as I pleased and didn't have to report to any authorities, not even to parents, now that no one really cared what I was doing or why I wasn't doing anything at all, instead of taking advantage of such an ideal situation to do things that were forbidden, or even those that were permitted, I did nothing. Somehow I couldn't figure out why I wasn't more inventive in doing something exciting. Many of my friends found themselves mates: Matched or not, they were getting married. I was just sitting there, knitting, or writing in my stupid diary, reliving the suffering all over again.

To break the anguish, I registered in school to start the spring semester. Meantime, with some of my friends, we tried to ponder many of the unanswered questions which survivors were asking themselves. "Why were we the ones to survive?" To me this question never made sense. I wasn't asking, "Why did I survive?" but always wondering, "Why did millions of innocent people die?" Only my pious friend, Regina, knew why: "It was God's will"; her answer to all my questions. She explained that the murdered Jews didn't die in vain, that they went on *Kidush Hasham* (that is, they died to sanctify God's Holy Name). Were they asked? Did they volunteer? Were they given a choice?

One day, our roommate Frida came back from visiting the shelter to see what was new. She had met a man who was looking for people from Warsaw. She had given him our address. A few days later, on a hot summer day in the early evening, the young man came over. I was sitting on the bed, my legs tucked under, and using yarn from an unraveled sweater, I was knitting a pair of socks.

"I heard all you girls are from Warsaw," the young man said, entering the room. "What part of town did you live in? Where did you survive?" he asked each of us separately.

The conversation ended at midnight. A few days later, the young man returned. A few friends dropped in. Seeing a new person, they started the usual conversation. He told us that his name was Jacob, and he was twenty-six. He told us where he had lived in Warsaw. It wasn't far from where I used to live. He knew more about Jewish life before the War than we did. He told us about his family, relatives, and friends, about his school, his life in the ghetto, and hiding under an assumed name; he also mentioned various camps he had been in. It was a long, appalling, complicated story.

Soon, he started visiting us more often. After some visits, Jacob and I became friends. He told me how one of the camp guards, a *Volksdeutsch*, had helped him survive, and also about his liberation.[68] I found out that he loved sports, and had played major-league soccer. We started meeting almost daily. By the time I heard his life story, and he mine, we were very much in love and very happy together. However, the situation in Poland was neither lovely nor happy. The country, trying to recover from the War, wasn't welcoming returning Jews. Anti-Semitism, although officially illegal, was widespread. Jacob, who had been liberated in France by the Americans, regretted his homecoming. He could have stayed in the West, but, coming from a large family, he had been sure that someone had survived. He had found no one.

When he heard that the Western Allies had opened DP (displaced person) camps in Germany, he decided to leave Poland. Jacob and I affirmed our vows and left together. We took a train to Szczecin, an old German port city on the Baltic Sea that was now part of the Polish "liberated territory." We were on our way towards new adventures, and more education for me.

XVIII. Berlin

On the train to Szczecin, Jacob and I discussed the issues that might be facing us on this trip and beyond. Our destination was Berlin, Germany. We spent a few days in Szczecin where other Jewish, Polish, and German refugees had assembled. At an agreed upon time a large covered truck picked us up and drove us through a forest and over the Polish-German border.

Germany was now a divided country. East Germany was Russian. The West was subdivided into three parts: American, British, and French zones. Berlin, once the capital city of "Intolerance, Destruction, and Hate," had transformed into a city of "International Love." People who merely a few months ago had enthusiastically *"Heiled"* Hitler, who had believed in the purity and superiority of the Aryan race, were now welcoming, with love and cheer, people of all creeds, races, and colors.

The city that was to be forever *Judenrein*, had become *Judenvoll* (full of Jews). Some were German Jews returning to their homeland to look for survivors and belongings. Many transit Jews, remnants of a once thriving European Jewry, and now homeless and destitute and bound for Western countries or Palestine, traveled through Berlin, too.

Most of them stayed in Ally-provided UNRRA-supported DP camps. The country that was to be of "pure blood" was packed with foreigners of many races, creeds, and colors.[69]

It was a time of resurrection in all of Europe. Enemies became friends. "Brotherhood of People" was the new motto replacing the slogan of "Pure Race." Fewer people were dying, hardly any were getting killed. Now babies were being born. It was a time of great hope and many expectations: "No more killings," "No more hate." People of all ethnic groups, persuasions, and creeds were to love one another and to live "Happily Ever After." This was the new "Public Opinion"—the opinion handed down to the public by the new leadership through the mass media.

While many European cities were still in ruins, and the smell of ashes and corpses still penetrated the nostrils, spiritual revival and physical reconstruction were in full swing.

Many older German people, while still mourning the death of their Führer, were reexamining the recent past. The younger generation was startled by the metamorphosis of their culture. They wondered what was happening to the "Hitler Epidemic" and to everything that they had been taught to believe in. The young German men who had survived the Front and the POW camps were returning to their devastated *Vaterland*. They had to be retrained and mainstreamed. Many had never known anything but hate and fighting. Very few had occupations, except as professional killers.

The years of hostilities and malice were over. Like a raging tornado, they had come, destroyed everything in their path, and then disappeared, leaving pain, sorrow, and desolation. Now, there was loving everywhere. People were kissing and hugging in the streets, in streetcars, in buses, in parks, in beds. Bars stayed open day and night. There were foreign bars, German bars, gay and lesbian bars— and all of them welcoming everyone.

Many girls of the "Master Race," who only a short time ago were lawfully obeying the Führer's "Pure Blood" doctrine, were now in love with everyone, especially everyone in uniform. They didn't discriminate against German POWs, nor even against the Jews. Not only did the Germans love everybody: The Americans loved the Russians, the French loved the British. All four Allies were riding in one jeep patrolling the streets of Berlin. Without knowing one other's language (for only the Americans and British had a more-or-less common tongue), all four communicated and seemed to understand each other quite nicely. These jeeps were driven through all four sectors of Berlin. The borders weren't guarded. Had it not been for the markers that indicated entrances to different sectors, no one would have known that they were crossing international borders.

Our first year in Berlin was eventful. We found living quarters in the city, started learning the German language properly, and got acquainted with many people, and we were expecting our first baby.

In September, when Jewish holidays came, I went with Jacob to a just reconstructed synagogue. It was my first time as a worshipper. Here, in the heart of Germany, I saw Jacob receive the honor of praying from the pulpit. He read from the Torah in Hebrew. Surprisingly, he still remembered things that he learned in his childhood. I sat in the back, reading through the translation. Many verses I didn't understand. The ones I did made no sense to me. They talked about a Merciful God, Full of Justice and Compassion. During the breaks and at the end of the service, the congregants talked about their war experiences. There were hardly any old people or children among the worshippers. Many of those present were German Jews who had recently returned from their hiding places or camps. A few had spent the War years in China, among them one named Herr Kaufmann.[70] He invited us to his home. He introduced us to his wife, and told us about his life in Berlin before the Nazis came to power. They talked about the time that they had spent in Shanghai. I told him about my Uncle Harry and Tante Trude. I thought, maybe, he might have known them. He didn't.

Herr Kaufmann offered Jacob a job in his delicatessen, which he had just reopened with some restoration money and, later, with the help of the Marshall Plan.[71] We were very thankful. Having a job, we could live in the city instead of in a DP camp.

In December, we celebrated Hanukkah and my birthday with Herr Kaufmann, his wife, and a few other survivors. As had happened at previous holidays, the celebration ended in crying. Right after the holidays, we had to move. Our landlady needed the room we lived in. Her husband had returned from a Russian POW camp. It was an emotional reunion. All of their relatives, neighbors, and friends came to see him. During the celebration, Jacob and I sat in our room, crying. Before we moved out, the man told us about his life on the Front and in the Russian prison camp. He hadn't been surprised at being treated harshly. "For what we have done to their people and the country," he said, "I only wonder they let us out alive."

The place we moved to was a two-room apartment. There was one multipurpose room and a kitchen. The toilet on the landing we shared with the Hömplers, our next-door neighbors. When the middle-aged Frau Hömpler first saw me, she became interested in my condition. She kept asking how I felt, if I had been seeing a doctor, if my mother was coming to help with the baby. I couldn't figure out what made her so interested. Then, right after the New Year holidays, she stopped me in the hall, wished me *"Ein Glückliches Neues Jahr"*—"Happy New Year"—and told me that on Christmas Eve, her twenty-year-old daughter, who lived in Vienna, gave birth to a baby boy. Inge was coming home with baby Michael as soon as the weather permitted.[72]

A few weeks later, our son was born. We invited our friends. We celebrated, and, as on all previous happy occasions, we cried.

At the end of April, Inge arrived with the baby. She was tall, slim, blonde, and blue-eyed—the perfect Aryan girl. The baby, a skeleton, had a large head and a bulging belly. It had taken her almost four weeks to get through the Russian zone from Vienna to Berlin.

When I first met her, we had a friendly conversation. In my broken German, I told her that had it not been for her mother, I wouldn't have made it to the hospital on time (my water broke at home). I had had no idea what to do. She said that she knew about me from Mutti's letters.

Inge and I started meeting often. At first, we talked about our blond, blue-eyed sons. After a while Inge's mother started "grand-mothering" both boys. I was breastfeeding mine, and providing some scarce food for hers. Inge and I became friends.

Jacob was gone a lot. Herr Kaufmann's store was busy. Many legitimate enterprises were reopening in the city, while trading on the black market was still going on. People were buying, selling, exchanging, trading. Americans were selling cigarettes, buying British coffee, French wine, and Russian vodka. The British were trading their coffee for American cigarettes, French wine, and Russian vodka. The

French were exchanging their wine for cigarettes, wine, and vodka. The Germans were trading gold and jewelry (most of which had been stolen from once—by them—occupied countries) for food, fuel, and other necessities. The Russians were buying anything that they could put their hands on and sending it to their starving relatives at home. Anybody who could match the buyers and sellers was rewarded with merchandise or foreign currency. The once almighty *Reichsmark* was useless.

Besides working, Jacob was spending a lot of time roaming the exciting city, meeting new people, and helping with the resettlement into DP camps of constantly arriving refugees from Eastern countries. But his time wasn't "all work, no play." With a few friends, he was trying to resurrect the disbanded *Berliner Hakoah*, the Jewish major league soccer club which the Nazis had expelled from German sports. Very few of the old *Hakoah* players returned from exile after the War. Those who survived the War were too sick or too old to play. It was a difficult job to assemble a new team.

Meanwhile, I was at home, spending a lot of time with Inge. While our boys were playing, we talked about children and the role of women and the responsibilities of mothers. We both came from girls' families—she had an older sister, I a younger one. We knew very little about raising boys, or how to discipline them. Inge came from a "Law and Order" totalitarian background. I, too, had had to listen and obey, but I'd had more freedom. I'd had the right to question "authorities," my parents and even grandparents. I could even disagree with them.

Inge and I also talked about school and music and the books we were reading, books that were translated into both Polish and German. We talked about our youth and our grandparents and, sometimes unwillingly, about politics and the War. No matter how much we tried to avoid this subject, it constantly came up. I told her about my life in the ghetto, on the farm and in camps; she told me about the years she had spent in the *Hitlerjugend*, and about her adventures during and after the War. In post-War Germany, there was hardly any German who would openly admit having knowledge about the Nazis. No German person had belonged to "The Party," or had known about "The Führer," or had heard about the crimes being committed. "Such bizarre actions couldn't have happened," said most Germans who had spent the war years in their own homes. They sincerely believed that "Such atrocities couldn't have been committed, especially not by our own people."

In order to make this wartime barbarism more undeniable, the Allies, as soon as they occupied Germany, required that all Germans, before receiving their ration cards, had to see the evidence for themselves. Those Germans living in the vicinities of Nazi concentration camps had to tour the locations of the former killing factories, the gas chambers, crematories, and the heaps of corpses and bones that were still on the ground and in trenches awaiting burial. Those Germans living in locations away from such camps had to watch the same scenes in documentary movies. They couldn't believe their own eyes. Those Germans who had witnessed or participated in those crimes firsthand had either run to foreign countries or changed their identities, or else had denied their past. Only after the Nuremberg Trials, when the captured Nazi leaders were presented with absolute evidence and admitted their crimes, did the general German population, reluctantly and with reservations, start accepting the undisputed truth of the atrocities committed in their name.[73]

On an individual basis, however, the Germans kept denying any personal involvement with Hitler or the Nazis.

Inge was the first person I met who told me that she had spent most of the Nazi years in a *Hitlerjugend Lager*. At first, she didn't give me any details about it. She only talked about her adventures, the discipline and education that she received in that organization. Later in our relationship, she told me that there was hardly a German child, especially a teenager, who hadn't belonged to some Nazi group. "If they didn't join through persuasion, they joined from peer pressure, or government requirements."

Since the day I met Inge, I was getting more educated daily. It was for the first time from her that I heard how many Germans were rationalizing and even justifying Hitler's policies and the War. I heard German propaganda in action. I learned about the economic and political conditions that had prevailed in Germany between World War I and World War II, about the economic depression and the conditions imposed by the Versailles Treaty, which eventually brought the Nazis to power.

I started going to classes and learning the language. I even began talking German to my baby so that he would be able to communicate with the people around him. I was getting acquainted with more German people, with their customs and culture.

I often wondered whether the Germans who had destroyed and occupied my country, killed my people, and put me into the camps, belonged to the same "race"—or even to the same species—as the Germans I was now meeting. Or if they were all Jekylls and Hydes.[74] I had wondered about it in Leipzig when I worked with the German *Frauen*. They, too, looked and acted like all other human beings.

Inge told me that she, too, wondered whether the Jews she was now meeting were the same Jews Hitler portrayed. According to her story, she knew only a few Jews. "There was a Jewish girl named Gertruda in my class," she told me. "When she stopped attending school, the teacher told us, 'Gerti moved out of town.'" Inge also knew a few merchants and a doctor who were Jewish. She thought that they lived well, and people liked them. She remembered the tumult of the *Kristallnacht* in Berlin, but she claimed that because of her age, she wasn't allowed into the street; she didn't understand what it was all about. She remembered seeing signs on many streets, gates and doors that said *Für Juden Verboten*. She knew that Jews weren't allowed into many public places, but she couldn't understand the problem since she couldn't even tell who was a Jew and who wasn't. When, years later, she was being courted by her son's father, Johann, he told her in one of their conversations of how his Hungarian-born mother was once pushed, cursed, and thrown out of a restaurant because she had been mistaken for a Jew. Inge said that until she met me she wasn't very interested in Jewish problems. She didn't really understand how bad it was to be Jewish until she became a German under foreign occupation.

I couldn't believe what I was hearing. "Had the Germans treated their subjects the way the Allies treat the Germans," I told her, "Hitler's thousand-year Reich might have become a reality."

Before and during the War everything to me had been very clear. I knew who the good people were, and who were the bad ones. Now I was confused. I found out that it was almost preposterous to assume that a Nazi was a special kind of long-horned beast with sharp tusks and a tail—an animal that could be spotted from a distance and identified. The Germans I had been meeting were for the most part very ordinary people: good parents, churchgoing Christians, patriotic citizens. They occasionally talked to me about the Nazi era. They claimed that economic conditions, the depression, and unemployment had been the main reasons for Hitler's coming to power; it was the same predicament which had been responsible for bringing communism to Russia. I was now able to see how otherwise average people, without questioning the party's principles, or without concern for the consequences, had joined the party for prestige, promotions, and for the honor such membership provided. Besides, swimming against the current is a difficult task, one that few are willing to undertake. According to my experience, most political persuasion starts in the stomach and the pocketbook.

That scared me even more. I realized that during crises, desperate people are prone to choose extreme measures in order to find quick solutions to complicated problems, and that the easiest ways to accomplish it is to find a scapegoat—to invent an enemy—and to create instant heroes for inspiration. With skillful propaganda, people can be persuaded to hate those whom they love, and love those whom they hate; the trick is to keep people's attention away from real issues and focused on empty promises. I am still apprehensive of "isms"—fascism, communism, socialism, capitalism, but mostly of extremism. I listen carefully to political speeches and baby-kissing politicians who promise their constituents a heaven on earth but who don't bother to explain how it will all come about.

Once I had such a conversation with Inge. I asked her what made the Germans hate Jews with such a rage. She didn't know. She said that she didn't hate anybody, not even the uncle who had brought shame to the family for being a communist, or the Polish cousin who was among the "undesirables" for being a Slav.[75]

"Haven't you learned anything in your camp about the Master Race and Nazi politics?" I once asked her, jokingly.

She thought for a while, and said, "Now that I think about it, it might have been taught to us somewhat indirectly."

Another time, the conversation took us to our respective history classes. It was astounding how differently the same incidents were presented in our books. It was hard to believe how our historical accounts conflicted, and how our "facts" differed. History books written only a few years earlier, during Inge's school years, were full of praises for Hitler and Nazi achievements. The new edition, just coming out, had only a few paragraphs about the whole Nazi era, including the War.

Villains and heroes, occupiers and liberators, aggressors and defenders, enemies and friends, all were in opposite order. We were astonished. We were finding out what most older people had known all along: not only can history be interpreted in different ways; it can be deliberately, or "unintentionally," distorted. And that's not all. Once it was written and adapted, it could, according to need, be changed at a later date. It can be rewritten under the auspices, or pretext, of a "New Revised Edition." The Russians say it best: "Our past is unpredictable."

We figured out that one can look at history as being my-story, your-story, her-story, or, as it is called, "his-story." Hidden somewhere among these is the actual story.

There were many things that made no sense to us. How does one make the rules of war? Is poisonous gas, which was used in World War I, and subsequently "banned" by the Geneva Convention (that set down the "rules" for war), more harmful than the atom bomb, which was used in World War II? Is a war played like a chess game? How can one operate Twentieth-Century Technology with Stone-Age Philosophy? Where do destitute countries get money to wage wars?

The more I mingled with the German people, the more complicated became my reasoning. Wasn't it only a short time ago that we were enemies? That we hated one another?

(I once told Jacob about my conversations with Inge. He said that we were hopelessly naive, or downright stupid. "What else could one expect from a couple of foolish women? People should stay away from subjects they know nothing about. Nobody," he said, "was going to change the world. Wars were fought before, and are going to continue." We got into a quarrel. I could never talk with Jacob the way I could with Inge. Besides, he was gone most of the time. Business was good. He had become the captain of the *Hakoah* soccer team. When the club added a girls handball team to their sports activities, I joined. There I met my teammates, other club members, and many people my age.)

My education continued.

We didn't always talk about complicated issues. We would often recall our happy childhood experiences, sometimes our sorrows. Squeezing a shabby teddy bear, Inge told me the story of this favorite toy.

"In early 1930," she said, "Vatti lost his job and joined the ranks of the unemployed. Every week, my sister and I walked with Vatti to the employment office to register. It took us an hour each way. (Streetcar fare was a luxury.) There, we had to stand in line for hours. Mother cleaned houses so that we could eat. We were living in an attic apartment. We had one room, a kitchen, and a hall. The hall my parents rented out to a young man from out of town. For my birthday, the young man gave me this teddy bear. It was my only toy. This bear kept me company when I was hungry, sad, or depressed." She sighed, then added, "If this bear could talk, he would tell many stories. Anyway, I was so glad when Vatti finally got a job."

I told Inge about my pre-War life, too. This was one of her favorites: "I was in the second grade. Our teacher, Miss Braff, who was the best-loved educator in school, broke a leg. We had a substitute. One day, out of boredom, I wrote a little secret song describing our sick teacher as an old maid who gave a lot of homework and liked to put kids in the corner. During a break, I shared these lyrics with a few girls in class. I kept the boys out of it. They didn't like this. While the girls were reading my song, one of the boys grabbed the paper and ran off with it. When, after a few weeks, our teacher returned to school, the boys handed her a sheet of paper. The teacher glanced at it, smiled, and put it on her desk under the inkwell. I turned crimson red. I was shaking, scared, and I burst into tears. That's how I betrayed myself. As it turned out, none of the boys knew who wrote that song." It was fun to reminisce.

We recalled our precious memories and talked about the horrors of the War. I knew many things about her past, including her involvement with the *Hitlerjugend*. About her parents' guilt or innocence during the Nazi era, I wasn't quite sure. From the simple way they lived, it was clear that they couldn't have benefited much from the War. Whether this was due to their anti-Nazi persuasion or to their inability to rise to higher ranks was hard to tell. I heard that her father, because of his age and World War I injuries, wasn't in military service during the Second World War. Since Germany lost the First War, there were no rewards, no victory parades, and no medals for those who fought it. Just before the Second War was to start, her father was called to military headquarters. He was very scared. He thought that he'd be questioned about his brother-in-law's communist activities. Instead, her father came home with a medal. He was told to wear it with pride, that it was for fighting in World War I, and was "long past due."

By the time the Second War started, her father had a medal to be proud of and a job that made him happy; her mother was working only part time. Inge joined the *Hitlerjugend* Camp, and her older sister joined another Nazi Pioneer movement. Things for the Hömplers started to look up.

From what Inge told me, they never took part in any anti-Semitic activities, but this was now the story of most Germans.

"When the Nazis first came to power," they claimed, "we didn't know the extent to which Jews and other 'undesirables' were being persecuted. When the dictator's grip tightened, no one dared to get involved. All news was censored. When the first stories about some bizarre atrocities started slipping in, most people thought that they were fabricated lies or, at best, enemy propaganda. When the Nazis were at the peak of power, it was too late to say or do anything. One could land in a concentration camp just for opening one's mouth. So," the Hömplers (like most other Germans) claimed, "we minded our own business. We still can't believe it. It makes no sense."

Whenever I hear this expression, I remember that young man in Warsaw's Missing Persons Office who said, "Don't try to make sense out of it. What happened here cannot be described or imagined in rational terms."

It still boggled the Hömplers' minds, how the Holocaust was possible. Since it did happen, they felt that those non-Germans who had helped in the killings should also bear some responsibility for this tragedy. Inge didn't mind if the guilty ones were punished, but most of the architects and executioners of the crimes, other than those caught and prosecuted in the Nuremberg Trials, were nowhere to be found.

One time she asked me if it was true that not long after Hitler came to power, many Jews wanted to emigrate but had no place to go. "Ships full of Jews cruised the seas, but no one let them in—*Keiner wolte die Juden* [No one wanted the Jews]." I knew that something like that happened. I remembered the story of the ship, the MS *St. Louis*, which, filled with Jewish refugees, cruised the seas.[76] I would overhear adults discussing such incidents.

"Sorry," I said, "but I don't have enough information about it. I only presume that had the countries in question known the extent of danger the Jews were in, the leaders would have bent their immigration laws, if only temporarily, and opened their doors to the wandering Jews." I liked to believe that it was true.

Inge said that she had never paid too much attention to Jewish issues until she met me. She hoped that I wouldn't be offended if we had a candid talk. She asked if I could tell her how long the Germans would be blamed for the War and for the Holocaust.

I didn't think she expected an answer. But I gave her one anyway.

"How history will treat Germany," I said, "and this is only my opinion, depends a lot on the circumstances. If the world finds another enemy soon, it might leave the Germans alone. I don't think anyone will ever forget what has happened. You see, governments don't relate to each other the way people do. People have friends. Governments have interests. If such a time comes that peace with Germany is in the best interest of the occupiers, Germany may, one day, even become one of the allies. How long will it all take? Well, my dear, your guess is as good as mine. Good Luck!"

In another discussion, I asked her how she felt about the *Hitlerjugend* movement, and whether she had changed any of her thinking since the War ended. She got into a lengthy explanation. "Going away to a Youth Camp and helping on farms was a special privilege, a patriotic duty. Only kids who made good grades and excelled in sports could participate. We were taught music, poetry, and, most of all, discipline. We learned table manners, work accountability, cooking, sewing, and comradeship. We were never left unattended, and, of course, were also taught ethics, morals, and—"

I interrupted. I could hardly believe what I was hearing: "Did you say Nazi ethics and morals?...How about the brainwashing?"

"Naturally," she said, "Now that I think about it, I realize that there were political undertones. This was to be expected from the prevailing authorities. You never get something for nothing. As a byproduct, we were also instilled with 'Respect for The Party,' 'Reverence for Law and Order,' and 'Love for *Volk, Vaterland,* and *Führer.*'"

"And wasn't it true," I asked, "they were teaching you that Germans were superior, that they were of a 'Master Race,' and weren't, therefore, to mix with the so-called *Untermenschen,* the sub-humans, people of inferior blood, which included everybody not classified as the 'Master Race'?"

To this, Inge said that I had it all wrong, that I was overplaying the reality. She knew, for a fact, that to every country the German troops went, the population was glad to have them. "People liked the Germans and their law-and-order policy. Our soldiers were greeted by enthusiastic crowds with flowers and outstretched arms."

She said she even had "proof" of it: She had seen pictures in the papers and magazines. It was even shown in the newsreels at the movies.

I was sure that she believed what she was telling me. I really hated to disappoint her, yet, in all fairness, I felt that I had to tell her how these movies and photos came about: I had seen some of them being made. So I told her about the bombing of Warsaw, and why the people she saw in the movies were coming to see the German troops marching in to occupy the city. "I was there," I said. "I saw the cameras rolling and the taking of pictures. The stretched-out arms were those of destitute people who were running from the fires to catch some bread that the soldiers were throwing from their army trucks. When the allotted bread was distributed, when people started cursing the invaders, the cameras stopped rolling." I could see the disappointment in her face. She still insisted that people in many countries were happy to see the Germans come.

There was quite a discrepancy between her "true facts" and my eyewitness account.

What kept Inge and me together was first of all our boys, who were growing to love each other. They were like brothers. They played and ate and fought together. Later, after Jacob and I moved to another apartment, and the Hömplers moved, too, Inge and I made sure that our boys attended the same preschool. We remained friends. We were always candid with one another, even when we disagreed.

Other Germans I kept meeting were also confident that their knowledge of the Nazi era and the war events were the absolute truths. Those who knew it wasn't so either weren't around any longer, or weren't talking. At least Inge was honest about her feelings. She said that she had loved the Third Reich, had thought whatever her people were doing was right. Now, in retrospect, many Germans could see things differently, but there was nothing that could be changed. Besides, most of the people, especially the young, didn't want to dwell on the past. They wanted to get on with life.

Some German girls who, for some time, had been dating Jewish guys, were now getting married to them—a disgrace to the "Master Race," as well as to the "Chosen People." A few of Jacob's friends were engaged to German girls who kept assuring their future husbands that they had had no Nazi involvement, that they had never belonged to any Nazi-affiliated group. I knew a few of them quite well.

One day, Inge and I had an interesting experience. Inge brought Michael on a visit. We were listening to records. The boys were playing on the floor with their toys. Unexpectedly, Gisela, the fiancée of Jacob's friend, came to the door. "I was just passing by," she said smiling, "and I thought I'd stop to see your new apartment."

I knew Gisela quite well. I invited her into the room to meet my friend. Inge looked at the guest. "*Guten Tag, gnädiges Fräulein,*" she said. "Good day, madam. I am quite sure I know you from somewhere...."

Gisela turned red, shaking.

"Weren't we in the *Hitlerjugend Lager* together?" Inge asked politely.

After Gisela's initial shock wore off, the two women had a long conversation. They recalled some events, and asked about some common friends. Gisela couldn't believe that knowing about Inge's past, I was her friend. Her eyes looked at me in disbelief. That's when I made it clear to her. "You see, Gisela, at least Inge was honest about her past; that's what I like about her. I wonder what Moshe knows about you."

Before Gisela left, I told her not to worry; I wasn't going to tell her fiancé what I knew, but I did suggest she tell him before he found out. I, personally, felt that people who kept secrets had something to hide.

After Gisela left, Inge, the kids, and I took a walk. On the way, she asked me why the Jews had been singled out as "special victims" of Fascism when, according to accounts now available, millions of other people, even many Germans, had also been victimized by the Nazis.

"I know that. Many of them were with me in Leipzig," I replied. "I thought that everyone who had lived through this period knew the answer, but it seemed that many still didn't. It's true," I said, "that many others suffered. Among them were religious leaders of many different denominations—doctors, writers, educators. POWs were killed, anyone whose opinion differed from that of the Nazis' was put into concentration camps, where they were starved and tortured and often killed. Jehovah's Witnesses, the handicapped, homosexuals, and other 'undesirables' were also among them.[77] The difference, however, was that these victims were charged with some kind of anti-Nazi crime, or whatever Hitler considered a crime. Only Jews, Gypsies, and the handicapped were victimized for no other reason than by virtue of their birth. They (men, women, children, the young and the old) were deliberately murdered. There were no accusations, no demands."

Inge always shook her head in disbelief whenever I talked about the Holocaust. She wanted to believe that some of my relatives, family members, or friends would still show up. I tried to believe it too; that's why Jacob and I kept going to the DP camps, to the Red Cross, and to other relief organizations where records had been kept, looking for survivors. We hoped to meet someone, even people who, at least, could give us a clue as to what had happened to all the people we had left behind.

One day Jacob came home from a visit to a DP camp. When he entered the room, I knew that something was wrong. After his anger subsided a bit, he said, "I just heard from the Jewish agency that in Kielce, some anti-Semites had carried out a pogrom on Jewish survivors who were returning from Russia.[78] Over forty Jews were killed, many more wounded. It was clear that the violence was professionally arranged, and that one of the underground right-wing organizations was responsible for the crime. Those Jews who escaped the slaughter were on their way to the DP Camps in Germany. We have to organize living quarters and support for them. The organizers asked me to help."

With horror in our eyes, we looked at each other, then at our peacefully sleeping baby. We were sure that our decision to leave Poland for good was right.

A few days later Inge brought a German newspaper with the headline, *"Das Pogrom in Kielce."* She handed me the paper and said, "I told you that the Germans couldn't have done all these terrible things by themselves."

Of course we knew that not all Nazis were German and that not all Germans were Nazis, but that didn't change the facts.

All Inge was asking for was that these Nazi helpers take some of the blame. She even admitted (now, in retrospect) that German bombings, killings, and occupation of other countries, were wrong; but, she added, "If it was so evil of the Germans, why did the Allies do the same to us?" She wasn't just saying this. She actually believed it.

It was hard for me to imagine her reasoning.

One time I praised the "Righteous Gentiles," those goyim (non-Jews) who had helped the Jews, as well as nations such as Denmark, Sweden, and Switzerland (the last two were neutral in the War) which, regardless of their political affiliations, didn't participate in the murdering (and even managed to save Jews from sure death), Inge told me that, according to her information, in each of these countries, the people loved the Germans.

Well, sometimes we agreed, sometimes we didn't, but we learned a lot from one another. We learned to question ideas, even "facts." We learned to read between the lines, and to listen to the words that aren't said. Among other things, we agreed that as dreadful as wars are, not everyone experiences them the same way. According to our logic, wars would be extinct were there no spoils— benefits that people don't like to talk about. But wars revive patriotism and nationalism, and fill people with immediate purpose. Wars create instant heroes and new idols. For those individuals and countries not directly involved in the fighting and destruction, for those who know how to use chaos and other people's misfortune to their own advantage, wars can be quite rewarding, even profitable.

After a few arguments, we also agreed that there are certain virtues in patriotism, but only as long as they do not turn to extremism, as long as they aren't synonymous with "Everything my government tells me is true; everything it does is right."

As a kid, I had associated patriotism with triumphant wars, heroic victories, bright medals, and glory for my country. In one of our friendly discussions, I told Inge that after hearing many stories about the First World War, I actually wanted to see a real war. She wasn't surprised. A week later I went out of town. In one of her lengthy letters, among other things, Inge wrote, "When World War II started, I was in the hospital with a broken knee. I can still recall how worried I was that I might miss the War. I was twelve then, and in my eyes, I imagined the War as a happy adventure. The things I heard from my father about the First World War didn't mean a lot to me. I was excited and patriotic."

Once, I, too, was patriotic. I thought that Poland was the best country in the world, the center of the universe. My first disappointment came in the fourth grade. It was in third-grade geography class that we had learned to read the map. Next to the blackboard was a map of Poland. It was almost twice a big as the blackboard. Poland was a huge country. We traveled over this map from the Carpathian Mountains to the Baltic Sea, from the German border to the Russian frontier. Nothing beyond Poland was visible on this map. But in the fourth grade, we studied Europe. What a disappointment it was to learn that mighty Poland was only one of many other countries, and that next to the Soviet Union it looked like a small speck. It was heartbreaking. By then, I also had learned that Russia and Germany weren't only our neighbors but also our enemies.

While Inge and I were exchanging memories, and hoping that from now on everyone would live "happily ever after," the love affair among the four Allies was coming to an end. Trouble between the former "comrades" was erupting. In April, 1948, the

Russians blockaded the three Western sectors of Berlin, stopping all land transportation of supplies and people to and from the city.[79] Berlin became an island surrounded by the Russian Zone. To deal with this situation, the three Western Allies started air-lifting all essential supplies to the city. I remember standing with Inge and the boys on an overpass by the Tempelhoff Flughafen, watching American planes land one every few minutes. This air-bridge wasn't only a way to get supplies into Berlin but also the only way to get in and out of the city. Those who could, tried to leave. The Jewish relief organizations Joint (or the American Jewish Joint Distribution Committee) and HIAS (Hebrew International Aid Society) were registering displaced people from DP camps for emigration.[80] A few Western countries were accepting applications from refugees. Jacob knew that his father's brother, Uncle Irwin, who left Poland in the 1920's, was living somewhere in the USA. We registered.

Joint and HIAS, in conjunction with the UNRRA (United Nations Relief and Resettlement Association), were taking care of the arrangements. UNRRA was to provide transportation, HIAS and Joint were to help with resettlement.

Meanwhile, our life in Berlin proceeded. We had many interesting experiences, the most exciting of which was Jacob's meeting with the German guard, the *Volksdeutsch*, who helped him survive the camp. It was an emotional reunion. We knew that the man was not only a hero to us but also an asset to humanity. We helped him with food and other necessities. Another interesting event was the reappearance of friend Wolf's dead wife—a situation that called for cheers and tears. The wife, with their four-year-old son, had survived in Russia. By the time she found her husband, he was married and had a daughter with his new wife. So much for the dead coming back to life.

During the time we spent in Berlin, the media were reporting war statistics, war crimes that had been hidden from the public, and all kinds of strange stories; and they were propounding many as yet unanswered questions: What had happened to our civilization? Where was the world when all the atrocities were taking place? Was it unaware, uncertain, unprepared, unable to deal with the problem? Had it underestimated the severity of the situation? Was the world undecided or unwilling to do anything, or was it all of the above? Could any part of this disaster have been prevented? Was this a lesson for the future?

Looking back at the War years, we who survived the horrors were trying to figure out How? and Why? We had more questions than answers. Even though the Nuremberg Trials took care of the major criminals, we still kept asking the question: Whom should we blame for such a human-made disaster? Do we blame: 1) only those who committed the crimes? 2) those who willingly participated? 3) those who unwillingly got caught up in the crimes? 4) all who happened to be of the same ethnic origin, nationality, or race as the perpetrators? 5) all of the above? 6) how about future generations? 7) how about those who knew of the crimes and atrocities but did nothing? For it is said that "All it takes for evil to triumph is for good people to do nothing." Well, we're still looking for answers. Does anyone want to help?

The trenches and ravines full of unnamed corpses and all the mass graves were slowly being identified by special markers. The ashes of the cremated bodies have, most likely, fertilized some barren soil. All those former human beings exist now only in the memories of the survivors. In our hearts and souls they will live until we, too, die. To those spared the direct suffering, and to those born afterwards, the period known as "The Holocaust" will only be another page in a history book, or an inscription on a recently erected monument. Some day, after all the eyewitnesses are gone, someone, somewhere, will issue a "Revised Edition" of the Holocaust history. The future of the Holocaust is unpredictable.

Although Germany was still an occupied country, it was hard to tell who the victors were, and who the losers. Most Germans lived better than did the victorious Allies.

As for us survivors, we were still looking for our families and trying to put our lives back together. We began to realize that no matter what had happened to us in the past, we couldn't live the rest of our lives looking backward. I remembered once reading somewhere that "Life must be lived forward, but it can only be understood backward." I finally understood the meaning of it. Oh, yes, we survivors were still crying and mourning and losing hope, and were getting depressed, but we knew that if we wanted to survive the peace the way we had survived the War, we would have to think about our future and that of our children. Most of us survivors clung together. We shared quarters, food, grief, and pleasures. Many of us talked about our experiences only with one another. Strangers wouldn't understand. Our children were too young to be burdened with our past. Besides, they learned by osmosis. We survivors became a family.

As in any family, we had differences and quarrels. It was our common past that bonded us and made us support one another. During Jewish holidays, which we observed as a family, we reminisced and cried and grieved, and planned for the future. During Passover Seder, instead of asking the traditional "Four Questions," we were asking our own: "What happened to God's miracles? Why, from all the peoples in the world, did God choose the Jews? And for what? Why did so many have to die? Where do we go from here?"

While most of us were waiting for visas to emigrate, Jacob kept busy with his club and work, and I went back to school part time. Inge helped me with the language; I helped her find a job.

Soon, some families started leaving Germany. The letters that we received weren't very encouraging. Even though refugees were being accepted into the USA, they weren't really needed, or welcomed, there. American troops were fighting in the Korean War (1950-53), and many of the young immigrant men were being drafted and sent to the front. Immigrants were called "greenhorns"; without language or profession, newcomers who found jobs were working for minimum wage or below, usually washing dishes in restaurants or doing janitorial work. News from other countries to which survivors were being accepted was about the same, even worse.

We knew that we wouldn't remain in Germany. We weren't citizens; we were classified as *"Staatenlosen"*—"stateless persons." Besides, we had many bad memories, and we felt that there was no future for us or our children in Germany. Moving would mean years of new adjustments, a new language, a new culture. Jacob was worried. For me, it meant new adventures and continuing education.

Midsummer, we received our application for a visa to the USA. We were called to the American consulate, where we had to fill out stacks of papers. We were asked a lot of "have you ever" questions: "Have you ever belonged to the Fascist Party? Communist Party? Have you ever had venereal infections, tuberculosis, or other contagious diseases? Have you ever been arrested or imprisoned?..." The last one needed a lot of explanation.

There were many other formalities to be dealt with before obtaining a visa. There was an interview with the American consul, a medical examination, a CIA investigation, and some miscellaneous odds and ends, such as the transference of our apartment to new tenants, getting police clearance papers, and paying all outstanding taxes.

While going through all these legal procedures, Jacob and I found out that we weren't married. The marriage papers we had from Lodz, Poland, weren't recognized by the American government as legal documents. A few weeks later, we did receive some good news: The American Consulate suggested arranging a communal wedding for us and a few other couples with the identical problem. Now, twice married, we were legally ready to go.

It was a cold, sunny November day when we took a taxi to the Tempelhoff Flughafen. Accompanying us was the whole Hömpler family and a few other friends. It was a sad farewell. We took pictures, reminisced over our years together, hugged and kissed and promised to write. Little Michael was crying. Simon, distracted by the oncoming plane with its whirling propellers, paid little attention to what was going on. When from the plane door, we waved goodbye to our friends, Michael was still crying. All others were waving goodbye.

The two-motor Pan-American plane took us over the Russian Zone to Bremerhaven in Northwestern Germany. There we stayed for almost two weeks in an American army barracks before the military ship, the *USS General Harry Taylor,* on its return voyage from Germany to the United States, took us to the Port of New Orleans.

The End

Accounting Page

Of the ninety-six (96) family members and relatives (not including friends) whose names I knew, and who were with me in Warsaw at the beginning of the War, fourteen (14) are accounted for.

Seven died of "natural causes":
1) Grandma Ester (72) died after getting sick in the bomb shelter.

2) Cousin Moniek (c. 30) died of typhus during the epidemic in the ghetto.

3) Aunt Dora (50s), Moniek's mother, died right after her son's funeral.

4) Cousin Abram (18-20) lost a leg during the bombing; he later died of complications.

5) Aunt Tova (40s), Abram's mother, died of depression after the death of one son and the unknown whereabouts of her other son, who had been taken away.

6, 7) Uncle Yakov and Aunt Rachel died of starvation and other ghetto-related conditions.

8) Dad's Uncle Pinchus died after a long illness.

9) Cousin Balka's death: accident or suicide.

All of the above have graves and headstones or markers. Some are buried at the Okopowa Cemetery in Warsaw. Others are at the Brudno Cemetery in Praga.

Survivors:

10) Cousin Mordekhei left for Palestine before the War in the mid-30s. His most cherished possession is a picture of his sister's wedding, a photograph of his immediate family that was sent to him just before the War started.[1]

11, 12) Cousin Sruel and his wife Mollie survived in the USSR

13) Cousin Luba also survived in the USSR *(All three live in Israel.)*

14) Oh, yes! I, too, survived....

All others, those who "volunteered" for work assignments, and those who were shipped for "resettlement," were taken away to "unknown destinations," and never heard from again. No photographs survive. Their names are registered with the Holocaust Museum in Washington, DC, and in the Yad Vashem in Jerusalem. *To them (may they rest in peace) I attribute my respect for life and my lack of hatred, for they taught me the gift of love.*

---

[1] He died in Israel. [added between composition of "Accounting Page" and final publication. *Editor*]

Inge and I continue our friendship to this day. We keep in touch through writing, phone calls, and occasional visits.

I am also in contact with a few of my camp friends, and with Greta and Moshe, who are still married.

Timeline

Date	Location	Fela's Life	World
Jan. 1933			Hitler appointed Chancellor
Feb. 1933			Nazi's burn Reichstag building
May 1933			Book burning throughout Germany
Sep. 1935			Nuremberg Laws passed in Nazi Germany
Mar. 1936			Germany occupies the Rhineland
Aug. 1936			Olympic Games in Berlin
Mar. 1938			German annexation of Austria (*The Anschluss*)
Nov. 1938			*Kristallnacht*
Dec. 1938	Warsaw	Chanukah; Birthday (12)	
Mar. 1939	Warsaw		Germany occupies Czechoslovakia

May 1939	Warsaw		MS *St. Louis*, with 937 Jewish refuges is turned away from Cuba, USA
Aug. 1939	Warsaw	**Book narrative begins** Returns from "Germany Experience"	
Sep. 1939	Warsaw	Germany invades Poland; Warsaw bombed	**World War II starts**
Oct. 1939	Warsaw	Poland surrenders to Germany	
Nov. 1939	Warsaw	Jews in Poland required to wear Yellow Star	
Dec. 1939	Warsaw	Chanukah (1st during war); Birthday (13)	
Feb. 1940	Warsaw	Jews deported from Germany to Poland	
Apr. 1940	Warsaw	Passover (1st during	Construction of Auschwitz

		War)	concentration camp in Poland; Germany occupies Denmark
May 1940	Warsaw		Germany occupies France; creation of Kraków Ghetto
Jun. 1940	Warsaw		Romania joins the Axis side
Sep. 1940	Warsaw		Signing of the Tripartite Pact (Germany, Italy, Japan), creating the Axis Powers
Nov. 1940	Warsaw Ghetto	Warsaw Ghetto sealed off	
Dec. 1940	Warsaw Ghetto	Chanukah (2nd during war); Birthday (14)	
Mar. 1941	Warsaw Ghetto		Bulgaria joins the Axis side
Mar. 1941	Warsaw Ghetto		Bulgaria joins the Axis side
Apr. 1941	Warsaw Ghetto	Passover (2nd during War)	Germany invades Yugoslavia and Greece

Jun. 1941	Warsaw Ghetto		Germany invades Russia
Jul. 1941	Warsaw Ghetto	Escapes to Sandomierz with mother	Construction of Majdanek concentration camp in Poland; Göring sends letter to Heyrich regarding "Final Solution to Jewish Question"
Sep. 1941	Sandomierz		First large scale of *Zyklon B-on* prisoners (in Auschwitz);Babi Yar massacres
Dec. 1941	Sandomierz		Bombing of Pearl Harbor, marking the entrance of USA into the War
Jan. 1942	Sandomierz	Chanukah (3rd during war); Birthday (15)	
Feb. 1942	Sandomierz	Sis and Aunt Naomi arrive in Sandomierz	Sinking of the SS *Struma,* killing 768 Jewish refuges traveling to Palestine

Mar. 1942	Sandomierz		Large scale gassing beings at Auschwitz
Apr. 1942	Sandomierz	Passover (3rd during War)	
May 1942	Sandomierz		*NY Times* reports over 100,000 Jews machined gunned in Eastern Europe
Jul. 1942	Sandomierz	Forced to relocate to Skarżysko	*NY Times, London Telegraph* report over 1,000,000 Jews killed by Nazis
Dec. 1942	Skarżysko	Chanukah (4th during war); Birthday (16)	Construction of Plaszów labor camp
Feb. 1943	Skarżysko		Germany loses the Battle of Stalingrad
Mar. 1943	Skarżysko		Conclusion of the liquidation of the Kraków Ghetto
Apr. 1943	Skarżysko	Passover (4th during War)	Waffen SS enters the Warsaw Ghetto; the Uprising begins
May 1943	Skarżysko		Liquidation of Warsaw Ghetto

Dec. 1943	Skarżysko	Chanukah (5th during war) Birthday (17)	
Mar. 1944	Skarżysko	Forced to relocate to Leipzig	
Apr. 1944	Leipzig	Passover (5th during War)	
Jun. 1944	Leipzig		D-Day— Invasion of Normandy
Jul. 1944	Leipzig		Closing of Majdanek concentration camp; attempt on Hilter's life
Aug. 1944	Leipzig		Liquidation of Łódź Ghetto
Dec. 1944	Leipzig	Chanukah (5th during war); Birthday (18)	Liberation of France
Jan. 1945	Leipzig		Germany loses in the Battle of the Bulge; Capture of Warsaw by Russians; Liberation of Auschwitz and Plaszów by Russians

Feb. 1945	Leipzig		Yalta Conference
Mar. 1945	Leipzig		Death of Anne Frank in Bergen-Belsen concentration camp
Apr. 1945	Leipzig	Passover (6th during War); Leipzig march	FDR dies; Mussolini is executed; Hilter commits suicide
May 1945	Leipzig	Liberation; bried period in Lignica	Unconditional surrender of Germany: end of war in Europe
Jun. 1945	Lignica	Moves to Łódź	United Nation Charter signed
Jul. 1945	Łódź	Jacob moves to Łódź	
Aug. 1945	Łódź		Atomic bombs dropped on Hiroshima and Nagasaki; Japan surrenders
Sep. 1945	Łódź		**World War II ends**; Berlin divided between allies
Nov. 1945	Łódź		Start of Nuremberg Trials

Dec. 1945	Łódź	Chanukah (1st after war); Birthday (19)	
Jan. 1946	Łódź	Moves to Berlin	
Oct. 1946	Berlin		End of Nuremberg Trials
Dec. 1946	Berlin	Chanukah (2nd after war); Birthday (20)	
Jan. 1947	Berlin	Son Simon born	
May 1948	Berlin		State of Israel created
Jun. 1948	Berlin		Start of Berlin Blockade / Airlift
May 1949	Berlin		End of Berlin Blockade; Israel joins the United Nations
Jul. 1951	Berlin		Kansas City, MO, flood
Dec. 1951	Berlin	Moves to Kansas City with Jacob and Simon	

Glossary

American Jewish Joint Distribution Committee (Joint. During the War, it was responsible for delivering food, medicine, and clothing to survivors of the Holocaust. It also administered a program for relocation to Western countries outside the former war zone. [editor]

Assassination attempt. There were numerous failed attempts on Hitler's life. Perhaps the one referred to here took place in Berlin on July 20, 1944. Hitler exacted terrible retribution on all of those implicated.

Bat-Mitzvah. A ceremony initiating a girl into adult responsibilities, usually performed at the age of twelve to thirteen (from the Hebrew for daughter + commandment; analogous to Bar [son] Mitzvah, performed at 13).

Black Market. In conditions of unreasonable restrictions, or in times of economic chaos, such as occurred in the Warsaw Ghetto, black markets always appear.
By his analysis, only Aryan or German blood was free from the taint of inferiority.

China. Roughly seventeen thousand German and Austrian Jews were able to reach China, specifically Shanghai, which at the time required no visas or passports.

Corridor. A strip of Polish land leading to the Baltic Sea, located between Germany proper and German Prussia.

Death camps. While some Jews were sent to slave labor, many others were shipped to camps, the sole purpose of which was extermination. Auschwitz, Treblinka, Belsec, Sobibor and Chelmno, and Mauthausen, were large ones, but others existed near Riga, Vina, Minsk, Kaunas, and Lwow. Many Russians and other "undesirables" were also killed in these camps.

Glossary

Droshka. A horse-drawn taxi.

Eastern Front. Germany had invaded the Soviet Union from the east. (The Western Front was the French border—and, in a sense, the English Channel.)

Eighth day. The reference is to ritual circumcision (bris), performed on Jewish males eight days after birth.

Exodus and Resurrection. Jewish and Christian miracles. Moses' leading of the "Children of Israel out of the Land of the Pharaoh" is one of the greatest events in Jewish history. Similarly, the raising of Jesus from the dead after the Crucifixion is the central event in Christianity.

Extended draft age. Owing to the tremendous losses of life in the War, particularly of young men, the age of draft eligibility was extended upwards.

Final Solution. From the German: *Endlösung.* The term refers to Hitler's policy for the extermination of all Jews. On January 20, 1942, Reinhard Heydrich, head of the SS security service, held a meeting in the Berlin suburb of Wannsee to plan the final extermination of all Jews in Europe.

Gestapo. Short for *Geheime Staatspolizei,* the feared "Secret State Police."

Goosestep. The formal, stiff-legged march step of the German army.

Gypsy. Gypsies, a nomadic people arriving in Europe from migrations from India in the fourteenth century would later become a target of Hitler's racial extermination policies.

Hanukkah. An eight-day festival commemorating the victory of the Maccabees over Antiochus Epiphanes and the rededication of the Temple at Jerusalem. Also called "Feast of Dedication" and "Feast of Lights," since the oil in the triumph of the

Maccabees, which was to burn for one day, actually lasted for eight days.

Hasidic Jews. Members of an ultra-conservative Jewish sect founded in Eastern Europe in the eighteenth century.

Hanukkah Gelt. Usually coins or chocolate money given to children as Hanukkah candles or oil menorahs are lit.

HASSAG. Hugo Schneider Aktien Gesellschaft. A German industrial conglomerate that manufactured weapons.

Inquisition. Egyptian Pharaohs (c. 1300 BCE) held Jews as slaves. Persian Hamman (c. 500 BCE) in what is today Iran, was a governmental official who sought the destruction of Jews. During the Spanish Inquisition (late 15th c.), Jews were forced to convert to Christianity; those who didn't conform were expelled from the country. All three refer to major persecutions of Jews.

Jehovah's Witnesses. A religious denomination founded in the United States during the late nineteenth century. It argues against war and governmental authority. In its evangelism, it preaches for the imminent approach of the Second Coming of Jesus Christ.

Jekylls and Hydes. A reference to the Robert Louis Stevenson story of the same name about a man of two opposing natures, the kindly Dr. Jekyll and the sinister Mr. Hyde.

Job. The Book of Job in the Bible recounts the story of an agreement between the Lord and Satan allowing the latter to "test" the pious Job to see if misfortunes will cause him to turn against the Lord. The sufferings are great and numerous, but Job passes the test.

K'riya. To execute K'riya or "cut Kinim" is to perform a prescribed ritual of mourning, in which the mourners have small cuts made in their clothing to symbolize the "rending of garments" in anguish for the departed.

Kapo. Abbreviation for *Kameraden Polizei* (Comrade Police). Prisoners, Jewish and non-Jewish selected by German guards to oversee prisoners in labor camps.

Kibbutz. A cooperative farming settlement in Israel in which all activities are done communally. Food, education, and childrearing are offered.

Kikes, Schwabs. Derogatory slang for Jews and Germans, respectively.

King's Palace. Former residence of Polish kings; now residence of the Polish President.

Kippah. A skull cap worn in accordance with the scriptural injunction to men to keep the head covered. *"Jude."* German: "Jew."

Kohen. By tradition, Kohen was the name of a priestly class, who, in addition to other rituals and practices, weren't to be in the presence of the dead. They had special religious privileges and responsibilities.

Kosher-keeping. Rules dealing with what foods may be eaten and how they must be prepared. The rigor of Jewish dietary laws varied with the orthodoxy of the practitioners. The basis for the laws is found in the Torah and centers around the separation of milk and meat in food preparation.

Kristallnacht. German: "Night of the Broken Glass." Destructive raids unleashed by the Nazis, November 9-10, 1938, in which numerous synagogues and other Jewish institutions were burned. Additionally, many Jewish-owned businesses were looted or destroyed.

Luftwaffe. The German air force.

Mezuzah. A piece of paper inscribed with a verse from the Torah placed into a small case, which is then put on the doorpost of a Jewish home. *Cantor.* The leader of sung prayers in a Jewish service.

Minyan. A minimum of ten Jews (or Jewish men only, in Orthodox belief) is required for a proper communal religious service.

Neutral zone. A strip of land between Poland and Germany belonging to neither.

Nuremberg Laws. Various laws passed by the Nazi regime that, among other things, banned marriage between Jews and non-Jews, stripped Jews of German citizen, and curtailed most employment opportunities once enjoyed by Jewish citizens. *Kristallnacht.* German: "Night of the Broken Glass." Destructive raids unleashed by the Nazis, November 9-10, 1938, in which numerous synagogues and other Jewish institutions were burned. Additionally, many Jewish-owned businesses were looted or destroyed.

Nuremberg Trials. The post-War trials of some major surviving Nazi officials. The Trials are noteworthy in legal history because they established that military and civilian officials couldn't use the defense that they "were just following orders" in committing genocide.

Palestine. Since 1948, the country of Israel. From early 1900 until 1948, it was a British protectorate. (It has also been known as Canaan, Land of the Hebrews, the Land of Milk and Honey, and The Holy Land.)

Pani. Polish: "Mrs." The male equivalent is *Pan.*

Passover. The most important holiday of the Jewish year, it is an eight-day observance that celebrates the Israelites' escape from Egyptian slavery (c. 1300-1200 BCE) *Kosher.* Foods conforming to the dietary laws enunciated in the sacred books of Moses (the Torah).

Pogrom. A systematic attack against Jews. The term is also used to describe a similar persecution or slaughter of other minority groups.

Potassium Cyanide and Zyklon. Gases used to kill people in the gas chambers of the extermination camps.

POW. Prisoner of War.

Praga. The "sister city" of Warsaw, across the Wisla River.

Pure blood." Hitler (like some geneticists at the time) believed blood carried genetic/racial traits.

Rabbe Gelt. Literally, "money for the rabbi"; idiomatically, "the cost of learning a lesson."

Red Army, the Soviet Army. "Red" being associated with revolution and communism.

Red Sea. The parting of the Red Sea, allowing the Jews to escape the onrushing army of the Pharaoh, and the sea subsequently swallowing up the Egyptian army, is recounted in the Book of Exodus.

Restoration money. Some of the Nazi-confiscated property was being returned to their owners. *Marshall Plan.* Popular name for the U.S.-sponsored European Recovery Program, which was designed to rehabilitate the economies of post-War European nations in order to create stable conditions in which free institutions could survive.

Revolt. The Jews held out until May 16, 1943, after which the ghetto was burned to the ground. Survivors of the Uprising met their deaths in the extermination camps. The 1944 Revolt was carried out by the Gentile population and was put down severely by the Nazis.

Sectors of Berlin. The four Allies divided Germany into four zones. The city of Berlin was in the center of the Soviet zone, but the city itself was divided into four sectors, which were occupied by troops from all four Allied countries.

Seder. The traditional feast commemorating the exodus of the Jews from Egypt. At the Seder, four traditional questions are asked by the youngest child (in Orthodox practice, by the youngest boy): Why is this night different? Why do we eat matzo? Etc. The father answers the questions according to Haggadah, the narrative of the Exodus.

"L'Shana Haba B'Yerushalaim"—"Next year in Jerusalem." Diaspora Jews had a wish (and a promise) to return to their homeland in Israel/Palestine.

Selection. The process whereby officials would choose who in a camp would live or die according to his or her medical condition. Usually determined by doctors.

Shtetl. Yiddish. A small market village in Eastern Europe or Russia with a substantial Jewish population.

Slav. A member of any group of people of Eastern or Central Europe (Czechs, Poles, Slovaks, etc.), considered by the Nazis to be *Untermenschen*, inferior people.

Spanish Civil War. 1936-39. A complex conflict in which an army general, Francisco Franco, led an insurrection against the newly installed Republican government. A testing ground for weapons and tactics used later in World War II, Franco's forces triumphed, and he quickly established an authoritarian, fascist rule.

The St. Louis. A German ship that sailed for Havana in 1939 filled with Jewish refugees. On its arrival, the Cuban government denied its landing permits. Eventually, the ship returned to Europe, where its passengers were distributed throughout England, Belgium, France, and the Netherlands.

Sukkoth. A Jewish holiday also known as "Feast of the Tabernacles" or "Harvest Holiday." A sukkah was a portable sanctuary carried by the Hebrews during their wandering. Jews, mostly men, eat in a specially constructed sukkah for the eight-day duration of the holiday. Children decorate the sukkahs, sing, and play.

Super Race. Nazi doctrines asserted that the Teutonic-German-Aryan "racial" group constituted a "super- or master-race," or, in German, *Übermenschen.* Of course, that idea meant that all others were *Untermenschen*, quite literally, sub-humans.

Tehillim. Prayers from the book of Psalms.

The Third Reich. The term given by Hitler to the projected thousand-year reign of the Nazi government. It lasted twelve years and four months.

Volksdeutsch. An ethnic German living outside of Germany; here, a German living in Poland.

Yellow stars. Jews of central Poland wore white armbands, with blue Stars of David. Yellow stars indicated Jews from outside central Poland.

Yiddish. The "common language" of European Jewry evolved from German in the Middle Ages and was spread by Jewish migrations.

Notes

[1] *Nuremberg Laws.* Various laws passed by the Nazi regime that, among other things, banned marriage between Jews and non-Jews, stripped Jews of German citizen, and curtailed most employment opportunities once enjoyed by Jewish citizens. *Kristallnacht.* German: "Night of the Broken Glass." Destructive raids unleashed by the Nazis, November 9-10, 1938, in which numerous synagogues and other Jewish institutions were burned. Additionally, many Jewish-owned businesses were looted or destroyed.

[2] *Neutral zone.* A strip of land between Poland and Germany belonging to neither.

[3] *Corridor.* A strip of Polish land leading to the Baltic Sea, located between Germany proper and German Prussia.

[4] *The insane painter.* A reference to Hitler, who in his youth aspired to be an artist. He was rejected by the Vienna Arts Academy.

[5] *Hasidic Jews.* Members of an ultra-conservative Jewish sect founded in Eastern Europe in the eighteenth century.

[6] *Spanish Civil War.* 1936-39. A complex conflict in which an army general, Francisco Franco, led an insurrection against the newly installed Republican government. A testing ground for weapons and tactics used later in World War II, Franco's forces triumphed, and he quickly established an authoritarian, fascist rule.

[7] *"Dzień dobry!"* Polish: "Good day!" *Pani.* Polish: "Mrs." The male equivalent is *Pan.*

[8] *Luftwaffe.* The German air force.

[9] *Tehillim.* Prayers from the book of Psalms.

10 *Mezuzah.* A piece of paper inscribed with a verse from the Torah placed into a small case, which is then put on the doorpost of a Jewish home. *Cantor.* The leader of sung prayers in a Jewish service.

11 *Oy Veh.* The humor here is that the expression is a common Yiddish/Jewish interjection for "Oh dear!" or "Oh me!" or even "Alas!" in order to register astonishment.

12 *"...cholera!"* A traditional Polish curse, used even by those who didn't know about the disease.

13 *Kippah.* A skull cap worn in accordance with the scriptural injunction to men to keep the head covered. *"Jude."* German: "Jew."

14 *Super Race.* Nazi doctrines asserted that the Teutonic-German-Aryan "racial" group constituted a "super- or master-race," or, in German, *Übermenschen.* Of course, that idea meant that all others were *Untermenschen,* quite literally, sub-humans.

15 *The Third Reich.* The term given by Hitler to the projected thousand-year reign of the Nazi government. It lasted twelve years and four months.

16 *Black Market.* In conditions of unreasonable restrictions, or in times of economic chaos, such as occurred in the Warsaw Ghetto, black markets always appear.

17 *Praga.* The "sister city" of Warsaw, across the Wisla River.

18 *Gestapo.* Short for *Geheime Staatspolizei,* the feared "Secret State Police."

19 *Yellow stars.* Jews of central Poland wore white armbands, with blue Stars of David. Yellow stars indicated Jews from outside central Poland.

20 *King's Palace.* Former residence of Polish kings; now residence of the Polish President.

21 *Aryan looks.* Blond or light hair, light skin, and blue eyes were typically considered "Aryan" traits.

22 *Bat-Mitzvah.* A ceremony initiating a girl into adult responsibilities, usually performed at the age of twelve to thirteen (from the Hebrew for daughter + commandment; analogous to Bar [son] Mitzvah, performed at 13).

23 *Hanukkah.* An eight-day festival commemorating the victory of the Maccabees over Antiochus Epiphanes and the rededication of the Temple at Jerusalem. Also called "Feast of Dedication" and "Feast of Lights," since the oil in the triumph of the Maccabees, which was to burn for one day, actually lasted for eight days.

24 *Hanukkah Gelt.* Usually coins or chocolate money given to children as Hanukkah candles or oil menorahs are lit.

25 *Passover.* The most important holiday of the Jewish year, it is an eight-day observance that celebrates the Israelites' escape from Egyptian slavery (c. 1300-1200 BCE) *Kosher.* Foods conforming to the dietary laws enunciated in the sacred books of Moses (the Torah).

26 *Seder.* The traditional feast commemorating the exodus of the Jews from Egypt. At the Seder, four traditional questions are asked by the youngest child (in Orthodox practice, by the youngest boy): Why is this night different? Why do we eat matzo? Etc. The father answers the questions according to Haggadah, the narrative of the Exodus. *"L'Shana Haba B'Yerushalaim"*—"Next year in Jerusalem." Diaspora Jews had a wish (and a promise) to return to their homeland in Israel/Palestine.

27 *Red Sea.* The parting of the Red Sea, allowing the Jews to escape the onrushing army of the Pharaoh, and the sea subsequently swallowing up the Egyptian army, is recounted in the Book of Exodus.

28 *Special identification.* Since it was easy to spot a member of the Hasidim by his or her traditional clothing and hair style, the compulsory wearing of the six-pointed Star of David was, at the least, redundant.

29 *Eighth day.* The reference is to ritual circumcision (bris), performed on Jewish males eight days after birth.

30 *Gypsy.* Gypsies, a nomadic people arriving in Europe from migrations from India in the fourteenth century would later become a target of Hitler's racial extermination policies.

31 *New social system.* Communism, which promised a classless society, state ownership of property, and full employment.

32 *Godless Society.* In the Soviet Union, formed by Lenin and the Communists following the Russian Revolution, atheism was the state policy in conformance to the idea of Marx that religion was the "opiate of the masses."

33 *Palestine.* Since 1948, the country of Israel. From early 1900 until 1948, it was a British protectorate. (It has also been known as Canaan, Land of the Hebrews, the Land of Milk and Honey, and The Holy Land.)

34 *Kibbutz.* A cooperative farming settlement in Israel in which all activities are done communally. Food, education, and childrearing are offered.

35 *Sukkoth.* A Jewish holiday also known as "Feast of the Tabernacles" or "Harvest Holiday." A sukkah was a portable sanctuary carried by the Hebrews during their wandering. Jews, mostly men, eat in a specially constructed sukkah for the eight-day duration of the holiday. Children decorate the sukkah, sing, and play.

36 *Jewish men.* In traditions of Judaism, men took the responsibility of praying. In Orthodox synagogues, women and men are still separated in services.

37 *Kohen.* By tradition, Kohen was the name of a priestly class, who, in addition to other rituals and practices, weren't to be in the presence of the dead. They had special religious privileges and responsibilities.

38 *Minyan.* A minimum of ten Jews (or Jewish men only, in Orthodox belief) is required for a proper communal religious service.

39 *Feminine features.* Orthodox Jewish men were forbidden to look at a "woman" (by definition, one who had passed through puberty).

40 *Job.* The Book of Job in the Bible recounts the story of an agreement between the Lord and Satan allowing the latter to "test" the pious Job to see if misfortunes will cause him to turn against the Lord. The sufferings are great and numerous, but Job passes the test.

41 *POW.* Prisoner of War.

42 *Hitler's funeral.* The implication of the sentence is that peace will come only with the deaths of the Axis leaders (Franco in Spain, Mussolini in Italy, and Hitler in Germany), of the communist leader of the USSR, Stalin, and all other heads of totalitarian regimes.

43 *K'riya.* To execute K'riya or "cut Kinim" is to perform a prescribed ritual of mourning, in which the mourners have small cuts made in their clothing to symbolize the "rending of garments" in anguish for the departed.

44 *Yiddish.* The "common language" of European Jewry evolved from German in the Middle Ages and was spread by Jewish migrations.

⁴⁵ *Kosher-keeping.* Rules dealing with what foods may be eaten and how they must be prepared. The rigor of Jewish dietary laws varied with the orthodoxy of the practitioners. The basis for the laws is found in the Torah and centers around the separation of milk and meat in food preparation.

⁴⁶ *Droshka.* A horse-drawn taxi.

⁴⁷ *Rabbe Gelt.* Literally, "money for the rabbi"; idiomatically, "the cost of learning a lesson."

⁴⁸ *Surprise German invasion.* In June, 1941, Germany invaded Russia, disregarding the 1939 "Non-Aggression Treaty."

⁴⁹ *Kikes, Schwabs.* Derogatory slang for Jews and Germans, respectively.

⁵⁰ *Shtetl.* Yiddish. A small market village in Eastern Europe or Russia with a substantial Jewish population.

⁵¹ *Red Army, the Soviet Army.* "Red" being associated with revolution and communism.

⁵² *Eastern Front.* Germany had invaded the Soviet Union from the east. (The Western Front was the French border—and, in a sense, the English Channel.)

⁵³ *Ukrainian uniforms.* With the German invasion of Russia, many Ukrainians allied themselves with the invaders. Hence, Ukrainians were enlisted to help in the "lower" duties of the Third Reich, such as becoming camp guards.

⁵⁴ *HASSAG.* Hugo Schneider Aktien Gesellschaft. A German industrial conglomerate that manufactured weapons.

⁵⁵ *Kapo.* Abbreviation for *Kameraden Polizei* (Comrade Police). Prisoners, Jewish and non-Jewish selected by German guards to oversee prisoners in labor camps.

⁵⁶ *Selection.* The process whereby officials would choose who in a camp would live or die according to his or her medical condition. Usually determined by doctors.

⁵⁷ *Final Solution.* From the German: *Endlösung.* The term refers to Hitler's policy for the extermination of all Jews. On January 20, 1942, Reinhard Heydrich, head of the SS security service, held a meeting in the Berlin suburb of Wannsee to plan the final extermination of all Jews in Europe.

⁵⁸ *Death camps.* While some Jews were sent to slave labor, many others were shipped to camps, the sole purpose of which was extermination. Auschwitz, Treblinka, Belsec, Sobibor and Chelmno, and Mauthausen, were large ones, but others existed near Riga, Vina, Minsk, Kaunas, and Lwow. Many Russians and other "undesirables" were also killed in these camps.

⁵⁹ *Potassium Cyanide and Zyklon.* Gases used to kill people in the gas chambers of the extermination camps.

⁶⁰ *Revolt.* The Jews held out until May 16, 1943, after which the ghetto was burned to the ground. Survivors of the Uprising met their deaths in the extermination camps. The 1944 Revolt was carried out by the Gentile population and was put down severely by the Nazis.

⁶¹ *Assassination attempt.* There were numerous failed attempts on Hitler's life. Perhaps the one referred to here took place in Berlin on July 20, 1944. Hitler exacted terrible retribution on all of those implicated.

⁶² *Exodus and Resurrection.* Jewish and Christian miracles. Moses' leading of the "Children of Israel out of the Land of the Pharaoh" is one of the greatest events in Jewish history. Similarly, the raising of Jesus from the

dead after the Crucifixion is the central event in Christianity.

63 *White handkerchiefs.* A universal sign of surrender.

64 *Goosestep.* The formal, stiff-legged march step of the German army.

65 *Evacuated.* That is, those who hadn't been moved into the eastern republics of the USSR before the German advance into Russia. *Stalingrad.* On the Volga River, the battle of Stalingrad (1942) is considered by historians to be one of the turning points of World War II, since the Russian army halted the German advance there and inflicted terrific losses.

66 *Extended draft age.* Owing to the tremendous losses of life in the War, particularly of young men, the age of draft eligibility was extended upwards.

67 *Inquisition.* Egyptian Pharaohs (c. 1300 BCE) held Jews as slaves. Persian Hamman (c. 500 BCE) in what is today Iran, was a governmental official who sought the destruction of Jews. During the Spanish Inquisition (late 15th c.), Jews were forced to convert to Christianity; those who didn't conform were expelled from the country. All three refer to major persecutions of Jews.

68 *Volksdeutsch.* An ethnic German living outside of Germany; here, a German living in Poland.

69 *"Pure blood."* Hitler (like some geneticists at the time) believed blood carried genetic/racial traits. By his analysis, only Aryan or German blood was free from the taint of inferiority.

70 *China.* Roughly seventeen thousand German and Austrian Jews were able to reach China, specifically Shanghai, which at the time required no visas or passports.

[71] *Restoration money.* Some of the Nazi-confiscated property was being returned to their owners. *Marshall Plan.* Popular name for the U.S.-sponsored European Recovery Program, which was designed to rehabilitate the economies of post-War European nations in order to create stable conditions in which free institutions could survive.

[72] *"Ein Glückliches Neues Jahr."* German: "A Happy New Year."

[73] *Nuremberg Trials.* The post-War trials of some major surviving Nazi officials. The Trials are noteworthy in legal history because they established that military and civilian officials couldn't use the defense that they "were just following orders" in committing genocide.

[74] *Jekylls and Hydes.* A reference to the Robert Louis Stevenson story of the same name about a man of two opposing natures, the kindly Dr. Jekyll and the sinister Mr. Hyde.

[75] *Slav.* A member of any group of people of Eastern or Central Europe (Czechs, Poles, Slovaks, etc.), considered by the Nazis to be *Untermenschen*, inferior people.

[76] *The St. Louis.* A German ship that sailed for Havana in 1939 filled with Jewish refugees. On its arrival, the Cuban government denied its landing permits. Eventually, the ship returned to Europe, where its passengers were distributed throughout England, Belgium, France, and the Netherlands.

[77] *Jehovah's Witnesses.* A religious denomination founded in the United States during the late nineteenth century. It argues against war and governmental authority. In its evangelism, it preaches for the imminent approach of the Second Coming of Jesus Christ.

78 *Pogrom.* A systematic attack against Jews. The term is also used to describe a similar persecution or slaughter of other minority groups.

79 *Sectors of Berlin.* The four Allies divided Germany into four zones. The city of Berlin was in the center of the Soviet zone, but the city itself was divided into four sectors, which were occupied by troops from all four Allied countries.

80 American Jewish Joint Distribution Committee. During the War, it was responsible for delivering food, medicine, and clothing to survivors of the Holocaust. It also administered a program for relocation to Western countries outside the former war zone. [editor]

www.ingramcontent.com/pod-product-compliance
Lightning Source LLC
LaVergne TN
LVHW011218080426
835509LV00005B/191